Accessible Libraries on Campus:

A Practical Guide for the Creation of Disability-Friendly Libraries

Edited by
Tom McNulty

Association of College and Research Libraries
A division of the American Library Association
Chicago 1999

The paper used in this publication meets the minimum requirements of American National Standard for Information Sciences–Permanence of Paper of Printed Library Materials, ANSI Z39.48-1992. ∞

Library of Congress Cataloging-in-Publication Data
Accessible libraries on campus : a practical guide for the creation of
   disability-friendly libraries / edited by Tom McNulty.
      p.   cm.
   Includes bibliographical references.
   ISBN 0-8389-8035-X (alk. paper)
   1. Library architecture and the handicapped--United States.
2. Academic libraries--United States.   I. McNulty, Tom.
Z679.8.A24 1999
027.6 '63' 0973--dc21   99-34534

Printed in the United States of America.

04 03 02 01 00 99   5 4 3 2 1

contents

introduction

Over the past few decades, but particularly during the 1990s, the library profession has made significant progress in extending its collections and services to people with disabilities. In fact, almost from the very beginning of our professional organization, librarianship's progress in this arena has been noteworthy. From modest beginnings—national and local collections of a few dozen braille-embossed titles, for example— libraries have capitalized on innovations and have attempted to exploit their potential for providing information to those previously deprived because of one or more physical, sensory, or cognitive disabilities. As we approach the millennium, the range of possible "access solutions" seems to grow exponentially. Although innovation is generally positive, it can also be overwhelming to the librarian, administrator, or other professional who is charged with developing and/or maintaining an access program in the college or university library.

Coinciding with the passage of the Americans with Disabilities Act (ADA) in 1991, numerous books and a plethora of journal articles have appeared in the professional library literature. Many of these efforts, not surprisingly, were and are intended to get libraries up to speed vis-à-vis their legal responsibilities to individuals with disabilities. Interestingly, a number of the authors of the chapters in this book have acknowledged legal issues surrounding the ADA and other legislation but see libraries' efforts to extend service and materials as more or less an extension of what librarians have been doing all along, not just for people with disabilities, but for all of our patrons: providing access to information. Without underestimating the power and importance of the "letter" of the laws, the premise here is more on addressing the "spirit" of disability law.

To contextualize some of the more specialized technical material that follows, the overview chapter briefly outlines, in a necessarily cursory fashion, some main points in the history of higher education and library service for people with disabilities. It explains that, for some groups (e.g., the visually impaired), the provision of information necessitated the development of entirely new and unique communication media (braille, audio books). More recently, efforts to "mainstream" students with disabilities at all educational levels have had the effect of altering the modern disabled student's expectations of what she or he can expect of our educational system, and perhaps more important, in the world of employment. Much of the change that has occurred can be related directly to significant pieces of national legislation, some of which are briefly described. Finally, the overview chapter explores the activities and impact of professional library associations, with particular emphasis on the ALA.

Although much professional and popular attention has been garnered by the idea of the "virtual library," we are all still buying books, journals, newspapers, and other "traditional" materials that are housed in more or less traditional physical structures. Independent and unencumbered access to the library, therefore, still means gaining access to, and being able to navigate, the library building. The first chapter offered by Susan Gilbert Beck addresses issues relating to the library as a physical structure. Issues of physical access, and the ADA guidelines governing the physical accessibility of libraries and other educational buildings, are explicated in this chapter, along with the often-overlooked aspect of ADA-compliant signage and other wayfinding aids for the library user or staff member with a disability.

What should the disabled library user expect to be able to use inside the building? Increasingly, the answer to this question is everything, and the goal of full access to all library materials by users with any number of disabilities is a potential reality. Bucking the trend to characterize our libraries as multimedia based, the truth is most of the typical librarian's day is spent helping people to use print (electronic and paper-based) resources. How, one might wonder, do people who can not see because of a visual impairment, or those who can not read because of a learning disability, keep on top of their reading? The chapter provided by Steve Noble of Recording for the Blind and Dyslexic (RFB&D) outlines the myriad alternatives to traditional print, including braille, large-print, recorded, and electronic texts.

Although alternative-format texts—particularly textbooks—are a lifeline for college students and other researchers, these materials have one inherent, and not insignificant, drawback: they are always produced after the fact, and in many cases they must be produced on demand. True access means access to everything physically housed in the library as well as everything made available electronically—whether locally on a stand-alone computer or remotely on the Internet—to the library's clientele. In their chapter, Dawn M. Suvino, a highly experienced assistive technology expert, and Janice O'Connor, career services specialist, examine the technologies available to achieve the goal of complete and independent access to the library's many printed resources. Emphasizing types of technologies rather than specific products and brands, Suvino and O'Connor offer guidance in the selection of specialized "adaptive" hardware and software for use by individuals with print-prohibitive disabilities. Speech output, large print, text-to-speech, and other technologies that can extend the world of traditional print and electronic resources are covered in detail, along with specific tips on training, troubleshooting, and other aspects of maintaining a program of adaptive technology in the academic library.

It would seem that the biggest hurdles to access—physical access to buildings by individuals with physical disabilities and access to print-based collections by people with visual or cognitive disabilities—have been overcome. However, libraries are more than just buildings with computers and books. In

Beck's second chapter, she offers guidance to the librarian serving patrons with deafness or hearing loss. In the past, libraries were probably less proactive in serving the deaf because deafness represents, for the most part, an invisible disability. However, many of the things we do involve audible speech and sound, including the traditional reference interview, more in-depth reference consultation, telephone reference and information, and so on. Beck provides concrete advice on how to interact with individuals who have various degrees of hearing loss. Included in her chapter is a discussion of technology available for the hearing impaired, including the TTY/TDD and other telecommunications aids.

Ironically, the very technology that is serving people with certain disabilities—the personal computer—is actually creating an entirely new class of disabled individuals, those with RSI (repetitive stress injuries), perhaps the most commonly known of which is carpal tunnel syndrome. In his chapter, Greg Shaw, a technology trainer and expert in voice input technologies, describes the needs of this large and growing population. College students, researchers, and other academic library users depend on the computer for all aspects of their work, from finding books in online catalogs to producing papers and other documents with word-processing software. How are students with RSI able to perform these indispensable tasks of the modern academic world? Many are using some of the hottest new technology around—voice input—which bypasses the need for keyboarding altogether. Shaw provides detailed information on how to integrate voice input technology into the academic library, from selecting hardware and software to training new users. Although the emphasis here is on high-tech solutions to access, Shaw also offers tips for making individuals with hand disabilities more comfortable in their use of the library, from providing book trucks to offering telephone renewal of library materials, inexpensive or even free accommodations that can make all the difference in the world to the person who has a hand-related disability.

Increasingly, libraries are not only acquiring information resources but also are involved in creating, or at least "packaging," information. Most academic libraries by now have a presence on the World Wide Web, and the contents of any library's Web pages—whether simple, descriptive "brochures" or more complex, unique finding aids and research tools—either are accessible or represent new hurdles for people with various disabilities. In the next chapter, Judith M. Dixon of the National Library Service, outlines some of the obstacles to full Web accessibility and offers concrete advice on the creation of disability-friendly Web page design. Noting that the Internet changes so rapidly that at least some of what we are writing today might be out of date as it comes off the press, Dixon provides a list of resources for keeping au courant in the field of Web accessibility.

In her general discussion of Web accessibility, Dixon identifies an online source called Bobby that can be used to provide a diagnosis of any page's accessibility. Created by the Center for Assistive Technology (CAST), Bobby is available free of charge to individuals interested in checking their sites' disability-friendliness. In the following chapter, Eric Stedfeld and I present Bobby's diagnosis of our own library's first page and discuss the measures taken to "fix" its access problems without changing its physical appearance even minimally.

All the technology in the world will not compensate for staff who are unprepared to integrate it into a comprehensive program of service for students and others with disabilities. In the last chapter, Courtney Deines-Jones provides a concise overview of how, and perhaps as important why, training is essential for both librarians and support staff (including student workers). Her overview of training includes goals and objectives, along with specific activities, for frontline public service staff (from reference librarians to circulation desk staff), library administration, and the library's sometimes-overlooked technical staff (Web designers, technical service personnel).

A series of appendices serve as "catchalls" for information and projects that I found much too compelling not to include, but that did not, in themselves constitute full-length studies or chapters. The program and project profiles were solicited via a number of library and disability related listservs. The response to my call for participation here was quite positive, and although a number of interesting profiles were suggested, only a sampling could be included. The resources directory—composed of print and electronic resources— is an overview of additional sources of information on the burgeoning field of disability in general and assistive technologies in particular.

Finally, I would just like to say a few words about the authors represented here. In the earliest stages of planning, I sketched out chapter titles/topics that I knew would be of interest to the library and disability communities. My list of authors was truly a "wish list" from which I hoped several would agree to author chapters. As one after another came on board without hesitation, my wish list became the book's finalized table of contents. Many thanks to all of you who have given so freely of your time, energy, and expertise!

Tom McNulty
New York University

disability in higher education:
An Overview

Tom McNulty

Introduction

Throughout history, people with one or more disabilities, whether sensory (blindness, deafness), physical, mental, or cognitive, have faced enormous obstacles and have been viewed and treated as being somehow outside the social norm. Before going on to consider the current state of library services for our target audience, this chapter presents a short overview of disability in higher education today. The integration of disabled individuals in primary and secondary education is touched on in passing, because access to the world of higher education is obviously dependent on progress in precollege educational institutions.

A complete history of societies' and cultures' treatment of their disabled members would surely comprise a many-volume work and in any case, is beyond the scope of this brief overview. Suffice it to say that beliefs and practices ranging from disability as a manifestation of evil to infanticide and imprisonment were not uncommon throughout the world in the first and well into the second millennium, and persist in many parts of the globe even today. Throughout history, until recent centuries, fear and superstition dominated social thought and practice vis-à-vis disabled persons and other disenfranchised segments of the population. This is not to suggest that the disability movement does not have a long way to go to reach its goal of universal access and equality of opportunity. But at least, as the twentieth century winds down, this once isolated population now represents an organized and powerful force with enough significant achievements to empower itself for the next millennium.

Coupled with the successful political organization of people with disabilities is a broad, if slowly evolving, change in social attitudes toward disability itself. It has often been noted that medical advances have prolonged life expectancy and that with a longer life, the chance that one will be disabled, or at least have one or more friends or family members count themselves among the ranks of the disabled, is a reality that all but the most fortunate of us should expect to encounter. "The increasing presence of people with disabilities in society, like the increasing proportion of elderly people in society, is a testament to the success of modern science."[1] But this success poses a challenge to virtually all of our institutions—including elementary, secondary, and postsecondary educational facilities—that will expand as the disabled population grows.

1

Early History of Education for People with Disabilities

Like so many contemporary institutions and social practices, the education of
people with disabilities has its beginnings in the mid-eighteenth century period called the Enlightenment. "Primarily French in inspiration and leadership, the Enlightenment brought about a revolution in the way people per-
ceived their world and their role in it. The philosophers built their theories
upon a combination of rationalism and empiricism that differed fundamentally from views that had prevailed earlier."[2] The French philosophers, including Diderot, Voltaire, Rousseau, and others, laid the groundwork for the
great shift in social thought that would characterize the next century. The
growing belief in the potential of humanity, and a slow, but steady, reversal of
power that had been heretofore maintained by the Church, resulted not only
in rudimentary attempts at educating individuals with disabilities but also,
and perhaps more significant, a belief in the importance of universal basic
education for all citizens.

Education of the Blind and Visually Impaired

To teach the written word to those with blindness, materials that could be
used via other senses—first touch, then hearing—had to be developed. As
noted above, France was the cradle of the revolution that set in motion some
of the most basic changes in our thinking toward education and laid the
groundwork for the advent of special education as we know it today. With the
publication, in 1749, of his *Lettre sur les Aveugles,* Denis Diderot is often credited with the specific empirical/scientific curiosity about the blind that engendered the revolutionary belief that this then-isolated population could
indeed be educated.

But teaching, then as now, relied on auditory and visual communications
media. Louis Braille's introduction of a systematic tactile reading code is be-
lieved by many to be the earliest successful attempt at developing the substi-
tute for the requisite visual medium (i.e., textbooks and other reading matter). But, in fact, although his is certainly the most enduring of the earliest
tactile reading systems, it was not the first nor was it without competition
over the past two centuries. Even the pre-Braille work of Valentin Hauy, often credited with the introduction of embossed reading, is most likely not
without precedent.[3] The importance of special format materials is under-
scored by the fact that the very first piece of federal legislation on education
for the handicapped, the *Act to Promote the Education of the Blind,*[4] led to the
creation of the American Printing House for the Blind (APH), whose work
in the provision of specialized materials continues to the present day. The
development of braille, then audio, and, most recently, electronic materials for
individuals who cannot see traditional printed texts is explored in much greater
detail in the chapter by Steve Noble.

Almost half a century elapsed before the founding of the New England
Asylum for the Blind (soon after renamed Perkins Institution and Massachu-

setts Asylum for the Blind), the first of its kind in the United States. Within the following ten-year period, an additional six schools opened in other states. However, it was not until well into the twentieth century that blind and partially sighted students entered day schools for the visually impaired, and later "regular" public and private schools with disability-specific instruction provided by specially trained itinerant teachers. Today, almost 50 percent of visually impaired persons between the ages of 3 and 21 attend "regular classes," and 53.9 percent pursue a postsecondary academic education.[5]

Education of the Deaf and Hard of Hearing

In the United States, the education of deaf students also began in the mid-nineteenth century. Deafness has the distinction of being the first formal specialization in American special education, and teachers of deaf persons were the first to form a permanent professional organization. This group, American Instructors of the Deaf and Dumb, founded in 1850, was the first formal national group of special education teachers in North America and is among the four oldest national educational organizations in the Unites States.[6]

Just as education of the blind required the development of an alternative to print, education of the deaf and hard of hearing required an alternative to the auditory lecture; that alternative, of course, is sign language. Institutional education supplied the basis of culture—a living language—and the residential schools furnished maximal conditions for the acquisition of sign, so that signing rapidly became an indicator of one's identity as a deaf person.[7] Early efforts at educating the deaf engendered a heated debate over the use of manual, or sign, language versus oral training, with Edward Miner Gallaudet representing the most noteworthy proponent of the former and Alexander Graham Bell the most vocal supporter of the latter.

Like students with blindness and other sensory disabilities, those with hearing impairments increasingly attend regular classes but are more likely to receive their precollege education in classes separate from their hearing classmates.[8] Major advances in technology have served to integrate this once-isolated population into mainstream educational institutions at all levels; these technologies are explored in detail in the chapter titled "Services for Patrons with Hearing Loss or Deafness."

Learning Disabilities

In recent years, many two- and four-year colleges, graduate and professional schools have experienced an influx of students with learning disabilities. One 1979 study reports that only 3.1 percent of college freshmen identified themselves as having a learning disability[9]; by some estimates, the percentage of first-year college students with learning disabilities has tripled since that time. Some individuals with learning disabilities do not identify themselves as such, making it impossible to project with any accuracy the true prevalence of this group of disabilities among the total student population.

Learning disabilities frequently go undetected, and perhaps for this reason, research in the field is primarily recent, compared with other disabilities. Often referred to as "word blindness" in the literature of the early Nineteenth century, learning disability is an umbrella term for a number of disorders. In 1990, the National Joint Committee on Learning Disabilities (NJCLD) defined learning disability as:

> a general term that refers to a heterogeneous group of disorders manifested by significant difficulties in the acquisition and use of listening, speaking, reading, writing, reasoning, or mathematical skills.

> These disorders are intrinsic to the individual, presumed to be due to central nervous system dysfunction, and may occur across the life span. Problems in self-regulatory behaviors, social perception, and social interaction may exist with learning disabilities but do not, by themselves, constitute a learning disability.

> Although learning disabilities may occur concomitantly with other disabilities (e.g., sensory impairment, mental retardation, serious emotional disturbance), or with extrinsic influences (such as cultural differences, insufficient or inappropriate instruction), they are not the result of those conditions or influences.[10]

Many of the technologies discussed throughout this book will be of value to the academic library user with a learning disability. Perhaps most important for the effective integration of this portion of our clientele, however, is Courtney Deines-Jones's chapter on the training of professional and support staff. As members of a largely invisible disability group, individuals with learning disabilities sometimes experience frustration in their use of the library. For example, decoding an alphanumeric call number can take an inordinate amount of time for some LD students, and only staff members with an understanding of the basics of learning disabilities will be able to provide the assistance needed with what can seem to be very simple tasks.

Mobility Impairments

When most people hear the term *mobility impairment*, they immediately envision someone in a wheelchair. In reality, the wheelchair user is just one of several groups considered to have a mobility, or orthopedic, impairment. Increasingly, those with hand-related disabilities are finding libraries a challenge. From searching a computer to lifting and carrying books can be painful, perhaps even impossible, for a surprising number of library users.

The early literature on disability and higher education had an obvious emphasis on physical access; indeed, many institutions' evaluation of their disability-friendliness dealt almost exclusively with physical access to buildings. Today, much more can be done to integrate people with various disabilities into the complete range of services, programs, and activities offered by institutions of higher education, including the academic library. Beck's chapter on wayfinding offers practical advice for planning physically accessible libraries, and Greg Shaw's chapter explores services and technologies for the hand-disabled library user in great detail.

Defining Disability Today

What is a disability? It might be temporary (a broken arm, for example) or permanent and lifelong; it might be psychological, physical/sensory, or cognitive; it might affect just about every aspect of one's life or present major or minor obstacles only in specific situations. The demographics of disability change as other populations change, but one thing seems certain: more than 40 million Americans are now characterized as disabled, and this population will certainly grow as the general population ages. The presence of disability on campus will also change, and our knowledge of our disabled users will help to ensure our continued ability to meet their changing needs.

Just as attitudes have changed toward disability, so has our approach to its very definition. Researcher Harlan Hahn, of the University of Southern California, notes that "in the past, disability was defined almost exclusively from a medical perspective that focused on functional impairment. Disability was considered a defect in the individual, and the primary emphasis was on the cause of organic condition .... The resulting preoccupation with diagnosis fragmented the disability community by stressing the functional traits that divided them rather than the external obstacles that they faced as a common problem." [11]

In the rehabilitation community, the strictly medical definition came to be superseded by an economic one, which "suggests that a disability can be described as a health-related inability or limitation on the amount or kind of work that can be performed." [12]

A great many of our most important government programs, including Social Security and major rehabilitation legislation of the earlier half of the twentieth century, took the economics-based definition of disability as their primary guiding force. Finally, Hahn notes the emergence of a sociopolitical definition of disability, which "implies that disability stems from a structured social environment to adjust to the needs and aspirations of disabled citizens rather than from the inability of a disabled individual to adapt to the demands of society." [13]

The ADA Definition

The definition of disability as presented in the ADA itself seems simple enough:

> The term disability means with respect to an individual: (a) a physical or mental impairment that substantially limits one or more major

life activities, (b) a record of such impairment, or (c) being regarded as having such an impairment.[14]

As this book goes to press, the issue of definition is receiving a great deal of attention in the news media as a result of one of three Supreme Court decisions handed down in late June, 1999. One of the more controversial cases involves twin sisters who want to pursue careers as pilots with a major national airline. The airline requires of its pilots uncorrected vision of at least 20/100; the plaintiffs, whose corrected visual acuity does not meet the requirement, have tested the legal definition of the law and the Court responded, by a 7–2 margin, with a restrictive view of the term "disability." According to Ohio State University law professor Ruth Colker, "The disabled have been losing more than 90 percent of the employment bias claims they file because they get defined out of the law.... 'Either they say you are so disabled that you do not meet the qualification to work, or if you can work, they say you aren't disabled.'"[15]

It is certainly advisable for librarians, faculty, and administrators in all areas of higher education to be knowledgeable about this and other aspects of disability legislation, but in their day-to-day work, and even with their somewhat defined user base, college and university librarians do not always know if the patron before them is registered for service and has supplied the requisite documentation for such service with the appropriate central office. How can we know if a user qualifies for an accommodation? There are no easy answers, as the details are, and will continue to be, worked out in the courts.

As an example, is an extreme fear of heights considered a disability under the Americans with Disabilities Act? For a person faced with retrieving a book from the stacks of a twelve-storied library with a cavernous atrium, this phobia is indeed a disability in this situation.[16] The requested accommodation is reasonable and appropriate, and one would like to think that it would have been deemed so long before passage of the Americans with Disabilities Act, or any other legislation for that matter.

Disabled Students' Services Campuswide

Probably in response to Section 504 of the Rehabilitation Act of 1973, many, if not most, institutions of higher education have by now undertaken the systematic review of their programs' and facilities' accessibility to persons with disabilities, and have instituted some form of Office for Students with Disabilities. In some instances, an individual in a larger Student Life Department serves as the point of contact for students and other members of the institution's population of persons with disabilities, whereas many larger institutions, both public and private, employ an entire staff of specialists in various disabilities, assistive technologies, and so on.

Most of us probably take for granted that a certain percent of the users of our libraries will be disabled, but this was certainly not the case just a few short decades ago. "One 1962 survey of 92 mid-western colleges and universities noted that 62 institutions would not accept wheel-chair bound students."[17] Summarily rejecting an individual from participation in higher education is now considered a major violation of that individual's civil rights, as a result of the Rehabilitation Act of 1973 and the more recent Americans with Disabilities Act, discussed below and throughout this book in relation to specific disabled populations.

Considerable research on how best to integrate disabled students into higher education was conducted during the 1970s, as colleges and universities struggled to devise ways of meeting their new legal requirements. One such study, conducted in Pennsylvania in the mid-1970s, surveyed the postsecondary educational status of disabled adults state-wide, and found that a full 33 percent attended college, trade, or business school full or part time, and of the 44 percent who never attended, about half expressed a desire to pursue their education.[18] But it is important to note that disability, in the 1970s, meant, for the most part, physical disability, according to Dr. Jack Gentul of New York University. "The campus self-evaluation, a Section 504 requirement, focused almost entirely on physical access to buildings. There was little else we could do for most disability groups."[17] Dr. Gentul goes on to characterize the change in our conception of our responsibility toward the disabled as "protecting students' right to fail as vigorously as we protect their right to succeed. It is far less likely for a student to be guided away from a desired course of study than it was in previous decades. At NYU, this has had the effect of changing not only who studies here, but what they study and how they manage to overcome the obstacles to their desired goals."[20]

Coordinators of Library Service for People with Disabilities

It has been noted that most, if not all, institutions of higher education have an office for students with disabilities. In some instances, this "office" might be a designated person in the Office of Student Affairs or a related division. Whatever the designation, most medium to large public or private institutions of higher education by now should certainly have an office that provides services, advises students on rights and responsibilities, serves as liaison with faculty, and so on.

But what about the library? Those institutions that do not have a designated "point person" to deal with disability-related library issues are probably the exception. For libraries just beginning to address the important issue of inclusion, there are probably many resources right in their own backyard. The college or university's Office of Disabled Students should be contacted because it is most familiar with the demographics of disability and is in the best position to advise on the specific programs, equipment, or materials that should be considered. The School of Education, a department of occupational therapy, community organizations not directly affiliated with the library or university, all might serve as good starting points for librarians in search of information, and expertise in access issues.

The possible accommodations are without limit, but that does not necessarily mean that your library *must* have a full-time professional to deal with what might be a small population, as in the case of a very small liberal arts college library, for example. By now your library should have information on its Web pages, in printed brochures, and so on that identify a contact person and map out the resources disabled users can expect to find in the library. If your campus does not have a great deal to offer in terms of expertise, any number of specialized electronic listservs can put you in touch with the myriad disability groups and professional organizations devoted to serving the disabled community. (See the directory of resources in the last chapter.)

In a later chapter, the issue of training is addressed in considerable detail. Because the field has grown in complexity, and because the population of disabled students is growing steadily, just about everyone who works in the library has some stake in the library's disabled readers' programs and services. In large, complex organizations, individuals must be prepared to take on routine tasks without having to rely on the disabled readers' specialist. The responsibility for training professional and support staff will most likely fall to the library's coordinator of disability services, but it will be time well spent if it results in enhanced service throughout the library.

What should be expected of the library's disabled users' services coordinator? She or he will probably be responsible for some or all of the following:

- selecting specialized equipment and training in its use;
- devising "work around" solutions to inaccessible facilities or services
- providing specialized orientation sessions, probably early in the year or each semester;
- designing and delivering training sessions for professional and support staff members;
- serving on university-wide ADA/504 Committees, if one is in place;
- serving as liaison with the Office of Disabled Students;
- advising on access issues throughout the library;
- advocating the rights of people with disabilities with vendors, electronic materials producers, and distributors.

Legislative Mandates for Inclusion in Higher Education

Several of the authors in the forthcoming chapters state, in various ways, that our efforts to extend our libraries to individuals with disabilities should be driven by other-than-legal mandates. Indeed, libraries' earliest efforts to reach out to individuals with disabilities are almost as old as the profession itself, and certainly predate by decades the several legal directives in place today. Whether we are striving to fulfill the letter or the spirit of disability-related legislation probably depends on whom one is talking to; the frontline public service librarian will most likely have a different take on the matter than the administrator who fears any sort of litigation. These differences notwithstanding, laws are in place and must be addressed in our planning efforts. In the following section, major pieces of national legislation affecting colleges and universities in general, and libraries in particular, are discussed.

Section 504 of the Rehabilitation Act of 1973
Public Law 93-112, Section 504, 29 USC, 794

It is probably safe to say that when the Americans with Disabilities Act was signed into law, most institutions of higher education already had at least some rudimentary access programs and initiatives in place. This is because most colleges and universities are recipients of federal funding and, as such, have been subject to the provisions outlined in Section 504 of the Rehabilitation Act since 1973. Note that "federal financial assistance" is not limited to large government grants but also includes "student financial aid (*Grove City College v. Bell*, 1984) and that receipt of federal monies by any department within a postsecondary institution triggers the accountability of the entire institution under Section 504 (Civil Rights Restoration Act of 1987)."[19]

Section 504 has had far-reaching consequences for persons with disabilities and, in fact, laid the groundwork for the Americans with Disabilities Act that was passed into law almost two decades later. Section 504 is short, and very broad in its mandate:

> No otherwise qualified individual with disabilities in the United States, as defined in section 706 (8) of this title, shall, solely by reason of his or her disability, be excluded from participation in, be denied the benefits of, or be subjected to discrimination under any program or activity receiving Federal financial assistance or under any program or activity conducted by any Executive agency or by the United States Postal Service.[22]

Under Section 504:

> Institutions were given until June 1980 to complete all architectural modifications. The regulations carefully emphasize that recipients are not required to make structural changes to existing facilities where other methods are effective in achieving compliance. As of 1979, 40.7 percent of all available spaces were reported accessible; few library-specific statistics are available, but open-stack reading room spaces in public institutions were reported to be 93.3 percent accessible and the equivalent spaces at private institutions came in at 89.9 percent accessible.[23]

In examining your institution's accessibility, noted expert Salome M. Heyward offers the following pointers:

1. There are very few concrete principles. The question is whether a reasonable person would conclude that unlawful discrimination has occurred.

2. Compromise must be uppermost in one's mind. The rights of the individual must be balanced against the duty to preserve the integrity of the program/service.
3. The spirit of the law must be adhered to, as well as the letter of the law.[24]

Americans with Disabilities Act

As noted earlier, many of our libraries have made significant progress vis-à-vis individuals with disabilities as a result of the requirement set forth in Section 504 of the Rehabilitation Act of 1973. The ADA has added mandates and has extended our responsibility to current and prospective employees (applicants). It also has established deadlines (many of which have passed) for the elimination of particular barriers in both private and public accommodations, including libraries of all sizes and types.

ADA makes extensive reference to a few key concepts that should be understood by all librarians; these include:

READILY ACHIEVABLE

Many access solutions can be achieved without incurring great cost, and in some cases, might not require any expenditure. ADA defines "readily achievable" solutions as "easily accomplished and able to be carried out without much difficulty or expense."[25] In determining whether an action is readily achievable, factors to be considered include:
- the nature and cost of the action needed under this act;
- the overall financial resources of the facility or facilities involved in the action; the number of persons employed at such facility; the effect on expenses and resources, or the impact otherwise of such action upon the operation of the facility;
- the overall financial resources of the covered entity; the overall size of the business of a covered entity with respect to the number of its employees; the number, type, and location of its facilities;
- the type of operation or operations of the covered entity, including the composition, structure, and functions of the workforce of such entity; the geographic separateness, administrative or fiscal relationship of the facility or facilities in question to the covered entity.

What might be considered a readily achievable accommodation for the academic library? Production of information bulletins in large print, using either large-font laser printing or the enlargement option available on most photocopy machines, would represent one such accommodation.

REASONABLE ACCOMMODATION

Depending on your clientele, budget, and other factors, some adaptations and services will invariably be categorized as "reasonable." In the 1970s, when a Kurzweil Reading Machine cost tens of thousands of dollars, many libraries' budgets would certainly have placed such an acquisition in the "unreasonable" category. Today, by contrast, some very good off-the-shelf, large-print software products can be acquired for as little as $ 300—certainly a reasonable purchase price for users with limited vision.

Note that the concept of reasonable accommodation is referred to throughout ADA. In title I, for example, an employment-related reasonable accommodation for a disabled employee might include job reengineering or transfer. Contrary to popular belief, accommodations are very frequently inexpensive and in fact might even incur no cost at all to the institution. In fact, "studies conducted in 1986 and in 1992 showed that more than half of the accommodations made for employees with disabilities cost nothing, while another fifteen percent cost under $500."[26]

Undue Hardship

Libraries and other institutions are required to make accommodations unless they present an undue hardship. Like reasonable accommodation, undue hardship varies greatly from institution to institution. The very small academic library might find the production of braille reading matter to present an undue hardship (i.e., this practice would consume an inordinate amount of the institution's budget).

In a nutshell, the ADA represents a combination of two movements that have evolved simultaneously. The first is the movement to integrate or "mainstream" people with disabilities in educational institutions, employment, and other areas. The second legislative movement to feed into the ADA is the civil rights movement.

It is important to note that the ADA is not affirmative action legislation; rather, it is the equivalent of other legislation that was designed to ban discrimination against individuals based on gender, racial, and ethnic identity. Many public and private institutions, particularly schools and colleges, already had many access programs in place when ADA was signed into law; However, many in the private sector that had not previously been covered under much earlier access legislation had a great deal of catch-up to do in order to become accessible on all levels. Indeed, much of the early press coverage of ADA was cautionary and pessimistic, often focusing on potential lawsuits under the act.

Although it provides some very comprehensive guidelines, the Americans with Disabilities Act is not a document that can be addressed "once and for all." Access issues, and options, evolve continually. Libraries are in a unique position to address this issue and to provide some highly visible leadership to the rest of the academic community.

Specifics of the Americans with Disabilities Act are provided throughout the following chapters. The statute itself, along with many supporting documents and guidelines, can be found on the Web at: The Americans with Disabilities Act Document Center, http://janweb.icdi.wvu.edu/kinder/.

Specific ADA complaints filed against institutions of higher education, along with some secondary interpretation of ADA, can be found at: EASI (Equal Access to Software and Information) http://www.rit.edu/~easi/.

Copyright Law Amendment, 1996
PL 94-197

Prior to the passage of the Copyright Law Amendment (1996), PL94-197, major producers of alternative format materials (braille, audio recording, etc.) were required to obtain permissions from publishers in order to carry out their mission of providing accessible materials to individuals with disabilities. Introduced by Senator John H. Chafee in 1996, PL104-97 provides an exemption for such "authorized entities" as Recording for the Blind and Dyslexic, the National Library Service for the Blind and Physically Handicapped (Library of Congress), and others. Note that "'Authorized entity' means a nonprofit organization or a governmental agency that has a primary mission to provide specialized services relating to training, education, or adaptive reading or information access needs of blind or other persons with disabilities."[27] Most of our own libraries, as nonprofits, are included here alongside the larger producers of alternative format materials.

PL97-197 has had a significant impact on the timely production of alternative format materials for the community of scholars with disabilities. It serves to shorten what was, prior to its enactment, a considerable waiting period before a qualified student was provided with textbooks and other reading matter in braille or audio format.

Professional Library Associations

The ALA continues to address the issue of access to information through several specialized bodies in a number of divisions. In this section, these activities are described in some detail. Note that, beyond the specialized bodies described below, disability has been among the association's priorities in recent years. For example, the recently adopted *Questions and Answers: Access to Electronic Information, Services, and Networks: An Interpretation of the Library Bill of Rights*[28] (adopted June 5, 1997 by the Intellectual Freedom Committee) contains two frequently asked questions of particular relevance:

- Does our library have to make provisions for patrons with disabilities to access electronic information?
Yes. The Americans with Disabilities Act and other federal and state laws forbid providers of public services, whether publicly or privately governed, from discriminating against individuals with disabilities. All library information services, including access electronic information, should be accessible to patrons regardless of disability.

Many methods are available and under development to make electronic information universally accessible, including adaptive devices, software, and human assistance. Libraries must consider such tools in trying to meet the needs of persons with disabilities in the design or provision of electronic information services.

Another point clarified in the FAQ on electronic information involves the sometimes thorny issue of who can have access to certain resources in our libraries. Academic libraries frequently have multiple "classes" of users with varying degrees of access to library resources. For example, faculty and students might have access to LEXIS/NEXIS, whereas Friends of the Library, referrals from other libraries, and other unaffiliated users do not.

• My library recognizes different classes of users. Is this a problem? The mission and objectives of some libraries recognize distinctions among classes of users. For example, academic libraries may have different categories of users (e.g., faculty, students, others). Public libraries may distinguish between residents and nonresidents. School library media centers embrace curricular support as their primary mission; some have further expanded access to their collections. Special libraries vary their access policies depending on their definition of primary clientele. Establishing different levels of users should not automatically assume the need for different levels of access.

What about access to the text-to-speech reading machine? Or the large print Internet terminal? Assuming there is only one of each, we can limit use to our own students, faculty, and staff, according to the FAQ. But should we? These kinds of questions must be answered on an individual basis, of course, and denial of access to, say, a reading machine is a detail that will most likely be worked out in the courts someday. Generally speaking, if a patron has access to your library, even on a temporary basis, it is a good idea to provide the greatest possible level of access.

The following represent just a few of the ALA bodies concerned with disability and libraries:[29]

Americans with Disabilities Act Assembly Committee
Mission: To facilitate communication among ALA units and other groups concerning the Americans with Disabilities Act—the legislation and its regulations; to foster coordination and cooperation of efforts to meet the challenges presented by the ADA legislation and its regulations among ALA units and other groups; to act as a clearinghouse of information concerning ADA issues such as employment and access to programs, services, and facilities for persons with disabilities; to report to and advise the ASCLA/LSSPS Executive Committee, the ASCLA Board, and the ASCLA Office on issues, activities, programs, and materials related to ADA legislation and its regulations, to be shared with all ALA units and other groups.

LIBRARIES SERVING SPECIAL POPULATIONS SECTION (LSSPS)

Mission: To improve the quality of library service for people with special needs, including those who are blind, physically handicapped, deaf, developmentally disabled, impaired elderly, in prisons or in health care facilities, or confined in other types of institutions; to improve library service for their families and professionals working with them; to foster awareness of these populations and their needs in the library community and among the general public. To carry out this charge, the section will provide forums, membership activity groups, and discussion groups to stimulate activities, discuss issues, and exchange ideas concerning high-quality library services for these special populations. The forums will assist libraries in initiating and improving these services, foster library programming, serve as a liaison with other agencies concerned with these populations, encourage instruction in library schools regarding these populations and services, serve as a clearinghouse for ideas and resources, develop standards of service, monitor legislation affecting library services for these populations, and encourage their participation in librarianship and the ALA.

LSSPS FORUMS AND DISCUSSION GROUPS

The following represent just a few of the more specialized forums and discussion groups of interest to academic librarians serving people with disabilities:

Academic Librarians Assisting the Disabled Discussion Groups (ALAD)

Mission: To provide a forum for sharing information and experiences concerning services to users with disabilities in academic libraries; to build an information network among those responsible for providing such services; to encourage their improvement; to promote dialogue between librarians and vendors regarding the needs of users with disabilities; and to increase the awareness and cooperation of all academic librarians in better serving this special population.

Library Service to Developmentally Disabled Activity Group (LSDDP)

Mission: To promote and extend effective library services to developmentally disabled persons at their level of need by sharing information among practitioners currently providing service to this population and by providing information and guidance to those librarians who have unserved or inadequately served populations of developmentally disabled persons in their area.

Library Service to People with Visual or Physical Disabilities Forum (LSPVPDF)

Mission: To extend and improve library service to those unable to read or use standard printed materials because of physical limitations; to provide a symposium for the exchange of ideas and personnel; to acquaint all librarians whose service communities may include blind and physically handicapped readers with a forum and to enlist their cooperation in meeting those objectives.

Library Service to the Deaf Forum

Mission: To promote library and information service to deaf persons by: fostering deaf awareness in the library community and in the deaf and hearing populations at large; monitoring and publicizing legislation and funding developments related to library and information services for deaf persons; encouraging employment and career opportunities for deaf persons in libraries and encouraging their participation in the ALA; stimulating the production, distribution, and collection of materials in formats that are readily accessible to deaf persons and that accurately portray deaf persons; and developing and operating a clearinghouse of information on services for deaf persons to assist libraries in collection development and programming. These functions shall be carried out in cooperation with other ALA units and national organizations, as appropriate.

ROADS TO LEARNING DISABILITIES INITIATIVE

Roads to Learning encourages linkages among libraries, community organizations, and service providers to improve service to learning disabled people, their families, professionals, and other interested people. The initiative's ultimate goal is to bring information about learning disabilities to the general public through libraries while increasing public libraries' capacity to serve their communities in this area.

The initiative is shaped with the help of a National Advisory Board. Members were drawn from both the library and learning disabilities communities. Their expertise ensures accuracy of information and a strong practical base for products and services developed.

Conclusion

As librarians and educators, we are now required by law to provide access to our programs and services to individuals with disabilities. This can seem a formidable task given the endless array of options available for various disability groups. Although much of the remainder of this book deals with the use of technology in academic libraries, technology should be considered only one aspect of the total library access program; a staff with adequate training, a good array of sensible service offerings, and proper orientation to the library might, in the long run, prove more valuable to the disabled library user than all the technology in the world. ▇

Notes

1. National Council on Disability, *Achieving Independence: The Challenge for the 21st Century* (Washington, D.C.: NCD), 13.
2. Margret A. Winzer, *The History of Special Education: From Isolation to Integration* (Washington, D.C.: Gallaudet University Pr., 1993), 39.
3. W.H. Illingworth, *History of the Education of the Blind* (London: Sampson Low, Marston & Co., 1910), 4.

4. U.S. Congress, *Act to Promote the Education of the Blind*, 1879.
5. U.S. Dept. of Health, Education, and Welfare, Education Division, National Center for Education Statistics, *Digest of Education Statistics, 1998* (Washington, D.C.: Government Printing Office, 1998), 67.
6. Winzer, *The History of Special Education*, 228.
7. Ibid., 104.
8. U.S. Dept. of Health, Education, and Welfare, *Digest of Education Statistics, 1998*, 67.
9. President's Commission on Employment of the Handicapped, *The Disabled College Freshman* ERIC, ED199-959 (Washington, D.C.: The Commission, 1979), 5.
10. National Joint Committee on Learning Disabilities. *Learning Disabilities: Issues on Definition.* January, 1990. Available at: http://www.ldonline.org/njcld/defn_91.html.
11. Harlan Hahn, "Toward a Politics of Disability: Definitions, Disciplines, and Policies." *Social Science Journal* 22, No. 4 (Oct. 1985).
12. Ibid., 90.
13. Ibid., 93.
14. PL 101-336, 104 STAT.327, *Americans with Disabilities Act*, Section 3(2).
15. Tony Mauro, "Disabled Issue Troubles Court Justices Try to Decide Who is Protected under Legislation." *USA Today.* Apr. 29, 1999, 3A.
16. NYU's Bobst Library is one such library, and at least one patron has materials retrieved because he has a fear of height.
17. J.L. Angel, Employment Opportunities for the Handicapped (New York: World Trade Academy Pr., 1969). Quoted in Charles Oliver Nale, The Need for University-Provided Services by a Sample of Students with Disabilities at the State-Supported Universities in Pennsylvania." (Ph.D. diss., The American University, 1993), 1. Unpublished.
18. Pennsylvania State Dept. of Education, *A Preliminary Survey of the Postsecondary Educational Status of Physically Disabled Adults*, ERIC Document. ED146-368, Aug. 1977.
19. Personal communication, Dr. Jack Gentul, Director of the Henry and Lucy Moses Center for Students with Disabilities, New York University.
20. Ibid.
21. American Occupational Therapy Association, Inc., *Educating College Students with Disabilities: What Academic and Fieldwork Educators Need to Know* (Bethesda, Md: AOTA, 1997), 1.
22. PL93-112, Rehabilitation Act of 1973, 29 USC, Sec. 794(a).
23. Rolf M. Wulfsberg and Richard J. Petersen, *The Impact of Section 504 of the Rehabilitation Act of 1973 on American Colleges and Universities*, ERIC, ED184-391 (Washington, D.C.: National Center for Education Statistics, 1979), 17.
24. Salome M. Heyward, *Access to Education for the Disabled: A Guide to Compliance with Section 504 of the Rehabilitation Act of 1973* (Jefferson, NC and London: McFarland, 1992), 6.
25. P.L. 101-336, 104 STAT. 327, *Americans With Disabilities Act*, Section 301(9).
26. Barbara A. Lee, "Reasonable Accommodation under the ADA." Available at: http://janweb.icdi.wvu.edu/kinder/pages/reasonable_accommodation.html.

27. PL104-197, *Copyright Law Amendment*, Section 121(c)(1).
28. American Library Association, Intellectual Freedom Committee, *Questions and Answers: Access to Electronic Information, Services, and Networks: An Interpretation of the Library Bill of Rights* (Chicago: ALA, 1997). Available at: http://www.ala.org/alaorg/oif/oif_q&a.html.
29. All mission statements appear in *The ALA Handbook of Organization, 1998-99*.

wayfinding in libraries:

The Importance of Universal Appeal and Universal Access

Susan Gilbert Beck

Introduction

Many statistical pictures describe the substantial life experiences that persons with disabilities long to experience and often reach for without success. For example, it is easy to find several statistics to show the unemployment of those with disabilities—or their success in being employed. But no one, to my knowledge, has done a study and extrapolated the number of people with disabilities who would use libraries by going to the library buildings—if only the buildings were accessible. This latter "accessible" might be qualified in terms of personal privacy in seeking information and finding it (a situation that is universal to those with or without disabilities) or simply in terms of having available accessible ramps, doors, bathrooms, and water fountains.

In today's world of electronic access to information, some people wonder if library buildings are necessary at all. Computer access to information is available from so many places other than libraries, including the comfort of one's own home, if one has the resources to support that access. More and more, people will be looking for full-text access online. Distance education, say some, will allow librarians and other educators to offer bibliographic instruction online. In addition, the large aging population will be less mobile. Using 1986 baseline data, researchers project that there will be a threefold increase (from 5.1 to 14.8–22 million) in the number of Americans with long-term disabilities by the year 2040 when baby boomers reach the age of 85+.[1] That generation was imprinted with finding information in bound books and enjoying their leisure time reading bound books. The electronic world is new, but increasingly familiar to them. Yet, in the year 2040, who knows what *Star Trek*-like technology or formats will allow that population to tie into information. So do we need library buildings at all?

The multiple answers as to why library buildings are needed are as various as the senses and sensibilities of the people who use them. Based in the democratic demands of the diversity of each human being, the answers involve favorite ways of learning, their imprinting, intellect, social need, physical need, and the economy—in other words, universal access. Well-designed libraries ensure better universal access to information for work and leisure. They make technology available to the general population who cannot afford

Thanks to C. Edward Wall, former editor of *Library Hi Tech*; Ken Wachsburger, editor of *Library Hi Tech*; Lee Pastalan of the School of Architecture at the University of Michigan; and Gregg Vanderheiden, Molly Storey, Bill Petersen, and Ron Mace for introducing me to the importance of universal design.

to have it at home. This universal access is often better because it is accompanied by librarians onsite who can guide users through the maze of unknown sources, assistive technologies if they are available, and searching strategies.

True universal access in libraries demands the best universal design. Universal design goes far beyond the minimum specifications and limitations of legislated mandates for accessible and barrier-free facilities.[2] It addresses quite practically the potential needs of all users. The best universal design, to be cost-effective, probably should be included at the blueprint stage of planning a facility. According to Gregg C. Vanderheiden, director of the University of Wisconsin TRACE, universal design has three components:

Universal Design-A benefits all: 100 percent of the population
Universal Design-A.1 benefits all people in all environments.
 Example: IBM ability to adjust the key repeat rate on its computer.
 Example: Door handles rather than door knobs.

Universal Design-A.2 benefits all people in some environments.
 Example: The ability to have a visual indication when sounds signal danger. In noisy areas such as trains or bus stations, for example, this is useful.

Universal Design-B broadens the base: 50 percent of the population will benefit in their lifetimes: 10–15 percent at any one time.
(of people who can use a product directly)
 Example: MouseKeys (using the number pad on the keyboard to control the mouse).
 Example: Dimples on the top of a McDonald's drink lid that indicate diet or regular pop.

Universal Design-C is compatible with assistive technologies: 50 percent of the population will benefit in their lifetimes; 10–15 percent at any one time.
 Example: Touch buttons or touchscreens can be operated with mouthsticks or artificial hands. This would be useful in the operation of kiosks.[3]

Work on easy access to kiosks and touch screens is done at Trace.[4] Not only do the features enable those with disabilities, they are innovations useful, for example, to drivers who cannot reach the screen easily or simply to those who might have forgotten their reading glasses. Screens are operated by dragging a finger in a prescribed direction. Actions desired must be confirmed by operating a green diamond-shaped key. The diamond shape of the key will be patented, says Vanderheiden, so that it may continue as a unique universal indicator.[5] It is useful to those with low vision or blindness. For those who cannot reach the screen, an alternative called Auto Scan also depends on the green diamond button (see figure 1). The items on the screen will be highlighted and/or announced one by one. One presses the green diamond button

Figure I

Accessible Touchscreen Kiosk Trace Center prototype

Introduction

This is a portable touchscreen kiosk which features the following:

- touchscreen;
- stereo sound;
- smart card reader / writer

Traditionally, such kiosks have required the user to be able to see the instructions on screen, to be able to reach and press individual buttons reliably. This prototype features EZ Access™ to provide access to people with disabilities...

Components added to this device for disability access

- EZ Access™ & EZ Access Green Diamond Button™
- Telephone-type handset for listening to voice prompts
- Headphone jack and volume control for listening to voice prompts

Disability groups who can use this device

This device can be used by people who...

- have difficulty seeing
- cannot see
- have difficulty hearing
- cannot hear
- have difficulty reaching, manipulating items or accurately pressing buttons
- have cognitive or language disabilities
- cannot reach the device at all
- cannot see or hear (effectively deaf-blind)

again to activate any item when it is highlighted.[6] The button is cutting-edge technology and one of many applications and ideas presented on TRACE's Web pages. These pages offer a deep view of what exists in assistive and adaptive technologies, an understanding of universal design from the engineer's perspective, and publications to highlight new research.

In an effort to describe the greater depth and breadth of today's user needs in terms of negotiating travel to and within libraries, this chapter reviews the architectural literature from the 1970s through the 1990s that examines wayfinding and universal access. Also, library literature and rehabilitation engineering literature from the 1990s concerning the construction and use of buildings and the existence and development of assistive technology and universal design in terms of service for users is included. Finally, the possible impact of the Americans with Disabilities Act of 1990 on wayfinding is highlighted, with an emphasis on persons with cognitive disabilities as well as those with mobility challenges.

The hypothesis is that public, academic, school, and special librarians have not identified or been able to address the total variation of needs within their service groups, and as a result, they are not serving all of the community. These client needs are seen and unseen, and they are common to users of any type of library. A basic need is that a person be able to find his or her way to the library and then to locate the services inside. Finding an exit easily—especially in an emergency—is important, too. User comfort in wayfinding is examined. Finally, recommendations on how to identify and create better wayfinding conditions in libraries, with the goal of universal access through universal design, are listed.

Background

In recent years, librarians have attempted to identify individual user needs. Librarians in the past have served their communities with people, rather than the storage of books and materials, as their top priority; however, in library and information science literature, user-centered theory is new. It offers a psychological/sociological depth that the practical literature, as late as 1990, fails to touch.

Even the respected *Planning Academic and Research Library Buildings*, published in the 1960s, presents the stereotypical librarian's concern with noise, distractions, and dangers to the collection:

> Library buildings are designed to be used, and use obviously implies traffic. One of the essential characteristics of a functional building is the accessibility of all parts with a minimum of effort and a minimum of disturbance.
>
> If planning is to produce satisfactory traffic patterns, it must take into account problems of supervision and control of the building and its exits, facilities for communication and vertical transporta-

tion, and means of minimizing noise and other distractions. Spatial relationships are also involved.[7]

If food is to be served in the library, the greatest care must be taken to provide for proper housekeeping, as cockroaches and mice tend to appear wherever there are food operations. This is one of the greatest objections to installations of snack bars.[8]

In the same book, however, user needs and behavior are examined in terms of the human condition and services needed. Some needs are recognized based on the past behavior of users:

The simple and successful traffic patterns in the new Olin Library at Cornell are noteworthy, Dr. Stephen A. McCarthy, the Director of Libraries, reports: 'The continuous study of traffic patterns in the Olin Library moved the entrance from the middle of the north side of the building to the west end; and this in turn dictated the location of the graduate study rooms and the conference rooms at the west end. The disposition of many of the facilities in the building flows naturally from the traffic patterns.' It might even be added that this was not an accident.[9]

The text does not identify who the users were who set the traffic patterns, nor does it discuss wanting or needing to attract the library nonuser. The user who, because of age or physical, mental, or emotional disability, encounters difficulties in ordinary transactions in the library is forgotten. This is representative of the difference between the library literature of the 1960s through the 1980s and that of the 1990s, which begins to recognize the population of persons with disabilities. One wonders if the planners thought beyond function to the diverse human being and his or her basic wayfinding needs.

Basic Elements of Wayfinding and Universal Access

Like many human functions, wayfinding requires the processing of information in advance. It is defined as a nonrepetitive, serial task and may be dependent upon several factors:

The age of the way finder, how the person is accustomed to using a building, the layout, whether an emergency exists, and what sorts of finder aids or maps and wall guides or signs are available, etc.[10]

It has been found that the length of time a person spends in a building does not necessarily indicate a total knowledge of its arrangement.[11] Also, often it is less stressful if a person is introduced to only those parts of a building necessary to his or her functioning. This is particularly true for the elderly, people with cognitive disabilities, and young children.[12] Actually, the initial acceptance of a service-based building, such as a library or a nursing home, probably depends in great part on how comfortable and successful users feel traveling through its halls and rooms, using the elevators, or climbing the stairs.

Not surprisingly, the age of the individual affects navigational and adaptive skills. For example, young children and the elderly are more spatially oriented. If they are presented with a model in which buildings are spread out on a field (spatial), and then with one in which the buildings are clustered together (objective) on the same size field, they are likely to choose the former.

A spatial design offers variation; it does not carry the flat characteristics that the objective design of a simple rectangular building does. The latter might have square windows, all the same, marking floors, but no other distinctive characteristics.[13] Spatial designs offer recognizable, unique landmarks. Examples would be a large, open staircase, a rug marking a specific area, or an unusual curve in the building. The spatial arrangement makes the very young and the elderly feel in control of the situation.[14]

On the other hand, people between the ages of seven and seventy seem comfortable with either spatial or objective arrangements. Unlike young children and the very elderly, they tend to feel more in control of their lives, new situations, and the tasks they perform. In fact, they may prefer objective arrangements.[15]

For all ages, visual accessibility enhances proficiency in finding the way. The more a person can see of the building, the easier it is to travel to desired points.[16] For people with blindness, it is knowing the measurements or how many steps it might take to get from one point to another that makes wayfinding possible. For all persons, knowing the shape, the vertical organization, and the horizontal organization of the building's exterior through real examination or through the simulated experience of a model or a film (author's note: for those with blindness, an audiotape) is helpful.[17]

Supporting this belief is Lynch's argument in 1960 that "a strong image of a physical setting may also serve as an organizer of activity and provide the basis for the ordering of knowledge and may help ... to establish an emotionally safe relationship between men and their total environment."[18]

In the interior, visual and nonvisual access is probably enhanced by a simple spatial layout. Such a layout requires less cognitive effort than more complex arrangements,[19] and "cognitive mapping is the basis for deciding upon and implementing any strategy of spatial behavior. The better the cognitive map, the more efficient will be the spatial behavior of the individual."[20] Here Ozel's and Garling, Book, and Lindberg's "spatial" holds a different meaning than the field-dependent indicator; within the context of their article, Garling et al. mean behavior patterns within a space. The idea is that keeping the layout simple will help field-dependent or spatially oriented persons to retain a sense of mastery in the wayfinding situation; field-independent persons (objective) feel they are in control of more complex environments and maintain good self-esteem.[21] None of the studies offer any distinctions of *measurable levels of confidence* that might define and describe the relative amounts of spatial orientation or objective orientation, and considering the 1990s approach to the individual user, such measures must be important.

One wonders, for instance, what spatial situations might cause discomfort for the middle group as they approach field dependency in the built environment. It was noted that people beyond the age of 50 have slower response patterns. The strong emphasis was that the responses were measured quantitatively, not qualitatively. A qualitative observation might have shown that the elderly were more cautious in movement because they knew their limitations based on the aging process.[22] Also, Michael E. Hunt and Leon Pastalan note that a voluntary move to a building by senior citizens, particularly those who are older seniors, makes adjustment easier and survival surer.[23] The right personal choice is the key to comfort. Once again, a certain caution seems instrumental to success. Aging not only slows physical response, it also reduces the ability to hear and see. For the older person, colors are not as visible—because of either the colors themselves or the lighting in the built environment.

Color, although it may be useful in signage, is not recommended as an aid in wayfinding. Even early studies warn against color indicators. Color blindness is one reason not to depend on various hues.[24] Apparently, visually stimulating patterns or colors also can confuse people with low vision or those who have problems with perception and cognition.[25] In addition, green and blue should be avoided for use in public areas because they are not seen easily by aging eyes.[26] So patterns of the building itself, the furniture and accoutrements within, and activity remain the important factors.[27] Nevertheless, in an effort to help users navigate, designers are likely to include signage as part of the pattern. The signage will facilitate navigation from the exterior to the interior of a building and back again. It offers the security of something familiar for all persons: comfortable reassurance through universal recognition.

SIGNAGE

It is generally agreed that buildings designed for service industries, including libraries, should have signs incorporated into their plans. Aaron Cohen and Elaine Cohen indicate that librarians are interested in effective signs because the messages make their work easier. Signs eliminate some of the directional questions that would be asked.

In opposition, architects may not approve of signage:

> Ironically, the people who design library buildings do not seem to understand the librarians' need for good signage systems. Many architects and interior designers seem to feel that a new library should be unencumbered by graphics of any sort. That is why a traveler to

different library facilities across the country may find the most exciting, iconoclastic buildings depending upon small pieces of paper pasted here and there to point out, say, the differences between the 600s and the 800s. Even stacks with beautiful end panels may be ordered without slots to hold identifying numbers—a necessity if there ever was one.[28]

It seems that both professions have support for their stands on using signs or not. In 1981, Bryan discovered that:

Many recent studies reveal people rarely rely on signage for wayfinding in buildings. Way-finding should be supported by other features of the environment. Only seven to eight percent of people reported noticing exit signage during emergency egressing.[29]

There are more subtle signs or cues to say a person is traveling in the right direction.

These other features or patterns should be either sequential or spatial: patterns of activity defined by the location of service desks; items of varying degrees of importance to the person such as favorite spots in the building; or elements bearing visual distinctiveness such as areas holding many green plants or sculpture or an area marked by unique flooring.[30]

If designers include all sensory possibilities, outdoor and indoor paths might be marked by the scent of growing plants and shrubbery. If a library building has ornamental gardens, paths should accommodate wheelchairs or even stretchers.[31] Raised planters allow the elderly and those in wheelchairs to touch and smell flowers. In fact, scent may signal to someone with blindness or someone distracted by a busy world where he or she is on the journey to the library's front door. Different paving materials also offer clues in wayfinding, but one should be careful not to create hazards that will catch wheels or the tip of a cane or a crutch.[32] Finally, where stairs introduce changes in the level of the landscaping, ramps and elevators should be considered and included.[33] Also, places for transfer from a wheelchair or a walker to a seat might be included by incorporating rails into the design. If reading courts are provided outside, benches and chairs should offer a variety of ergonomic comfort, and proper shelter from the elements is a good idea, too.[34]

When libraries incorporate signs in addition to patterns, Jackie Kinder and Catherine Eckman recommend preliminary planning.[35] It is a good idea, they advise, to walk through the building and try to experience it from the user's perspective. Input from staff concerning user behavior is important: What are the general traffic patterns? What directional questions are asked most often? After those basic observations are made, the number and type of signs should be selected with careful attention paid to the size and type of lettering.

Colors chosen are important. In a study reported by Bryan in 1983, more people remembered red lettering on white signs (50.4%) than green lettering on white (30.6%).[36] In a 1990 study reported by Mikellides on twenty-four subjects (who were not identified in any way beyond that), there was no difference in reaction to red and/or blue conditions. Research history on the experiment disclosed that it is not hue but, rather, chromatic strength that affects reactions to colors. More vibrant colors elicit stronger reactions.[37]

Whatever colors and patterns are chosen should coordinate with the library's design and colors, but it should be remembered that persons with vision problems need "a strong contrast between lettering and background—highly reflective lettering on a darker, more absorptive background."[38] Also, a library will want to use universal signs. These are the signs used everywhere in the world, recognizable by all for their simplicity (e.g., a silhouette of a woman in a dress marks the women's bathroom; a wheelchair indicates an accessible ramp). However, although these signs transcend language, graphics alone do not constitute a serviceable sign. Audio and tactile signs should accompany the visual. Beyond the latter criteria, sign messages should be consistent with library handouts. Maps on the wall, for instance, should match handheld maps.[39]

MAPS

Some special attention should be given to wall maps and to the maps that are beginning to appear on the World Wide Web. In a study of hospital mapping, people were asked what they would most likely do if they had to find a place in a complicated building such as a library. They also were asked to rank the order in which they would use three aids to navigation. Seventy-two percent said they would first look at a wall display showing a floor plan. The second choice was to ask someone. Sixty-one percent made the third choice, which was to browse until they saw a relevant sign. In contrast, 74 percent of the subjects preferred handheld maps rather than wall maps for use in places such as exhibitions. Only 34 percent preferred to use handheld maps in a shopping precinct.[40] In any case, visibility, maintenance/costs, and user-friendliness are important. Signs should be visible from the entrance, from a reasonable distance, and from any direction. It is a good idea to have a building cross-section sign visible from the entrance to help orient the user to the building. "You Are Here' signs are helpful. Signs in braille should be included.[41] If these caveats are met, and the spatial/objective approach to design is remembered, the modern libraries should be inviting and usable as well as easy to navigate.

Maps on the Web are useful to those who have computers at home or who may want to travel from a computer or kiosk in one building to use another. Mike Myatt's accessible map at the University of Michigan not only offers locations of buildings, but it also tells which doors are accessible and where one is likely to find an elevator. He was inspired by the maps created at the University of Washington and encouraged by the support of Pam Hamblin and Jim Knox at the University of Michigan. The map began as a team effort, but Myatt, as a student employee, took the major responsibility for the finished product. (See Mike Myatt's case study at the end of this book.)

Given all the foregoing information on design and access, one wonders what the state of library buildings is in 1999. The following section discusses the modern library building and offers some important economic indicators.

The Popular Libraries

Library Journal reports that 81 new library buildings and 116 renovations/additions were completed between July 1, 1997, and June 30, 1998. The dollar figure for this year is down from the previous year, from $662.1 million to $542.8 million.[42] That comparison misses, of course, the comparisons of materials used or size or location. Either figure equals a lot of money. The figures indicate that people feel the need for library buildings in times of distance learning, electronic databases, and electronic text.

The December 1992 and 1993 issues of *Library Journal* showed academic and public library designs of many kinds. In that variation of space and style, a deceptive simplicity was the common theme.[43] In 1998, enormous space and artistic grandeur characterized the mix of objective and spatial styling in buildings. One can return to the buildings, new in 1992 and 1993, to observe that they are the nascent examples for the architectural directions of the 1990s.

Figure 2

Blueprint of the Queens College Library

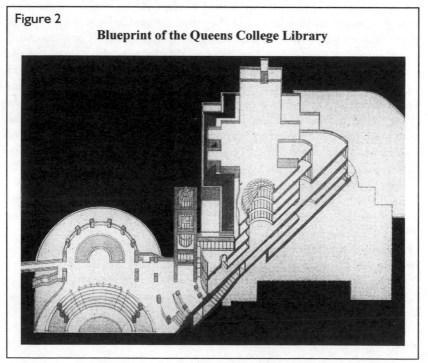

An illustration in point, offered in December 1992, describes the remarkable transition of the "reviled" old library at Queens College. The old library "provided a blueprint for the new one"[44] (see figure 2). The architects, engineers, and librarians learned something about wayfinding from the old, inconvenient library. Together, they asked and addressed the following questions:

- How can we situate the library to emphasize its central role on campus?
- How can a building's layout contribute to a logical presentation of services and collections so that even a first-time user can function effectively?
- How can the library accommodate growing collections and new technologies without having to resort to building additions or electronic retrofitting?[45]

To begin, the architects answered the questions by redefining the library in terms of its placement on the campus:

By making the library the focal point along the central mall of the campus, Peter Samton began the process of establishing the building as the new symbol of Queens College. The triangular library, six stories tall, stands in a commanding position at one corner of the central mall. The library and the landscaping extend and complete the quad and form a new raised semicircular plaza that serves as a climax to the open space and creates a "forecourt" for Rosenthal and the new Science Building that faces it. The Chaney Goodman Schwerner Clock Tower effectively echoes earlier structures on campus and marks the entrance to the Library (see figure 3).[46]

The description of the interior of the library continues the spatial effect (versus the objective) for the wayfinder. Architects provided a strong visual orientation, using glass to expose all levels of the library. Layouts on each level are uniform/ similar so that people need not use maps or directories much at all.[47]

Exterior and interior features of the Queens College Library are

Figure 3
Exterior Shot of the Queens College Library

(Architect: Grunzen-Samton, Architects, Planners and Interior Designers LLP; photographer: Norman McGrath)

readily observable and facilitate wayfinding. Like the libraries granted awards by the Library Administration and Management Association of the American Library Association, this academic library has spatial appeal. The appeal is intrinsic in the variation of the structure. Once again, the award-winning libraries have interior views of high visibility so that users can see where they wish to go.[48]

Another example from the early 1990s, obviously meant to build community involvement and use, was designed for Hanson, Massachusetts. Architects created a combination public library/senior citizens' center (see figure 4). Once again, spatial orientation prevails from the exterior to the interior. Bookshelves are placed around the perimeter of the library (this area on the schematic looks objective but may be altered by plants, the shape of furniture, art of signage). In this way, visibility is increased. If someone stands at the entrance to the library, he or she can see the entrance to the children's room and the circulation desk, spot a friend reading at a table, and see directly back to the historical collection. The senior citizens' center is less of an open arrangement than the library, allowing for the (spatial) comfort of more compact space, as does the historical collection.[49] This was done because the elderly like a smaller amount of personal space; younger people like greater areas of personal space.[50]

While discussing personal space and spatial needs in school libraries offering equal access, Linda Lucas Walling says that students with disabilities like library structures that offer visibility; they feel more comfortable when entering a section if they can see what is happening there.[51] Given the universal design scenario (A.1, according to Vanderheiden's definition and examples), the student with disability(ies) is no different from anyone else; however, wayfinding for those with disabilities demands some unusual accommodations.

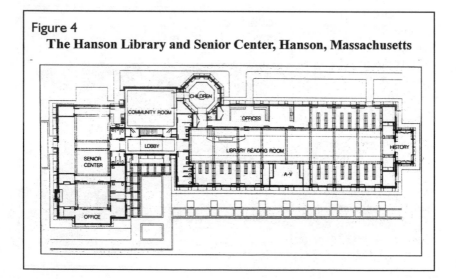

Figure 4
The Hanson Library and Senior Center, Hanson, Massachusetts

Wayfinding from Different Dimensions:
The Wayfinder with One or More Disabilities

Ever since the inception of the Americans with Disabilities Act (ADA) of 1990, service institutions and businesses have been forced to look carefully at the individual client's needs:

> Title III of the ADA extends nondiscrimination policy beyond the employment context to the broader range of building and facility accessibility, thus enabling individuals with disabilities to participate more fully in the mainstream of society with improved physical access to hotels, convention centers, entertainment and sporting events, commercial establishments and other areas.[52]

In a survey done by Susan Gilbert Beck, Rise Smith, and Susan Goodman of Michigan public librarians' reactions to the demands of the ADA, the response indicated that the breadth of the requirements of the act was a worry to many directors in 1992–1993. They wondered where they would find money in their budgets to meet the service needs of people with a wide variety of disabilities. Many turned to consultants for help in deciphering the law and identifying its requirements.[53]

Now it has been eight years since Congress affirmed the ADA. The law remains a worry for library administrators and for the architects who build libraries. It is crucial that both groups be aware of all the components of the ADA. Several agencies have jurisdiction over parts of this civil rights law. The Equal Employment Opportunity Commission handles regulations, technical assistance, and Title I. The department of Justice oversees Titles II and III and can certify that a state or local accessibility code is equivalent to the ADA's requirements for new construction and alterations. The Department of Transportation deals with regulations, technical assistance, and enforcement of transportation requirements under Titles II and III. The Federal Communications Commission presides over Title IV. Finally, the U.S. Architectural and Transportation Barriers Compliance Board, or the Access Board (which is an independent federal agency), reviews the technical design guidelines and offers technical assistance on architectural, transportation, and communications issues.[54]

In the early days of the ADA architects, according to Robert Campbell, were concerned. He says:

> An entirely typical suggestion from the draft guidelines states that architectural barriers that are structural in nature must be removed from existing facilities "when such removal is readily achievable, i.e., easily accomplishable and able to be carried out without much difficulty or expense." Read that carefully three times and then figure out what your precise responsibilities are going to be under the new law.[55]

So it is not surprising that over the years, in an effort to clarify the language of the ADA, several accessibility guidelines have been issued.

The Uniform Federal Accessibility Standards (UFAS) are Issued by the General Service Administration, the U.S. Postal Service, the Department of Defense, and the Department of Housing and Urban Development for the Architectural Barriers Act. UFAS is based on the Minimum Guidelines and Requirements For Accessible Design, which are developed by the Access Board. UFAS is also the minimum standard for the Rehabilitation Act. Within ADA, private and commercial entities must follow the Justice Department's Standards for Accessible Design based on The Access Board's "Americans with Disabilities Act Accessibility Guidelines for Buildings and Facilities" (ADAAG) or a certified equivalent. State and local governments can follow either ADAAG or UFAS. For the "Fair Housing Act," architects can heed the "Fair Housing Act Accessibility Guidelines," issued by HUD, or CABO/ANSI A117.1 as a reference on accessibility. Not surprisingly, a large part of the confusion among architects is the plethora of regulations and guidelines.[56]

It is true that if a library does not comply with the current law, the legal remedies are the same as under Title VII of the Civil Rights Act of 1964:

Individuals may bring private lawsuits to obtain court orders to stop discrimination. Individuals can also file complaints with the U.S. Attorney General, who may file lawsuits to stop discrimination and obtain monetary damages and penalties. It should be noted that, unlike Sections 501 and 503 of the Rehabilitation Act of 1973, the ADA is not an affirmative action statute.[57]

But taking a less legal view of the human condition, as Campbell points out, one of his favorite acronyms is "TAB: Temporarily Able-Bodied. In other words, we are all in this together."[58] Keeping all the intricacy of the law and the vulnerable human condition in mind, "good faith" is an important term in reference to the ADA and its requirements. It means that a library may show that it is offering service to the best of its budgetary and/or resource ability. Indeed, a library may take some simple measures, expensive or not, to help persons with disabilities in wayfinding. Of course, the best possible scenario brings the benefits of universal design to everyone. Then, too, some applications cannot serve at that universal level.

For instance, the Queens College Library offers rampways on two levels and dedicated elevators. (Because this library was so new, one may hope that tactile tape and braille indicators marked the entryways and elevators.) Many users with (remember the effects of spatial and objective designs that would affect all) disabilities may appreciate the visibility offered by the glass enclosures, but other conditions are not so simple.[59-60] For example, the college library was also designed to absorb, distribute, and deflect noises for clients' comfort.

Paradoxes in help and accommodation are common. People wearing hearing aids may or may not benefit from noise control. The hearing aid meets various needs in pitch and volume that may or may not handle all the challenges for that person in specific environments. It is unfortunate, but true, that the needs created by one disability may conflict with those of another.[61] When lights flash more than four times per second, for instance, they may elicit seizures in some people. Yet, for the person with hearing loss, a flashing light may be necessary to warn that he or she should take emergency egress.[62]

RESEARCH AND DEVELOPMENT

Although difficulties created by trying to serve all user needs may seem daunting, remember that research and development for assistive technology have produced some useful wayfinding devices. The Smith Kettelwell Eye Research Institute, for instance, has produced Talking Signs, meant to aid persons with blindness in locating rooms or areas within a building. The person carries a remote control unit that ties into a unit placed on the wall and announces the location as he or she approaches.[63] This kind of unit is listed in the HyperAbleData Web pages under LOVE LIGHTS TALKING SIGNS. Its generic name is Voice Output Sign, Access Sign and the description is as follows:

> The Talking Signs is an access sign and orientation system for the persons with blindness or low vision. It supplies the information contained on printed signs as precisely beamed modulated infra-red transmissions containing recordings of the sign message that is detected and spoken by a receiver carried by the user who could not otherwise read the sign. Transmitters have ranges of a few inches for building directories, transit schedules, etc. to hundreds of feet for street names, transit system facilities, etc. The receivers speak the messages recorded on the signs and inform the user as to the general direction of the sign to enhance navigation. Demonstration versions are in operation on the streets of San Francisco and at the National Rehabilitation Hospital in Washington, D.C. [64]

Another device, in research and development in the mid-1990s, is much like a hearing aid. The aid ties into a satellite and announces the person's position wherever he or she happens to be in the outside world.[65] This kind of wayfinder may eventually eliminate the need for tactile and "voice" signs outside library buildings. Reg Golledge, at UCLA, is working on this project. One can see him with the navigation system at http://www.psych.ucsb.edu/~loomis/nb.html, on a Web page updated in 1998. He walks the campus with a microcomputer, worn in a backpack, that tells him which buildings are to his right, to his left, behind him, and before him. He asks the computer for the information by tilting his head in the appropriate direction and receives a voice response.[66] "The investigators are taking advantage of three advanced technologies in an innovative way," says Michael Oberdorfer, branch chief of the Visual Processing Program at the National Eye Institute, which is funding the research. The principal technologies are global positioning using the military's space-based satellites, a computer-based geographical information system, and a virtual acoustic display.[67]

In further examination of potential needs, it is found that users with perceptual and cognitive disabilities become confused by complexity and need stable, predictable, noncomplex environments. This is, once again, a spatial orientation. For some, wayfinding needs include "multiple coding" to reinforce their senses of orientation and location. For example, they may need to see the International Library symbol, the library's address, and a sign that says "Library" in order to reassure themselves that they have come to the right place.[68]

Another device that architects may use to reduce the complexity of a building is the tracking system. In July 1998, *PR Newswire* carried an article on the Technor tracking system. The system uses a terminal, communication servers, and a remote control system that allows an agency to instantly locate a person or an item. The position of the person or item is shown on a map on a PC. The system might be used, amazingly, from anywhere in the world to lock and unlock doors, to report personal threat, fire, theft, or other disasters.[69]

Imagine, in a future world (perhaps not so far away), the help this might be to persons with blindness, deafness, quadriplegia, or any other challenging physical conditions who wish to examine the contents of the stacks of a large research library with personal freedom. The system, if one imagines far enough, might be centralized at varying levels—from the central security office to the switch on the chair of the person with quadriplegia. Perhaps the automated catalog will have tracking devices that will lead people directly to books and materials misshelved. This latter would certainly be an ultimate condition of universal design. We all look for misshelved items.

Of course, with the advances in technology, users, disabled or not, may stay in their homes to use library databases and reference tools; or they may spend less time at libraries because they can take information home in a usable format. For example, at the Library of Michigan, clients with blindness may download citations in voice form from the library's ANSWER (online catalog) system. Beyond that, a Kurzweil Reader makes all print materials accessible through voice translation.[70] These technical abilities force librarians to think about wayfinding and the education of their patrons in navigation. It is true that when the paradigm changes, reliance on human help seems the first answer for the unusual situation. Although people might appreciate help in finding whether to use the Kurzweil Reader or the automated catalog, the user needing immediate assistance in an emergency might be the crux of public relations for any library.

EMERGENCY EGRESS

Studies show that when an emergency condition exists, evacuees are not likely to use signage. They may move toward a familiar, but not necessarily safe, route; or they may follow someone else, again perhaps a familiar, but not a safe, situation. Prior experience with a similar emergency is helpful in recognizing danger and responding to it in a positive fashion. For instance, in the case of a fire, previous training in the environment may play an important part in recognition and survival.[71]

As a precaution beyond training staff and users in safety practices, library staff and administration should make sure that areas are uncluttered. Furniture should have rounded corners. Glass should be marked so that people do not miss and bump into it.[72] Safety glass is essential. Provided that the way is uncluttered, the blind, the very old, and the very young will most likely follow a particular path or a leader. In the case of fire and smoke, many persons may be blinded and follow a particular path or a leader whether the built environment is complex or simple. Interestingly, in 1980, Canter noted that "some insurance companies give discounts for the simplicity of a layout."[73]

No matter how simple the layout, users will remember complete or incomplete cognitive maps of a building.[74] Not surprisingly, those who have seen models of the interior structure of a building are more likely to have a better concept of exit paths.[75] One hopes that in the case of a library emergency, the staff would be likely to have more complete cognitive maps of the structure; therefore, it is reasonable for the employees to be the wayfinding leaders.

In fact, staff may be viewed as powerful in terms of building usage. Residents of one nursing home were admonished daily by nurses not to use exits with emergency labeling. When a fire occurred, *only six of 100 residents* used the labeled doors.[76] In another nursing home example, a more experienced resident helps people who are suffering emotional bereavement and disorientation or disablement to locate their rooms when he finds them wandering.[77] In an emergency, this person would have the power of previous trust.

In some scenarios, library staff with whom users are familiar would be viewed as having the same strength of power and control. When they are preparing for emergencies, that strength, along with the practical knowledge offered in this chapter, should be uppermost in the minds of the library administrators and staff. If the staff is prepared to be in control, the likelihood of the survival of users and staff in emergencies will be greater.

CONCLUSION

It is clear that the individual library user is cognitively, affectively complex—a potentially stressful condition for the public budget; however, in meeting humanity's general needs, service industries may address many needs of a single entity. It is important to recognize spatial versus objective orientation and the age groups most comfortable with each style. The impact of color and aspects of signage are crucial to ways in which people may use a library. Color may not be seen by some and may confuse others depending on the mix and/ or chromatic strength. Signage is only useful if it can be seen and read or the pictures easily understood. In fact, visibility, the alignment of patterns inside and outside the building, and other objects of demarcation are often likely to help library users find the way more readily than signs. In support of the total service, library staff should stand ready to help patrons find the way if all else fails. Finally, it is important to note the individual differences among all patrons—not only those identified by the Americans with Disabilities Act.

The basic recommendations for highly usable, easily navigable library buildings, designed by architects committed to universal design and access, have evolved from the studies reported here. They are based in the knowledge and information drawn from the background reading and from the experience of the librarian writing this article. Libraries vary widely in structural designs and budgets; therefore, some of these suggestions may be immediately useful and some not, depending on the library and its community. All the suggestions should be goals for every library. They should be observed with the access guidelines published by the U.S. government in mind. Basic ADAAG (Americans with Disabilities Act Access Guidelines) guidelines for libraries follow the summary recommendations below. The complete guidelines are available on the Web at: http://www.access-board.gov/bfdg/bfdg.htm.

Finally, the chapter closes with some very practical advice from the kiosk Web pages at TRACE.[78] It holds the rhythm of human need in poetic suggestion, reminding us all that our own needs are part of that kaleidoscopic challenge that we face in making anything accessible for ourselves and for everyone.

Recommendations for Highly Usable, Easily Navigable Library Buildings

The prospective user population should be surveyed regarding their cognitive, functional/navigational, and intellectual/informational needs.

The library staff and the community should be educated on the importance and convenience of universal design and assistive/adaptive designs.

Universal design applications should be introduced, whenever possible, at the blueprint stage of the building/renovation process.

The exterior and interior of the library should be synchronized for highly visible, spatial, or objective arrangements designed to help individuals find their way to the library and the services inside.

Librarians and architects should tour the library, looking for logical or natural places in which to place location indicators and signage.

Signs should be designed in strongly contrasting colors (not green or blue), with clear, simple graphics and appropriately sized characters. Multiple media signs, including tactile, graphic, print, and audio messages, are important to the function of the blind or the learning-disabled user.

Signs should be placed so that they are visible from as many locations as possible. Day and night lighting should be taken into consideration.

Specific needs of the user with disabilities should be served whenever possible. Staff should be trained in sensitivity and to aid people in a dignified fashion with wayfinding. One author recommends that those with mental disabilities need library staff who have good judgment, tact, poise, initiative, creativity in administrative techniques, emotional stability, and good health. These qualities are listed by the ALA as desirable.[79] Models of the public areas of the building should be available. Some models might be loaned to student groups, agencies, or individuals. Simulated models have been shown to support excellent wayfinding.[80] They are important to introduce new buildings or renovations. Maps on the Web may serve this purpose.

Staff should be trained to offer group and individual tours of the building, either in reality or in helping users to decipher simulated models. For example, in helping a patron with blindness, the staff member would guide the person's hands over the model[81] or assist him or her in finding braille or talking computer access to the online map.

In-house cable television or, in the case of the public library, public cable television may show spots in which directions are given to the library and to the services within the structure. CD-ROM technology may be used to combine motion pictures of the library and its activity patterns linked to library services.

Administrators and staff should keep abreast of as much new technology for universal applications, assistive/adaptive applications, and wayfinding as possible.

Administrators, the library's legal representative, and architects employed must be aware of the laws and changes in laws regarding access for persons with disabilities.

ADAAG (Americans with Disabilities Act Access Guidelines) Guidelines for Libraries (Complete Guidelines Available on the Web: http://www.access-board.gov/bfdg/bfdg.htm)

8. Libraries

8.1 General. In addition to the requirements of section 4, the design of all public areas of a library shall comply with 8, including reading and study areas, stacks, reference rooms, reserve areas, and special facilities or collections.

8.2 Reading and Study Areas. At least 5 percent or a minimum of one of each element of fixed seating, tables, or study carrels shall comply with 4.2 and 4.32. Clearances between fixed accessible tables and between study carrels shall comply with 4.3.

8.3 Check-Out Areas. At least one lane at each check-out area shall comply with 7.2(1). Any traffic control or book security gates or turnstiles shall comply with 4.13.

7.2 Sales and Service Counters, Teller Windows, Information Counters. In areas used for transactions where counters have cash registers and are provided for sales or distribution of goods or services to the public, at least one of each type shall have a portion of the counter which is at least 36 in (915 mm) in length with a maximum height of 36 in (915 mm) above the finished floor. It shall be on an accessible route complying with 4.3. Such counters shall include, but are not limited to, counters in retail stores, and distribution centers. The accessible counters must be dispersed throughout the building or facility. In alterations where it is technically infeasible to provide an accessible counter, an auxiliary counter meeting these requirements may be provided.

8.4 Card Catalogs and Magazine Displays. Minimum clear aisle space at card catalogs and magazine displays shall comply with Fig. 55. Maximum reach height shall comply with 4.2 (see above), with a height of 48 in (1220 mm) preferred irrespective of approach allowed.

8.5 Stacks. Minimum clear aisle width between stacks shall comply with 4.3, with a minimum clear aisle width of 42 in (1065 mm) preferred where possible. Shelf height in stack areas is unrestricted (see Fig. 56).

4.2 Space Allowance and Reach Ranges.

4.2.1* Wheelchair Passage Width. The minimum clear width for single wheelchair passage shall be 32 in (815 mm) at a point and 36 in (915 mm) continuously (see Fig. 1 and 24(e)).

4.2.2 Width for Wheelchair Passing. The minimum width for two wheelchairs to pass is 60 in (1525 mm) (see Fig. 2).

4.2.3* Wheelchair Turning Space. The space required for a wheelchair to make a 180-degree turn is a clear space of 60 in (1525 mm) diameter (see Fig. 3(a)) or a T-shaped space (see Fig. 3(b)).

4.2.4* Clear Floor or Ground Space for Wheelchairs.

4.2.4.1 Size and Approach. The minimum clear floor or ground space required to accommodate a single, stationary wheelchair and occupant is 30 in by 48 in (760 mm by 1220 mm) (see Fig. 4(a)). The minimum clear floor or ground space for wheelchairs may be positioned for forward or parallel approach to an object (see Fig. 4(b) and (c)). Clear floor or ground space for wheelchairs may be part of the knee space required under some objects.

4.2.4.2 Relationship of Maneuvering Clearance to Wheelchair Spaces. One full unobstructed side of the clear floor or ground space for a wheelchair shall adjoin or overlap an accessible route or adjoin another wheelchair clear floor space. If a clear floor space is located in an alcove or otherwise confined on all or part of three sides, additional maneuvering clearances shall be provided as shown in Fig. 4(d) and (e).

4.2.4.3 Surfaces for Wheelchair Spaces. Clear floor or ground spaces for wheelchairs shall comply with 4.5.

4.2.5* Forward Reach. If the clear floor space only allows forward approach to an object, the maximum high forward reach allowed shall be 48 in (1220 mm) (see Fig. 5(a)). The minimum low forward reach is 15 in (380 mm). If the high forward reach is over an obstruction, reach and clearances shall be as shown in Fig. 5(b).

4.2.6* Side Reach. If the clear floor space allows parallel approach by a person in a wheelchair, the maximum high side reach allowed shall be 54 in (1370 mm) and the low side reach shall be no less than 9 in (230 mm) above the floor (Fig. 6(a) and (b)). If the side reach is over an obstruction, the reach and clearances shall be as shown in Fig 6(c).

4.3 Accessible Route.

4.3.1* General. All walks, halls, corridors, aisles, skywalks, tunnels, and other spaces that are part of an accessible route shall comply with 4.3.

4.3.2 Location.
1) At least one accessible route within the boundary of the site shall be provided from public transportation stops, accessible parking, and accessible passenger loading zones, and public streets or sidewalks to the accessible building entrance they serve. The accessible route shall, to the maximum extent feasible, coincide with the route for the general public.
2) At least one accessible route shall connect accessible buildings, facilities, elements, and spaces that are on the same site.
3) At least one accessible route shall connect accessible building or facility entrances with all accessible spaces and elements and with all accessible dwelling units within the building or facility.
4) An accessible route shall connect at least one accessible entrance of each accessible dwelling unit with those exterior and interior spaces and facilities that serve the accessible dwelling unit.

4.3.3 Width. The minimum clear width of an accessible route shall be 36 in (915 mm) except at doors (see 4.13.5 and 4.13.6). If a person in a wheelchair must make a turn around an obstruction, the minimum clear width of the accessible route shall be as shown in Fig. 7(a) and (b).

4.3.4 Passing Space. If an accessible route has less than 60 in (1525 mm) clear width, then passing spaces at least 60 in by 60 in (1525 mm by 1525 mm) shall be located at reasonable intervals not to exceed 200 ft (61 m). A T-intersection of two corridors or walks is an acceptable passing place.

4.3.5 Head Room. Accessible routes shall comply with 4.4.2.

4.3.6 Surface Textures. The surface of an accessible route shall comply with 4.5.

4.3.7 Slope. An accessible route with a running slope greater than 1:20 is a ramp and shall comply with 4.8. Nowhere shall the cross slope of an accessible route exceed 1:50.

4.3.8 Changes in Levels. Changes in levels along an accessible route shall comply with 4.5.2. If an accessible route has changes in level greater than 1/2 in (13 mm), then a curb ramp, ramp, elevator, or platform lift (as permitted in 4.1.3 and 4.1.6) shall be provided that complies with 4.7, 4.8, 4.10, or 4.11, respectively. An accessible route does not include stairs, steps, or escalators

4.3.9 Doors. Doors along an accessible route shall comply with 4.13.

4.3.10* Egress. Accessible routes serving any accessible space or element shall also serve as a means of egress for emergencies or connect to an accessible area of rescue assistance. See definition of "egress, means of" in 3.5.

4.3.11 Areas of Rescue Assistance.

4.3.11.1 Location and Construction. An area of rescue assistance shall be one of the following:
1) A portion of a stairway landing within a smokeproof enclosure (complying with local requirements).
2) A portion of an exterior exit balcony located immediately adjacent to an exit stairway when the balcony complies with local requirements for exterior exit balconies. Openings to the interior of the building located within 20 feet (6 m) of the area of rescue assistance shall be protected with fire assemblies having a three- fourths hour fire protection rating.
3) A portion of a one-hour fire-resistive corridor (complying with local requirements for fire-resistive construction and for openings) located immediately adjacent to an exit enclosure.
4) A vestibule located immediately adjacent to an exit enclosure and constructed to the same fire-resistive standards as required for corridors and openings.

5) A portion of a stairway landing within an exit enclosure which is vented to the exterior and is separated from the interior of the building with not less than one-hour fire-resistive doors.
6) When approved by the appropriate local authority, an area or a room which is separated from other portions of the building by a smoke barrier. Smoke barriers shall have a fire-resistive rating of not less than one hour and shall completely enclose the area or room. Doors in the smoke barrier shall be tight-fitting smoke- and draft-control assemblies having a fire-protection rating of not less than 20 minutes and shall be self-closing or automatic closing. The area or room shall be provided with an exit directly to an exit enclosure. Where the room or area exits into an exit enclosure which is required to be of more than one-hour fire-resistive construction, the room or area shall have the same fire-resistive construction, including the same opening protection, as required for the adjacent exit enclosure.
7) An elevator lobby when elevator shafts and adjacent lobbies are pressurized as required for smokeproof enclosures by local regulations and when complying with requirements herein for size, communication, and signage. Such pressurization system shall be activated by smoke detectors on each floor located in a manner approved by the appropriate local authority. Pressurization equipment and its duct work within the building shall be separated from other portions of the building by a minimum two-hour fire-resistive construction.

4.3.11.2 Size. Each area of rescue assistance shall provide at least two accessible areas each being not less than 30 inches by 48 inches (760 mm by 1220 mm). The area of rescue assistance shall not encroach on any required exit width. The total number of such 30-inch by 48-inch (760 mm by 1220 mm) areas per story shall be not less than one for every 200 persons of calculated occupant load served by the area of rescue assistance.

EXCEPTION: The appropriate local authority may reduce the minimum number of 30-inch by 48-inch (760 mm by 1220 mm) areas to one for each area of rescue assistance on floors where the occupant load is less than 200.

4.3.11.3* Stairway Width. Each stairway adjacent to an area of rescue assistance shall have a minimum clear width of 48 inches between handrails.

4.3.11.4* Two-way Communication. A method of two-way communication, with both visible and audible signals, shall be provided between each area of rescue assistance and the primary entry. The fire department or appropriate local authority may approve a location other than the primary entry.

4.3.11.5 Identification. Each area of rescue assistance shall be identified by a sign which states "AREA OF RESCUE ASSISTANCE" and displays the international symbol of accessibility. The sign shall be illuminated when exit sign illumination is required. Signage shall also be installed at all inaccessible exits and where otherwise necessary to clearly indicate the direction to areas of rescue assistance. In each area of rescue assistance, instructions on the use of the area under emergency conditions shall be posted adjoining the two-way communication system.

4.13 Doors.

4.13.1 General. Doors required to be accessible by 4.1 shall comply with the requirements of 4.13.

4.13.2 Revolving Doors and Turnstiles. Revolving doors or turnstiles shall not be the only means of passage at an accessible entrance or along an accessible route. An accessible gate or door shall be provided adjacent to the turnstile or revolving door and shall be so designed as to facilitate the same use pattern.

4.13.3 Gates. Gates, including ticket gates, shall meet all applicable specifications of 4.13.

4.13.4 Double-Leaf Doorways. If doorways have two independently operated door leaves, then at least one leaf shall meet the specifications in 4.13.5 and 4.13.6. That leaf shall be an active leaf.

4.13.5 Clear Width. Doorways shall have a minimum clear opening of 32 in (815 mm) with the door open 90 degrees, measured between the face of the door and the opposite stop (see Fig. 24(a), (b), (c), and (d)). Openings more than 24 in (610 mm) in depth shall comply with 4.2.1 and 4.3.3 (see Fig. 24(e)).
    EXCEPTION: Doors not requiring full user passage, such as shallow closets, may have the clear opening reduced to 20 in (510 mm) minimum.
4.13.6 Maneuvering Clearances at Doors. Minimum maneuvering clearances at doors that are not automatic or power-assisted shall be as shown in Fig. 25. The floor or ground area within the required clearances shall be level and clear.
    EXCEPTION: Entry doors to acute care hospital bedrooms for in-patients shall be exempted from the requirement for space at the latch side of the door (see dimension "x" in Fig. 25) if the door is at least 44 in (1120 mm) wide.

4.13.7 Two Doors in Series. The minimum space between two hinged or pivoted doors in series shall be 48 in (1220 mm) plus the width of any door swinging into the space. Doors in series shall swing either in the same direction or away from the space between the doors (see Fig. 26).

4.13.8* Thresholds at Doorways. Thresholds at doorways shall not exceed 3/4 in (19 mm) in height for exterior sliding doors or 1/2 in (13 mm) for other types of doors. Raised thresholds and floor level changes at accessible doorways shall be beveled with a slope no greater than 1:2 (see 4.5.2).

4.13.9* Door Hardware. Handles, pulls, latches, locks, and other operating devices on accessible doors shall have a shape that is easy to grasp with one hand and does not require tight grasping, tight pinching, or twisting of the wrist to operate. Lever-operated mechanisms, push-type mechanisms, and U-shaped handles are acceptable designs. When sliding doors are fully open, operating hardware shall be exposed and usable from both sides. Hardware required for accessible door passage shall be mounted no higher than 48 in (1220 mm) above finished floor.

4.13.10* Door Closers. If a door has a closer, then the sweep period of the closer shall be adjusted so that from an open position of 70 degrees, the door will take at least 3 seconds to move to a point 3 in (75 mm) from the latch, measured to the leading edge of the door.

4.13.11* Door Opening Force. The maximum force for pushing or pulling open a door shall be as follows:
1) Fire doors shall have the minimum opening force allowable by the appropriate administrative authority.
2) Other doors.
   a) exterior hinged doors: (Reserved).
   b) interior hinged doors: 5 lbf (22.2N)
   c) sliding or folding doors: 5 lbf (22.2N)

These forces do not apply to the force required to retract latch bolts or disengage other devices that may hold the door in a closed position.

4.13.12* Automatic Doors and Power-Assisted Doors. If an automatic door is used, then it shall comply with ANSI/BHMA A156.10-1985. Slowly opening, low-powered, automatic doors shall comply with ANSI A156.19-1984. Such doors shall not open to back check faster than 3 seconds and shall require no more than 15 lbf (66.6N) to stop door movement. If a power-assisted door is used, its door-opening force shall comply with 4.13.11 and its closing shall conform to the requirements in ANSI A156.19-1984.

Strategies for Addressing Users' Needs
<http://trace.wisc.edu/world/kiosks/itms/needs.html>
If the user cannot see the device, make it *say things* so they can use their ears. If the user cannot understand things that are said by the device, let them change the way it says it.
   CHANGE THE WAY IT SAYS IT.

Change the way it says it.

Change the *WAY* it *says it!*

If the user has difficulty seeing the device, let them *change the way it looks.*

If the user cannot locate the buttons on the device, let them *use a list* with only 3 buttons.

If the user has difficulty hearing the device, let them *change the way it sounds.*

If the user cannot hear the sounds from the device, *show the sounds visually.*

If the user cannot be sure of pressing the right button, allow them to *confirm button presses.*

If the user cannot provide speech input, allow them to *use buttons instead.*

If the user cannot reach or touch the device, let them *give commands by speech.*

If the user can see, but can only use one or two switches for input, let them *step around the buttons using scanning.*

If the user wants to use their own customized type of input and output, let them use *Remote Control.* ■

Notes

1. S.R. Kunkel and R.A. Applebaum (1992), quoted in Michael L. Jones and Jon A. Sanford, "People with Mobility Impairments in the United States Today and in 2010," *Assistive Technology* 8, no. 1 (1996): 51.

2. Ronald L. Mace, "Perspective: Universal Design in Housing," *Assistive Technology*, 10, no. 1 (1998): 21.

3. Gregg C. Vanderheiden, "The ABCs of Universal Design," A Concurrent Session at RESNA '98: Universal Design and Assistive Technology: Different Approaches with Common Goals, June 29, 1998.

4. ———, available at: http://trace.wisc.edu/docs/ez_access_brochures/ezaccess.htm.

5. ———, "The ABCs of Universal Design."

6. ———, at: http://trace.wisc.edu/docz/ez_access_brochures/ezaccess.htm.

7. Keyes D. Metcalf, *Planning Academic and Research Library Buildings* (New York: McGraw Hill, 1965), 75.

8. Ibid., 221.

9. Ibid., 96.

10. Filiz Utsakarci Ozel, "The Computer Model" 'BGRAF:' A Cognitive Approach to Emergency Egress Simulation. (Ph.D. diss., Univ. of Michigan, 1987), 61.

11. Ibid.

12. Michael E. Hunt and Leon Pastalan, "The Relocation of Older People: A Case for Environmental Learning." Unpublished paper.

13. Tommy Garling, Anders Book, and Erik Lindberg, "Spatial Orientation and Wayfinding in the Design Environment: A Conceptual Analysis and Some Suggestion for Postoccupancy Evaluation," *Journal of Architectural and Planning Research*: 3, no. 1 (Feb. 1986); Mardelle McCluskey Shepley, "Age Changes in Spatial and Object Orientation as Measured by Architectural Preference and EFT Visual Performance." (Ph.D. diss., Univ. of Michigan, 1981).

14. Shepley, "Age Changes in Spatial and Object Orientation as Measured by Architectural Preference and EFT Visual Performance."

15. Ibid.
16. Garling, Book, and Lindberg, "Spatial Orientation and Wayfinding in the Designed Environment."
17. Hunt and Pastalan, "The Relocation of Older People."
18. K. Lynch. *Image of the City* (Cambridge, Mass: MIT Pr., 1960), 4.
19. Garling, Book, and Lindberg, "Spatial Orientation and Wayfinding in the Designed Environment."
20. Ozel, "The Computer Model 'BGRAF,'" 54.
21. Ibid., 47–48.
22. Shepley, "Age Changes in Spatial and Object Orientation as Measured by Architectural Preference and EFT Visual Performance."
23. Hunt and Pastalan, "The Relocation of Older People."
24. Metcalf, *Planning Academic and Research Library Buildings.* Ozel, "The Computer Model 'BGRAF,'" 56.
25. Linda Lucas Walling, "Granting Each Equal Access," *School Library Media Quarterly* 20, no. 4 (summer 1992): 219.
26. Leon A. Pastalan, "Designing a Humane Environment for the Frail Elderly," in *Aging in Place: Supporting the Frail Elderly in Residential Environments*, Ed. David Tilson (Glenview, Ill.: Scott, Foresman & Co., 1990), 276.
27. Hunt and Pastalan, "The Relocation of Older People."
28. Aaron Cohen and Elaine Cohen, *Designing and Space Planning for Libraries* (New York: R.R. Bowker Co., 1979), 197.
29. Ozel, "The Computer Model 'BGRAF,'" 56 and 75.
30. Ozel, "The Computer Model 'BGRAF,'" 218.
31. I know of at least one user in Michigan who comes to the library on a stretcher.
32. Thomas D. Davies Jr., and Kim A. Beasley, "Walks," chap. 3 in *Accessible Design for Hospitality: ADA Guidelines for Planning Accessible Hotels, Motels & Other Recreational Facilities* (New York: McGraw-Hill, Inc., 1994), 43.
33. ———, "Recreational Facilities," Chapter 8 in *Accessible Design for Hospitality*, 131.
34. Ibid.
35. Jackie Kinder and Catherine Eckman, "Where Do I Go from Here?" *ACRL News* 54, no. 2 (Feb. 1993): 80.
36. J.L. Bryan. "An Examination and Analysis of the Dynamics of the Human Behavior in the MGM Grand Hotel Fire," National Fire Protection Association N.LS-5, April, 1983, 24.
37. Byron Mikellides, "Color and Physiological Arousal," *Journal of Architectural and Planning Research* 7, no. 1 (spring 1990): 13–19.
38. Pastalan, "Designing a Humane Environment for the Frail Elderly," 276.
39. Jackie Kinder and Catherine Eckman, "Where Do I Go from Here?" 79.
40. Patricia Wright, Audrey J. Hull, and Ann Lickorish, "Navigating in a Hospital Outpatient's Department: The Merits of Maps and Wall Signs," *Journal of Architectural and Planning Research* 1, no. 1 (spring 1993): 76–89.
41. Kinder and Eckman, "Where Do I Go from Here?" 79.
42. Bette-Lee Fox, with Emily J. Jones, "Library Buildings, 1998: Another Year, Another $543 Million," *Library Journal* 123, no. 20 (Dec. 1998): 41.

43. Matthew Simon, "The Popular Library—by Design," *Library Journal* 117, no. 21 (Dec. 1992): 82; Bette-Lee Fox and Corrine O. Nelson, "Library Construction Hits the Ceiling," *Library Journal* 118, no. 2 (Dec. 1993): 53+.
44. Simon, "The Popular Library—by Design," 82.
45. Ibid.
46. Ibid., 83.
47. Ibid., 82–85.
48. Karen Muller, "Temporary Use, Conversion, and Expansion Characterize Building Award Winners," *American Libraries* 24, no. 4 (Apr. 1993): 298–99.
49. "Frame for Reference," *Architectural Record* (Feb. 1993): 78–83.
50. Shepley, "Age Changes in Spatial and Object Orientation as Measured by Architectural Preference and EFT Visual Performance," 18.
51. Walling, "Granting Each Equal Access," 217.
52. Henry Perritt, *Americans with Disabilities Act Handbook,* 2d ed. (New York: John Wiley & Sons, Inc., 1991), 131.
53. Susan Gilbert Beck, Susan Goodman, and Rise Smith, "A Survey on the Americans with Disabilities Act of 1990 and Its Impact on Public Libraries in Michigan" (Ann Arbor, School of Library and Information Studies, Apr. 1993). Unpublished.
54. Nancy Solomon, "Technology: Understanding Accessibility Laws: While the Courts Are Considering the Liability of Architects for ADA Compliance, the Federal Government Is Reviewing and Revising Design Guidelines," *Architectural Record* 186, no. 7 (July 1998): 109.
55. Robert Campbell, "It's Accessible, But Is It Architecture?" *Architectural Record* (Aug. 1991): 42–43.
56. Solomon, "Technology: Understanding Accessibility Laws," 109.
57. Nancy Pack and Donald D. Foos, "Library Compliance with the Americans with Disabilities Act," *RQ* 32, no. 2 (winter 1992): 256.
58. Campbell, "It's Accessible, but Is It Architecture?" 44.
59. Unless the person also has a fear of heights.
60. Simon, "The Popular Library—by Design," 83.
61. Ibid., 84; Walling, "Granting Each Equal Access," 217.
62. Walling, "Granting Each Equal Access," 218.
63. Telephone conversation with Donna Heiner, director of the Living Learning Resources Center, Lansing, Mich., Apr. 28, 1993.
64. http://trace.wisc.edu/conet-bin/xad (site updated 9/97), read 1/16/99. Love Electronics Inc., 395 Vosberg Lane, Goldendale, Wash. 98620-3415. Telephone: 509/ 773-5958.
65. Telephone conversation with Donna Heiner.
66. Roberta L. Klatzky, Reginald G. Golledge, and Jack M. Loomis, "Nonvisual Navigation by Blind and Sighted Assessment of Path Integration Ability," *Journal of Experimental Psychology* 122, no. 73 (Mar. 1993): 91.
67. Available at: <http://www.techreview.com/articles/apr95/TrendsBlind.html>.
68. Walling, "Granting Each Equal Access," 220.
69. "Technor International Inc. Retains Broker Relations Specialists to Inform Wall Street Brokers about Its Digital Cellular Asset Location System," *PR Newswire* (July 15, 1998): 715; CHW004, on the InfoTrac Custom Database, Nov. 5, 1998.

70. Telephone conversation with George Ossentjuk, teacher of the blind and physically handicapped, Kalamazoo Valley Intermediate School District, Kalamazoo, Mich., Apr. 28, 1993. Ossentjuk is a man with blindness who is active on committees at the Library of Michigan and who travels the country offering workshops on the condition of having a disability.

71. Ozel, "The Computer Model 'BGRAF,'" 307.

72. Walling, "Granting Each Equal Access," 220.

73. David Canter, ed., *Fires and Human Behavior* (New York: John Wiley & Sons, 1980), 307.

74. Ozel, "The Computer Model 'BGRAF,'" 61–62.

75. Hunt and Pastalan, "The Relocation of Older People.".

76. Ozel, "The Computer Model 'BGRAF,'" 73.

77. Leon Pastalan and Valerie Polakow, "Life Space over the Life Span," *Journal of Housing for the Elderly* 4, no. 1 (spring 1986): 80.

78. "Strategies for Addressing Users' Needs." Available at: <http://trace.wisc.edu/world/kiosks/itms/needs.html>.

79. Della Pearlman, *No Choice: Library Services for the Mentally Handicapped* (London: The Library Association, 1982), 29.

80. Hunt and Pastalan, "The Relocation of Older People."

81. Ibid.

accessible text formats:

From RFB&D to In-House Production

Steve Noble

Introduction

From the days of the earliest known libraries in ancient Sumer to the present high-tech era, culture has advanced because mankind saw the immense benefit provided by the creation of organized, accessible collections of written documents. And all of the bells and whistles of the modern library notwithstanding, libraries continue to be places where people go primarily to find books or other forms of printed texts. Even the vast majority of information retrievable on the Internet—arguably a true "global library"—exists as virtual words on a page.

One of the fundamental issues that must be addressed in any discussion of accessibility of libraries for individuals with disabilities is just how to ensure that users can access the information contained in the millions of pages of books in the typical library. Some library users lack the ability to hold or turn the pages of books. Others have little or no usable vision, meaning that they may not be able to see the words on the pages even with magnification and high-level lighting. Still other library users have adequate vision but, because of a learning disability, are unable to effectively process information in print formats. The academic library, like other libraries, has a profound obligation, and with the passage of the Americans with Disabilities Act a legal mandate to provide the accommodations necessary to make their holdings—whether traditional print or computerized—accessible to all library users, regardless of the type of disability the individual may have. It is important to remember that a modern campus library with a collection that exceeds one million volumes might have nothing on its shelves for a student with a disability to read if hard-copy print is the only medium available.

To address the issue of access to texts in academic libraries, this chapter surveys common access problems and take a look at solutions that currently exist, before looking at what the future might hold in store. Because adaptive technology is the focus of other chapters of this book, this chapter does not deal with that subject in detail, although these technologies are mentioned where appropriate. The chapter begins by looking at the advantages and disadvantages of various access strategies and accessible text formats. Considerations involved in locating and obtaining text selections from outside suppliers, as well as in-house production, also are explored, and some specific accessible text libraries available to persons with disabilities are surveyed.

Accessible Text Formats

This section discusses the primary accessible text formats: large print, braille, audio recordings, electronic texts, and digital audio. For the sake of completeness and a full comparison, the simplest and most typical access technique—the use of personal readers—will be mentioned as well. It is sometimes difficult to distinguish between access techniques and accessible text formats. For the purposes of this chapter, an *accessible text format* is defined as anything other than standard-size print on paper or other visual medium, and an *access technique* is defined as some secondary accommodation (typically using technological or human intervention) that may be used to transform an inaccessible text format into an accessible one. Generally speaking, however, printed text might be considered an accessible format for the majority of library users who do not have a print-related disability, although such individuals would probably not use an accessible format as it is defined here.

For example, an accessible text format such as braille would not truly be an "inaccessible" format to a sighted person with adequate finger sensitivity and agility because the individual could learn to use braille just as someone who is blind. So whereas braille could theoretically be used by both sighted and nonsighted individuals, printed text is a truly inaccessible format for those without adequate vision. On the other hand, a sound recording of a modern poet reading her own works will be totally useless to a library patron who is deaf, but the printed copy will probably suit his or her needs quite well. So it is important to understand that the description "accessible text format" should be qualified within the context of the user's needs and that the limitations of any one medium to adequately address all disability access concerns should always be taken into consideration.

Personal Readers

The human reader/assistant must be considered in any discussion of access to printed texts. If only as a historical note, we must remember that having someone else read books, journals, and other printed matter aloud was, until quite recently, the only way many people with certain disabilities could access written information. Libraries have traditionally utilized this most basic of accommodations for their patrons with disabilities, although the limitations of this approach are numerous and obvious. In some rare cases, however, it may actually be the preferred accommodation for both user and library staff. For instance, it is an ideal method for handling access to large and seldom used reference works where the occasional user is interested in just a very few definitions or bibliographic citations.

The advantages of the personal reader include the fact that this is a natural accommodation used in everyday life. For example, it is common for a professor to read a short passage from a book to make a certain point during a class session. This is usually done because it is simpler and much more effective than making numerous photocopies of the passage and distributing them to students to read on their own.

Moreover, besides being a natural accommodation, using a personal reader can be very flexible. The reader can zero in on just the paragraph or two the user needs to hear or may be able to compare the definitions for the same word in four different dictionaries within the same short visit to the library. Flexibility is also afforded because this accommodation requires no technology, specialized training, or skills, and can be done utilizing existing staff.

However, the disadvantages of using personal readers are many. Though it may be a natural accommodation and well suited for occasional use, in most cases it is so impractical as to be useless for daily reading. Generally speaking, monographs, journal articles, and even most encyclopedia entries cannot be effectively accessed this way. In addition, individuals with "hidden" print-related disabilities such as dyslexia may naturally feel very uncomfortable asking library staff to read to them. In the case of this disability, a personal reader may often be considered an "unnatural" accommodation.

Also, despite the aforementioned flexibility, depending on personal readers limits an individual's ability to explore a variety of texts and ties his or her library visits to the presence of a second person. And finally, personal readers might work well for quick access to general subject materials, but there are potential problems in having a reader work with highly specialized materials in a field with which he or she is unfamiliar.

LARGE PRINT

From a similar historical standpoint, large- or "enlarged" print text should also be considered in the discussion of accessible text formats. Though large-print has been a viable access medium for about as long as printed texts have been used, the commercial large print book industry did not materialize until around 1965. For individuals who have some degree of usable vision but are unable to utilize standard print even with corrective lenses—often referred to as having "low vision"—large print is often the preferred access medium. Though the defining size of large print seems to be a matter of opinion, standard print is typically 10- or 12-point font, whereas large print is usually 16- or 18- point font. Books in type sizes up to 24 point—often described as super giant print—can be found, although they are scarce. At the 24 point size, a person who has a visual acuity of 20/200 (just at the border of the legal definition of blindness) can still read the text without magnification. As one would expect, the larger the type size, the greater the number of low-vision users who will be able to read the text, but with a corresponding increase in the size and cost of the book.

Large print is alive and well in the publishing industry, although most of the production is geared toward recreational reading rather than academic materials. This is because the greatest number of large-print users are in the 55-year-plus age range, where failing vision is a often a consequence of conditions common to aging. Several commonly used book vendors (such as Baker & Taylor) can supply large-print titles. For titles that are not readily available in large-print format, a library may utilize the services of an after-market printer such as Library Reproduction Service. These printing services can be sent any clean copy of a book for conversion to large print. Large-print copies of the most commonly used reference works would be a good investment for any library. The same can certainly be said for classic literary works. For works anticipated to be used only moderately, it is generally considered more appropriate to use in-house enlarging accommodations, such as enlarging photocopy machines, high-power magnifying equipment, or closed-circuit television (CCTV) readers. Yet another option would be for library patrons to order large-print texts though the National Library Service for the Blind and Physically Handicapped (NLS), providing they qualify for service.[1]

Braille

Braille texts are composed of series of raised dots on heavyweight paper that can be read with the fingers by people who lack sufficient eyesight to work with printed material. Braille is not a language but, rather, functions as a code for reading various languages, mathematical notations, and even music. In each case, however, the code must be deciphered differently by the reader. One major drawback, however, is that standard format braille alone cannot convey organizational cues commonly accomplished in print through the use of spatial changes such as centering, indentation, and varying sections of white space separating printed sections. Nor can braille convey meaningful elements of typography such as bold print or italics. Moreover, it is very difficult to format braille in such a way as to allow the reading of high-level mathematical formulas and may be almost impossible to use for many advanced science and engineering subjects.

Braille is commonly used within the blind and very-low-vision populations, although the level of reading competency among blind adults may vary widely. Individuals experiencing blindness after childhood often do not learn how to use braille successfully. However, braille is the medium of choice for individuals who are deaf-blind. Braille has the distinct advantage of being transportable (although it is much bulkier than standard printed text) and providing independent access for the reader. However, it does require a degree of dexterity and finger sensation, so it may not be ideal or even possible for all blind readers.

Braille books in the United States are published primarily by the American Printing House for the Blind (APH), which also tracks production of braille texts through many smaller publishing sources. Although APH is mandated by federal legislation to provide braille textbooks for children up to the senior year of high school, there is no corresponding mandate to provide college-level texts. However, it is still possible to find a few appropriate reference books at the college level in braille format.

The availability of braille books has always been rather low due to the fact that complete braille texts can be very expensive to produce and very cumbersome for people to carry and handle. With the advent of computer-based optical character recognition (OCR) scanning and conversion software, it is now generally considered more effective for libraries to provide the means to produce in-house braille copies of portions of texts when they are needed. Production of hard-copy braille is not exactly spontaneous however, as braille embossers are notoriously slow—especially the small- and medium-duty embossers typically used in most libraries. The machines are also very loud, which can create other complications in a library or lab setting. Braille users who are fairly computer literate often prefer to use a refreshable braille display to access the electronic text file created in the scanning process, thereby eliminating the need for a hard copy. Refreshable braille, and other access technologies for visually disabled individuals, is reviewed in greater detail in the next chapter.

Audio Recordings

The concept of providing access to printed information through audio technology is not such a new idea. This was clearly in the mind of Thomas Edison from the very inception of his first phonograph machine in 1877. In the patent application, Edison states that his invention could be used to produce "phonograph books that will speak to blind people without effort on their part."[2] This early recording technology proved to be a bit too cumbersome to really expedite text access, but the development of longer-playing records eventually led to the creation of the Talking Book program in 1931 to supplement the Library of Congress braille library.[3] In addition to Talking Books provided through the NLS, the other major producer of audio books is Recording for the Blind & Dyslexic, a national nonprofit organization founded by volunteer readers in 1948. Whereas the NLS primarily produces audio versions of books of fiction, periodicals, and various ephemeral selections, RFB&D primarily records textbooks at all educational levels, as well as major resource works for the postgraduate professional.

Nearly all producers of recorded books have phased out their holdings of slow-speed flexible vinyl discs, as most distribution of recorded books switched to 4-track cassette tapes recorded at 15/16 inches per second in the late 1960s. This new format allowed entire books to be recorded on a modest number of cassettes, actually making the audio version of a book smaller and lighter than the original printed text—a much handier alternative to large and heavy books in braille. Audio books are also cheaper and easier to produce than braille, which has been helpful in trying to fill the "book gap" for readers with print disabilities.

One of the finest qualities of audio recordings as an access medium is the very broad population of individuals who can benefit from them. Other than people who are deaf, just about anyone can use recorded books. Although blind- and low-vision readers have been the traditional users of audio books over the years, people with learning disabilities now make up the bulk of special users of recorded texts. In the case of RFB&D, more than 62 percent of its membership has a learning disability.[4]

Interestingly, the decade of the 1990s has witnessed the rapid growth of the consumer retail audio book market, according to the Audio Publishers Association an increase of 250 percent per year since 1991.[5] Although audio books have not been marketed as aids for individuals with disabilities, the growth of this industry has nonetheless increased the availability of accessible texts by some 75,000 titles. These audio books, which are marketed by firms such as Talking Book World, can usually be bought for a little more than the price of a first-run hard-back book or simply rented by consumers and returned. Audio books produced for the commercial market are distributed on standard two-track stereo cassette tapes or on compact discs, negating the need for specialized players, though many may be severely abridged. Commercially produced audio books have become quite common in public libraries but other than recordings of plays or poetry are generally scarce in the academic library.

Unlike braille, recorded texts require little training to use, other than some initial practice at using a 4-track cassette tape deck. Moreover with the use of optional switching devices, 4-track machines can be modified for use by individuals with moderate to severe mobility impairments. And although taped texts do require tape decks to play them, these machines are fairly inexpensive and very transportable, affording the user the ability to transport and use them in almost any location.

Despite the many benefits of audio books, however, there are some limitations. One fundamental problem with recorded books is that production of the text itself is not spontaneous, and if the book does not already exist in audio form, it may take a significant amount of time to record it. This naturally limits the usefulness of audio texts for research use, particularly in disciplines where currency is important. There are also availability constraints arising from the need to locate readers who have a high degree of familiarity with more complex subject areas.

Another drawback to the audiotaped book is that it cannot be used in all of the ways we traditionally use printed books. For example, it is impossible to "browse" through a conventional analog audio recording in the same way a print user can flip through the pages of a book. Access to the text is basically linear, making it difficult to find a particular section of the text or to jump to a specific page number. The use of beep-tone indexing—a common practice among most major special audio book producers—does aid in locating page breaks and chapter divisions, but this requires readers to listen to long sections of text in the fast-forward search mode until the correct number of tones has passed. Despite these drawbacks, however, recorded texts still represent the greatest number of accessible book titles in the world today, perhaps more than 250,000 volumes of complete texts in English alone, and are relied on by many students and other readers with print-prohibitive disabilities.

ELECTRONIC TEXTS

Electronic text, often simply called e-text, owes its existence to the ability to store and retrieve information via computer technology. Thanks to the parallel development of desktop computers with word-processing capability and sound synthesizers able to mimic the human voice, the "computerized book" has now become an important access medium. Synthetic speech technology has advanced significantly over the past fifteen years, and many speech programs are now available that allow readers to use their own home multimedia computer without additional specialized hardware.

In addition to speech output, computerized texts can be displayed as enlarged type on a screen or output to a printer as a large-print document. And of course, e-text can also be output to a refreshable braille display or run through a braille conversion program to produce hard-copy braille on an embosser. This ability to provide for multiple output methods makes e-text a good access format for individuals who are blind or deaf-blind, as well as those having low vision or mobility impairments. However, e-text is not usually considered a good match for those with dyslexia or learning disabilities because listening to synthetic speech output requires a higher level of concentration than listening to human voice recordings.

In addition to the flexibility of output options afforded by this exciting new medium, e-text allows the user to increase his or her reading rate (up to three times normal speed) and also facilitates quick and precise navigation within the text. Providing that a sufficient amount of structural tagging and formatting has gone into the e-text product, a user can search for specific chapters, pages, subject headings, or key words within the body of the text with a speed and accuracy unparalleled in any other accessible text format now available. Creating an electronic text is much easier than producing a braille or large-print document and, depending on the subject matter and origin of the source file, might even be easier and quicker than producing the text in audiotape format. These qualities are offset by two realities of the medium: to make best use of e-text, the user must have regular access to a computer and at least a moderate level of computer proficiency.

Although many millions of documents across the globe exist in some type of computerized format, the number of full-text monographs available in an accessible electronic environment is comparatively quite low. Part of this is due to the fact that computer technology is relatively new (compared to the other text access forms so far discussed), but much of the problem rests with publishers and other copyright holders who have been very reluctant to make their books available in an electronic form for fear of loss of book revenue through illegal copying. Public domain books, on the other hand, are being made available in ever-growing numbers at several e-text libraries on the Internet.

Not surprisingly, there have been very few suppliers of recently published books in e-text format. The first major attempt to produce e-text books as an alternate access format led to the founding of Computerized Books for the

Blind (CBFB) by George Kerscher in the mid 1980s. CBFB secured copyright clearances from publishers and was allowed to sell electronic books to consumers at about the same price as the published printed book. CBFB eventually merged with Recording for the Blind in 1991, which currently continues to be the major supplier of electronic books under copyright protection.

The time it takes to produce an e-text title can vary substantially depending on the origin of the electronic file and the level of formatting desired in the finished product. Because virtually all publishers now use computerized texts at some point in the printing process, it is reasonable to conclude that all books published in the past few years must exist somewhere in electronic form. However, few publishers are willing to release their files even to an organization such as RFB&D. And even when the file is obtained, a significant amount of editing work still has to be done before a useful e-text copy can be produced. Files obtained from publishers are usually laden with specialized print codes, and files received from different publishers may require very different editing routines to produce the final e-text product. When obtaining the source files is not possible, or utilizing the files obtained is impractical, computerized files can be produced by the use of a scanner and OCR software, or even by simply rekeying the text into a computer.

After a clean copy of the ASCII text file is finally produced, a good bit of work still has to be done to render a high level of utility to the text. The e-text must be formatted to retain structural elements found in the original text, and additional descriptive text must be added wherever graphical material is used in the book. Once complete, e-text files can be placed on floppy disks or transmitted electronically. Due to the ease of copying computer files, e-text titles are generally sold, rather than lent, by RFB&D and other producers.

E-text provides a very effective medium for some books that could not be made easily available or very useful in other formats. Computer hardware and software manuals, lexicons, bibliographies, and dictionaries are just a few of the types of books that make good candidates for e-text format. As an example, an unabridged English dictionary would be all but impossible to use in audiotape format, regardless of how the tapes were arranged or the number of search tones included in the recording. Nor would such a dictionary be practical to use if available in braille. However, if properly formatted, such a dictionary could be very easy to use in e-text form. Indeed, a number of CD-ROM dictionaries and encyclopedias are commercially available for purchase through a variety of publishers, but care must be taken to ensure that these off-the-shelf reference works are compliant with your computer's magnification, speech, and braille output software. However, any e-text title available in ASCII form, should function properly with all computer accessibility programs.

Digital Audio

Digital audio as an access medium is a very recent development, that creates what is in essence a hybrid format of electronic text and audio recording. Although still in the early design stages, RFB&D began developing a digital audio system in 1996. The digital audio system was originally called AudioPlus, but a process is currently in place to rename the product. In the absence of more specific trademark product names, the currently used industrywide terminology for a digital audio text is a Digital Talking Book or DTB. Generally speaking, digital audio links an e-text file with a digitally recorded audio file of a human voice reading the same words, while at the same time allowing for structural navigation throughout the text. In this way, digital audio combines the benefits of audio books using a natural human voice rather than synthetic speech, with the advanced searching and navigation capabilities of e-text. Digital audio books will allow people who cannot effectively read standard books due to a variety of print disabilities to move easily between chapters, sections, subsections, and individual pages just as with standard e-text but will also provide the additional advantages of the human voice—namely, higher clarity and intelligibility coupled with the ability to describe graphical materials found within a printed book. In addition, because digital audio full-text titles will contain e-text, it provides for the same additional output media common to e-text, such as braille printing. It should be noted, however, that many digital talking books will be produced in a structured audio format that does not include the full electronic text. This will be particularly true with literary titles for which e-text may be deemed superfluous. In this case, nonaudio outputs will not be possible, though full structural navigation will remain intact.

With digital audio full-text format the human voice is digitally recorded and stored in a computer audio file. In addition to the audio information, "time-stamp" markers are stored linking specific recorded material to a specific location within the electronic text in much the same way that search tones are placed in taped audio recordings. These time stamps make it possible to know where each page begins or where a new section starts. Although the e-text portion of digital audio books will be produced much the same way as standard e-text (scanning, converting publisher files, or rekeying) these files will then be structured using hypertext mark-up language (HTML), or in the near future in XML (extensible mark-up language). By using a standardized document tag definition (DTD) that is now being developed for digital talking books by the DAISY (Digital Audio Information Systems) Consortium and NISO (National Information Standards Organization), the electronic text can be formatted in such a way as to provide for very powerful search capabilities as well as allowing for the direct linking of the audio files to the correct locations within the electronic text.[6]

Because readers will have the ability to break in and out of their own computer's synthetic speech, digital audio users can hear the correct letter-by-letter spelling of any word in the text. Other functions include the ability to highlight text on the screen as it is being read—possibly a valuable tool for users with learning disabilities. Perhaps one of the most important benefits of digital audio is the ability to have the same descriptive detail provided by human readers currently found only in audiotape recordings. This will ultimately allow access to high-level math and science texts because graphical materials and complex notations will be explained by human readers.

Although this is still a technology in the development stage, RFB&D has plans to begin marketing its CD-ROM format digital audio books within the next few years. These books can be read using a standard multimedia computer and commercially available Web browser software, such as Microsoft's Internet Explorer or Netscape. Besides using digital audio books on a PC, a handheld digital talking book player can also be used. These handheld players will allow structural searching of the text and with some further development will soon have the more powerful full-text searching and synthetic speech available to a PC. Though they will only be available initially as CD-ROM products, books created in this new format could eventually be issued in high-capacity digital video disc (DVD), hard-card memory (as used in the current "flash memory" devices), or simply distributed over the Internet.

Accessible Text Libraries

Although campus libraries have the specific duty of making the books on their shelves accessible to patrons, usually with the help of numerous access technologies, a number of sources of accessible texts are already available to our users. Library staff can serve their disabled patrons well by making them aware of these accessible text libraries and, even better, by facilitating the searching for these texts within your own library through access to the Internet. Although not an exhaustive listing, some of the best sources of accessible texts are discussed here.

THE NATIONAL LIBRARY SERVICE
The National Library Service Library of Congress
Washington, D.C. 20542
E-mail: nls@loc.gov
http://LCWeb.LOC.Gov/nls/nls.html
TEL: 202/ 707-5100
The Library of Congress (LOC) administers a free national library program of large-print, braille, and recorded materials through the National Library Service for the Blind and Physically Handicapped. The NLS selects and produces a number of new books, magazines, and musical scores each year. These materials are circulated through a network of more than a hundred regional and subregional libraries across the United States. Through a special federal appropriation given to the U.S. Postal Service, borrowers are able to receive and return their materials through the mail free of postage requirements.

To be eligible for service through NLS, a person must either be certified as legally blind; have a degree of vision better than that required for the legal definition of blindness, but yet be certified by a competent authority as having a visual or physical disability that would prevent use of standard print; or be certified as having a reading disability sufficient to prevent the normal use of printed texts. In addition, users of the NLS must be American citizens or legal residents of the United States.

The NLS Talking Book program is still very popular among blind readers in particular. The NLS selection criteria focus on titles of broad general appeal including novels and other fictional works, biographies, and self-help and instructional books. About seventy popular magazines are available through free subscription, and many regional libraries produce accessible versions of magazines of local interest. The NLS also provides books on music and musical scores in braille and large print, and some music instructional materials in recorded formats.

In addition to the texts themselves, the NLS lends the specialized players needed to utilize their recordings. Registered NLS patrons can borrow the flexible disc machines that will play the special format 8 rpm and 16 rpm records, and specially equipped cassette decks are available to play the 4-track cassette tapes. Additional ancillary devices are available to individuals who need extra amplification or special switching devices.

For Internet access to NLS, users may connect via Telnet, FTP, or the World Wide Web. For individuals preferring Telnet access, the Library of Congress Information System (LOCIS) can be reached at locis.loc.gov.

The NLS Union Catalog of some 240,000 volumes may be searched from this site by choosing the "Braille and Audio" selection from the main menu. Although this connects directly to a very powerful search engine, the interface is quite complicated and may present quite a challenge to users. For instructions on using this search engine, users are encouraged to acquire the document *Union Catalog Online: SCORPIO Files BPHP and BPHI* which is available from the NLS in print, braille, computer disk, or audiocassette format, or online from the NLS FTP site as ftp.loc.gov/pub/nls/online.search.guide. The FTP site also contains reference documents, newsletters, annual catalogs, bibliographies, and other items under the /pub/nls/ directory.

Individuals with access to the Web will probably prefer this mode of Internet connection, which can be found at http://www.loc.gov/nls. The NLS Web site contains a forms-based search engine which most users will find much easier to use than the Telnet equivalent. The Web site also provides access to numerous helpful documents and links to other important sites.

The American Printing House
The American Printing House for the Blind
1839 Frankfort Avenue
P.O. Box 6085
Louisville, Ky 40206-0085
E-mail: info@aph.org
http://www.aph.org
Tel: 800/223-1839

The American Printing House for the Blind (APH) is the oldest national agency established especially to serve the needs of blind individuals in the United States. As mentioned previously, APH has a legal mandate to provide educational materials for school-age children and provides these materials through appropriate state agencies. APH also manufactures a wide array of special materials, tools, and equipment for use by blind people, and has an ongoing research and development program to design new products.

Located at APH's site on the Web is a catalog of accessible texts called Louis. The Louis database tracks the holdings of some 200 nonprofit and government agencies as well as commercial producers of most forms of accessible texts, including large print, braille, recordings, e-text, and tactile graphics. The Louis database features a high level of bibliographic information for each text and is equipped with a forms-based Web interface that allows easy searching. The database can be accessed at http://www.aph.org.

Recording for the Blind & Dyslexic
Recording for the Blind & Dyslexic
20 Roszel Road
Princeton, N.J. 08540
E-mail: info@rfbd.org
http://www.rfbd.org
Tel: 800/221-4792

For readers who need to use academic textbooks and research literature, the largest producer of educational audio books is the national nonprofit organization Recording for the Blind & Dyslexic. RFB&D was originally founded as Recording for the Blind in 1948 to serve the needs of blinded veterans who had enrolled in college after World War II. In the 1960s, RFB began to broaden its user base to include individuals with other forms of print disabilities, such as dyslexia or mobility impairments, that prevented them from effectively using printed books. In recognition of the fact that the composition of RFB's user base had changed since its inception, RFB changed its name to Recording for the Blind & Dyslexic in 1995. Currently, people with dyslexia make up over 60 percent of RFB&D's consumer population.

RFB&D relies on thousands of volunteer readers, monitors, and e-text editors who work at thirty different studio locations across the United States. Most of RFB&D's texts are available as audio books in 4-track cassette tape format, although about a thousand titles are now available in e-text form. RFB&D functions primarily as a lending audio library for individuals with a documented print disability, and requires both an initial registration fee and a small annual fee to receive member services. Educational establishments may also apply for an annual institutional membership (AIM), which enables them the flexibility of borrowing at different levels based on their students' needs. E-text products cannot be borrowed, however, and are, instead, available for nonprofit sale to consumers. In addition, RFB&D stocks 4-track cassette machines and accessories for nonprofit sale. For additional information on services, consult RFB&D's Web site or use its toll-free phone number.

Recording for the Blind & Dyslexic primarily records textbooks and other books of professional or educational value for kindergarten through postgraduate-level use. E-text books are primarily computer science and reference works. RFB&D's Web site contains an easy-to-use forms-based search engine that lists both the audio and e-text formats available or in progress.

Commercial Vendors

BAKER & TAYLOR
2709 Water Ridge Parkway
Charlotte, N.C. 28217
E-mail: btinfo@baker-taylor.e-mail.com
http://www.baker-taylor.com
Tel: 800/775-1800

LIBRARY REPRODUCTION SERVICE
14214 South Figueroa Street
Los Angeles, Calif. 90061-1034
E-mail: lrsprint@aol.com
http://lrs-largeprint.com
Tel: 800/255-5002
Talking Book World
9496 Magnolia Avenue
Riverside, Calif. 92503
E-mail: information@talkingbooks.com
http://www.talkingbookworld.com
Tel: 800/403-2933

Notes
1. James L. Thomas and Carol H. Thomas, *Library Services for the Handicapped Adult* (Phoenix, Az.: Oryx Pr., 1982), 128.
2. Peter B. Putnam, The Eyes of the Mind (Princeton, N.J.: Recording for the Blind, 1992), 4.
3. Ruth A. Velleman, *Meeting the Needs of People with Disabilities: a Guide for Librarians, Educators, and Other Professionals.* (Phoenix, Az.: Oryx Pr., 1990), 183.

4. John Kelly, Recording for the Blind & Dyslexic: LearningThrough Listening for Half a Century, *Perspectives* 24 , no. 3 (1998): 28.

5. Press release, Southfield, Mich., Talking Book World, Apr. 14, 1997.

6. Library of Congresss, LC Information Bulletin (Washington, D.C.: LOC, 1997), 82–83.

access systems for blind and partially sighted pc users:

An Overview

Dawn M. Suvino and Janice O'Connor

Introduction

Just a few short years ago, when Microsoft Windows began to emerge as the dominant PC operating system, blind and partially sighted users worried that their ability to access standard applications software would be severely compromised. The visual nature of the graphical user interface (GUI) and its seeming reliance on an external pointing device would confront access developers and end users alike with a series of unprecedented operational challenges. During the initial years of Windows popularity, a large number of visually impaired consumers were reluctant to abandon their use of DOS, which had a relatively simple, text-based command-line interface. Indeed, many of the well-known access developers seemed equally reluctant to abandon this familiar environment. Thus, it was not until the Windows revolution was well under way that any reliable access technology was born. Many early releases of Windows-based synthetic speech output and screen-magnification systems were so technically unstable that blind and partially sighted users had little choice but to continue working under DOS.

Now, however, with virtually all the technical problems either solved or on their way to being solved, reliable access to modern PC technology is once again available to all users. Not only are there a number of exciting new access products on the market today but, ironically, Windows's popularity may have actually increased the potential accessibility of most off-the-shelf systems and software. Hardware configurations now regularly include sound cards, high-resolution video adapters, and other multimedia capabilities that facilitate speech output and screen magnification; access systems no longer need to rely on proprietary hardware support. Windows itself contains a set of accessibility options that individual end users can adjust to accommodate various sensory and cognitive disabilities. In some regards, accessibility is more readily attainable today than it was in the pre-Windows computing environment.

This chapter discusses modern trends in technology, defines accessibility with regard to the visually impaired user, and describes methods by which blind and partially sighted individuals interact efficiently with the GUI. By outlining a set of system specifications, training guidelines and staff requirements, the authors hope to provide readers with a prescription for the successful integration of assistive technology in standard academic computing environments.

Historical Overview: From DOS to Windows

The IBM personal computer first appeared in the American marketplace in 1982. By today's standards, it was a slow and inefficient device for which few useful applications had yet been developed. Its "operating system," or the software component responsible for interpreting keyboard commands and processing instructions, was a relatively simple program called DOS.

Written and developed by a then very young Bill Gates, DOS was purely text based and entirely command-line driven. Early versions of the product used no graphics and had no menus or online help facilities. For the average PC user in the 1980s, working under DOS was confusing at best, often frustrating, and sometimes even scary.

But despite its shortcomings with regard to user-friendly features, DOS proved readily accessible to the visually impaired user. From a technical standpoint, the operating system was straightforward and efficient. It was text based and relied on a simple one-to-one numeric code when writing information to the screen; access developers were able to resolve the technical translation process quickly. The first screen-magnification, synthetic speech output, and refreshable braille systems were developed within two years of the PC (see figure 1). And by 1986, any number of sophisticated and reliable access systems were on the market.

Figure 1

Refreshable Braille
ALVA Braille Terminal, by Humanware, Inc., converts computerized text to braille by way of its dynamic strip of tactile "pins."

Throughout the 1980s and into the early 1990s, blind and partially sighted users gained access to virtually all commercial software packages then in popular use. Running under MS DOS, most word-processing, database, spreadsheet management, and telecommunications applications were highly compatible with a variety of access systems. Rapid advances in technology had contributed not only to a growing commercial computer industry but also to the development of new electronic aids for the visually impaired user. By the early 1990s, handheld note takers, stand-alone reading machines, sophisticated CCTV systems, and peripheral devices such as CD-ROM drives, braille embossers, and optical character recognition (OCR) systems were widely available. Again, after the technical issues surrounding PC access were resolved, product developers had no difficulty designing new assistive technologies that could stand alone or interface with standard computer configurations. Unfortunately, however, the key to providing visually impaired users with reliable access to computer technology, the common denominator among access systems, the technical standard of the era, was DOS. As previously described, the simple, text-based nature of this operating system had rendered DOS exceedingly friendly where the technical aspects of synthetic speech output, screen magnification, and refreshable braille were concerned.

Earlier attempts at developing access products for use with Apple computers and the Macintosh operating system had met with limited success due to the complex, graphically oriented nature of the software interface. The IBM PC, on the other hand, relied on an operating system that used no graphics, was command-line oriented, and did not regularly incorporate WYSIWYG (what you see is what you get) features; DOS required all users to function on a purely textual level. Thus, now equipped with an appropriate access system, blind and partially sighted users were able to interact with the operating system and its applications as efficiently as their sighted colleagues did. But DOS would eventually give way to Windows as Microsoft sought to answer user complaints about the cryptic commands, unforgiving syntax, and functional limitations of its operating system.

It is ironic indeed that some of the very elements that had rendered DOS readily accessible to the visually impaired user contributed to its ultimate demise. As a 16-bit, text-based operating system, DOS was severely limited where technical development and end-user support were concerned. Its screen-write method did not facilitate display enhancements. Its command-line interface required users to memorize text strings and specific syntactic structures in order to launch applications and execute system commands. As technology advanced and the PC became increasingly popular, users would first demand a friendlier interface and eventually a more powerful operating system as well.

Early versions of Microsoft Windows attempted to resolve the user-interface difficulties. Running under DOS, Windows 3.X and its antecedents offered PC users a more visually intuitive approach to computing.

Following Macintosh's successful lead, Microsoft designed its own GUI. Icons and menu bars increased visual mnemonics; a Program Manager helped users launch applications and organize files; a mouse was added to the system configuration; and on-line help was easily available. Although the PC and its applications achieved a friendlier "look and feel" with early versions of Windows, the program remained buggy and fairly unstable as long as it ran under DOS. It was not until Microsoft developed Windows into a full-blown operating system in the mid-1990s that the PC was again a stable environment for the average user—and for the visually impaired user in particular.

Although a number of fairly reliable screen-magnification software packages began to appear with early releases of Windows 3.X, the technical complexities involved in producing accurate synthetic speech output under a GUI delayed access to the totally blind user for several years. It was not until Windows 95 was released that stable synthetic speech output systems were again widely available. Similarly, refreshable braille displays did not emerge again as viable output systems for the blind user until the late 1990s. To this day, a "dual-modality" approach with regard to assistive technology remains difficult under Windows. Not all access systems will be fully compatible with one another; many screen readers, for example, will not function properly in tandem with screen-magnification software and refreshable braille displays. So, although it would be erroneous to assert that the visually impaired user cannot easily access modern, graphically oriented software packages, it would be equally false to claim that Windows is fully accessible to all blind and partially sighted user populations. Product developers, assistive technology instructors, technical support personnel, and end users alike should remain cognizant of the limitations inherent in current access systems. Pending the resolution of various technical difficulties, the visually impaired computer user may require some degree of creative instruction and support where access to standard applications is concerned.

Leaving aside the technical immaturity of modern access systems, it is important to recognize that the visually impaired user has not been disenfranchised by the GUI as was earlier predicted. Windows, though highly charged with visual metaphors and graphic design features, is nevertheless conceptually accessible to most blind and partially sighted users. Moreover, it has proven functionally accessible as well, despite its icons, button bars, menus, and mouse. This latter device, often a red herring in discussions of access technology and vision impairment, has in point of fact imposed few functional limitations on the visually impaired user because Windows itself includes keyboard alternatives for virtually all mouse commands. Users can access the desktop icons via shortcut keys, activate menus and make selections using accelerator keys, and execute most frequently used program functions by means of easy-to-remember hotkeys.

Thanks to the so-called Windows Programming Standard, modern PC applications now exhibit a higher degree of consistency than DOS-based applications did; thus, users will have less difficulty memorizing keyboard commands, navigating unfamiliar environments, and learning new programs. Given a reliable access system and the appropriate training, blind and partially sighted users will likely find the GUI an exceedingly friendly environment. And although access developers must continue working to improve their products, blind and partially sighted users should not remain fearful of Windows and its applications. Although the familiar DOS prompt is still and always will be available as an option off the Windows Start Menu, fewer and fewer visually impaired users are compelled to return to it because of the instability and functional inadequacy of their access systems.

Technical Overview: Accessing the GUI

In the preceding section, the term *access system* has been used generically when referring to any software package or hardware device designed for blind and partially sighted users. However, the authors have not defined the term explicitly. What constitutes an access system where the visually impaired computer user is concerned?

Because most blind and partially sighted users will not have any difficulty learning to touch-type, accessing the system keyboard is not generally at issue. And, as explained above, Windows's keyboard alternatives allow users to bypass the mouse. Therefore, input is not a problem. On the other hand, system output is problematic because visually impaired users will have little or no access to the computer screen.

There are three primary screen access methods designed to accommodate the visually impaired user: screen magnification, speech output, and refreshable braille. Screen-magnification programs allow users to change the size and shape of system fonts, enlarge icons, enhance the mouse pointer, and alter screen colors. Modern systems regularly include a secondary speech output feature that augments access for many low-vision users.

Speech output is itself composed of two distinct elements: a hardware synthesizer and a screen-reading program. The screen reader captures information as it is sent to the video display, runs it through a text-to-speech translation process, and then routes it to the synthesizer. The synthesizer then sends it out through an external speaker.

It is worth noting that the GUI has complicated the text-to-speech translation process significantly because text printed on the screen is no longer linked to a simple one-to-one ASCII correspondence but, rather, to an indistinguishable matrix of pixels called a bit map. Modern screen readers must therefore intercept information before it is printed on the screen and store it in a memory construct known as the off-screen model or OSM. The OSM, though designed to simplify the translation process, actually increases the technical complexity of the screen reader. In fact, it is this increased technical complexity that renders Windows-based screen readers somewhat less stable than their DOS-based predecessors.

Refreshable braille systems translate output data into Grade 2 braille and display it dynamically along a 40- to 80-cell external device. Refreshable braille displays, though expensive, are a favored access method among users who like to proofread text and verify document formatting independently. For deaf/blind users, refreshable braille may be the only viable access system. Note that refreshable braille systems do not generate hard copy; braille embossers (discussed below) are used for hard copy production. Refreshable braille, on the other hand, is an interactive output method that allows the blind user to actively review information as it appears on the video display.

Many visually impaired users will benefit from a dual-modality approach to screen access. Two access systems are generally better than one where Windows is concerned. The rich visual imagery of the GUI and overall "busyness" of its screen formats may be difficult for low-vision users to navigate using screen magnification alone. It is perhaps for this reason that virtually all Windows 95/98 screen-magnification software packages now include an optional speech component. Though insufficient to meet the needs of a totally blind user, the screen-reading features of modern magnification products are fairly robust. Most low-vision users will find speech output a practical accompaniment to screen magnification. Learning disabled users, too, will do best with a dual-modality approach; although magnification may not be at issue, programs that enable video enhancements, automatic text scrolling, and speech output can augment computer access for learning disabled users.

Though an expensive access solution, blind users may prefer a speech–braille combination. Speech output, though fast and efficient, is not as intimately interactive as is refreshable braille. Reviewing information aurally may be quick and easy given the power and sophistication of modern screen readers, but many users will benefit from a braille "backup" just the same. Although refreshable braille is a somewhat slow and awkward access method, requiring users to remove their hands from the system keyboard in order to read the display, many users prefer this method when studying text or editing their own work. Most Windows 95 screen readers support the use of a braille display, but some do not. Thus, compatibility is always an issue when purchasing adaptive software. As previously stated, many dedicated screen readers will not function properly in tandem with screen-magnification systems. Users who require equal access via speech and large print may find a stable configuration difficult to attain. But despite their frequent incompatibility with one another, Windows-based access systems are generally less proprietary in design than their DOS-based predecessors were. Modern screen-magnification and screen-reading programs require little or no unusual hardware support. Using less memory and storage space than most Windows applications, they are fully compatible with standard system configurations. Some screen readers are slightly incompatible with a handful of video adapters, but these conflicts may be easily resolved. Because computers are now factory installed with a sound card and speakers, speech output is readily available on virtually any PC.

Because Windows takes a multimedia approach to computing, peripheral devices such as CD-ROM drives and scanners are often included in a standard hardware configuration. Although these devices can be instrumental in helping blind and partially sighted users gain increased access to electronic text and print matter, off-the-shelf CD-ROM products and commercial OCR software packages often prove incompatible with speech output and refreshable braille systems in particular. The low-vision user may have little difficulty adjusting his or her screen-magnification software to function properly in these environments, but the blind user will likely require greater training and support.

Proprietary OCR systems, sometimes called reading machines, are still somewhat more reliable for blind users than their commercial counterparts are. Considerably more expensive than commercial programs, OCR software that has been specifically designed for the blind user is well worth the expenditure. Optical character recognition is a complex process in and of itself; introducing a screen reader into the mix can complicate the process further and result in technical inaccuracy and user frustration. OCR software designed specifically for visually impaired users generally incorporates sophisticated screen-magnification, speech output, and braille translation features directly into the program, offering users a fully integrated, "triple-modality" approach.

Another popular product group that has begun to emerge in the Windows marketplace is voice input. Like the mouse, voice-recognition products are designed to offer users more flexibility with regard to input. And although most blind and partially sighted users will be able to access the system keyboard efficiently, some, of course, will not. Individuals with multiple sensory, cognitive, and neurological disabilities may benefit from a voice input system. Recently, a number of reliable products have appeared in the commercial market; the extent to which they will function properly with screen-magnification and speech output systems is largely dependent upon the processing speed and memory of the computer itself.

Finally, there are a number of peripheral devices and stand-alone systems that will assist blind and partially sighted users in accessing electronic text and/or print matter. As mentioned above, braille embossers, used in conjunction with a Grade 2 translation package, facilitate hard copy production. Like standard ink printers, most braille embossers interface with the PC via a parallel port; indeed, one can use an A/B switchbox to connect both an ink printer and braille embosser to the same PC. In this way, users may select multiple hard copy formats on the fly—standard or large-print, Grade 1 or 2 braille, and depending on the sophistication of the braille translation program itself, raised-line graphics and Nemeth code.

The closed circuit television or CCTV (see figure 2) has been a popular access system among low-vision users for many, many years. More or less mechanical in nature, CCTVs use a high-resolution camera mounted above a moveable X/Y table to project a magnified image of virtually any print document or graphic image onto a video display. Most systems allow users not only to magnify the image but also to adjust color, contrast, and polarity. CCTVs may be purchased as stand-alone units with their own dedicated displays or as peripheral devices designed to interface with the PC monitor. When used in tandem with the PC and a screen-magnification program, modern CCTVs enable split-screen presentations whereby the user can view both the computer applications screen and information placed under the camera simultaneously. This feature is exceedingly useful where copy typing is concerned. Unlike OCR systems, however, CCTVs do not permit users to store data electronically. Information placed under the CCTV camera is neither scanned nor recognized by the computer; rather, it is merely projected onto the screen where the image may be reformatted visually. CCTV technology does have the advantage of allowing users to magnify any and all print matter from handwritten notes to textbooks to newspapers to photographs and maps. OCR systems are considerably less versatile in this respect.

Though perhaps only tangentially related to the current discussion, the portable note taker bears mention. Highly popular among blind users, portable note takers are similar in function to today's electronic organizers and "wizards." Lightweight, handheld devices that store data electronically, some note takers use a standard QWERTY, keyboard whereas others rely on a braille input method. Designed specifically for the visually impaired user, note takers typically do not include a video display; instead, a synthetic speech output system and/or refreshable

Figure 2

CCTV
Optelec's ClearView CCTV is just one of many easy-to-use closed-circuit video enlargement

braille display is employed. In this way, blind users can easily take down class notes, phone numbers, and meeting schedules without recourse to sighted assistance. Moreover, this information may subsequently be transferred to any number of accessible formats. Because virtually all portable note takers are capable of storing data in ASCII format and because they generally include a serial port and/or external disk drive, information may be easily transferred from the note taker to a printer, a braille embosser or a PC.

As technology advances and the computer industry itself continues to expand, access developers will be increasingly able to refine current products and design new ones. Thus, one could predict that many of the stability issues and compatibility conflicts identified above will shortly be resolved. In fact, full-blown accessibility may eventually be integrated into the operating system itself. Remember that Windows already contains a series of accessibility options that can augment access for many low-vision users; Microsoft reports that future releases will include a simple screen reader as well. Called Narrator this feature will provide blind users with access, albeit limited, to any PC "straight out of the box." As the multimedia approach becomes more and more popular, it is likely to engender many such exciting additions to the standard computing environment. One might anticipate voice input and OCR technology eventually being incorporated into the operating system as well. At the moment, however, it is important to recognize that Windows is in fact highly accessible to the visually impaired user. The methods by which blind and partially sighted PC users interact with the GUI may differ from those employed by sighted users, but access to the operating system and its applications has nevertheless been attained.

Establishing Access: System Specifications

In seeking to establish one or more accessible workstations in the academic computing environment, one must consider potential user populations as well as the availability of funds and staff resources. The following sections delineate three distinct levels of accessibility, providing readers with system specifications for what the authors have defined as a basic, mid-level, and high-end configuration. These sections also offer suggestions regarding appropriate staff support for each level of access.

Basic Configuration

Given the power and sophistication of modern hardware configurations, basic access is now readily attained on virtually any off-the-shelf PC. Note that the system specifications outlined below are entirely standard but for the 17-inch monitor and large-print keyboard; however, these devices will not increase system cost significantly. In fact, many manufacturers now regularly include a 17-inch monitor in their standard hardware configuration. Large-print keyboards, sold by most adaptive technology vendors, are generally available for less than $150; alternatively, stick-on key labels may be purchased for under $20. Thus, the hardware requirements defined below will not typically exceed $2,000; indeed, the PC's ever-increasing popularity annually engenders widespread reductions in cost.

- Pentium II processor, minimum 266 MHZ
- minimum 64 MB RAM
- minimum 2 GB hard disk
- CD-ROM drive, sound card, and speakers
- 17-inch SVGA monitor
- mouse
- system keyboard with large print keys
- high-speed modem (This device is, of course, optional but may be required if Internet access is to be offered.)
- Microsoft Windows 95/98 operating system

This basic system configuration will easily support any number of screen-magnification software packages and synthetic speech–based screen readers. Many screen-magnification programs now cost under $500; screen readers range in price from $500 to $900. Thus, full-blown access for both low-vision and totally blind users may be realized for less than $1,500. Remember, though, that the secondary speech functions built into some screen-magnification systems will not be entirely sufficient for all low-vision users. Some users will benefit from a dual-modality approach; therefore, one should investigate potential product incompatibility carefully before purchasing any access systems that are to be used in conjunction with one another.

A stand-alone, black-and-white CCTV also might be included in the basic system configuration. Although this device will not increase PC accessibility, it will augment print access for the low-vision user considerably. A low-end CCTV may be purchased for less than $1,500. Therefore, the overall cost of providing visually impaired users with basic accessibility will be approximately $3,000 above the price of a standard hardware configuration.

Mid-level Configuration

A mid-level hardware configuration will, of course, adhere to the system specifications outlined above but may include increased processing speed, hard-disk capacity, and RAM. The cost of this additional hardware will vary according to the extent to which the configuration is upgraded. Note, however, that none of the access systems described below requires additional hardware support. But because Windows-based applications will always operate more efficiently with increased RAM, you may wish to purchase additional memory if your budget permits. A 20-inch monitor may also be added to the hardware configuration; however, this device will increase system cost substantially. A high-quality 20-inch monitor may easily exceed $1,500. In addition to a screen-magnification software package and screen reader, the mid-level access configuration will include an OCR system. This device will typically cost between $1,800 and $2,200. Low-end voice recognition also may be included, along with simple word predictors and other tools that will assist learning disabled users in accessing PC applications. These packages may increase cost by an additional $250 to $500.

In the mid-level configuration, a color SVGA CCTV may replace the black-and-white, stand-alone unit identified above. A high-quality color CCTV will range in price from $2,800 to $3,200. Most SVGA CCTVs will easily interface with the PC monitor, helping to offset the seemingly prohibitive cost of a 20-inch video display. Discussed in further detail below, training materials and staff who can provide end-user support for the mid-level accessible workstation may contribute to the project's overall cost. But staff and resource development costs aside, the equipment needed to provide visually impaired users with mid-level accessibility will require an additional $5,000 to $7,000 above the basic accessibility configuration described above.

HIGH-END CONFIGURATION

Whereas the mid-level system configuration might engender a hardware upgrade, the high-end accessibility option will necessitate increased processing speed, hard-disk capacity, and RAM. Again, the cost of these hardware upgrades will vary widely from one manufacturer to another but, generally speaking, an additional $1,000 to $2,000 may be required. Indeed, at the high end, facilities may wish to provide multiple workstations, each of which may be outfitted with various access systems. Note that the hardware specifications outlined below will be required to support a full-blown voice input/speech output configuration. If voice input is not at issue, hardware upgrades may not be required.

- Pentium II 366 MHZ
- minimum 128 MB RAM
- 4 to 6 GB hard disk

At the high end of accessibility, a sophisticated voice input system may cost anywhere from $500 to $800 and will likely require a fair bit of system maintenance and user support.

Refreshable braille and hard–copy production also may be added; a refreshable braille display will range in price from $4,500 to $6,500. Grade 2 translation software, used to generate hard copy, will not exceed $300, but a high-quality braille embosser will likely cost upwards of $2,500. Note, too, that braille paper is fairly expensive as well.

To provide low-vision users with unencumbered access to print materials at all times, the authors urge the acquisition of at least one stand-alone CCTV as well as another unit that interfaces with a PC that has itself been installed with screen-magnification software. Two CCTVs, one a low-end, black-and-white, stand-alone unit and the other a high-quality color SVGA device, would cost approximately $4,500. As the access configuration becomes more complex, system maintenance and end-user support will become more costly as well. At this level, at least one full-time staff member who is well versed in all aspects of adaptive technology, hard-copy production, technical troubleshooting, and end-user support should be available at all times. Indeed, the high-end accessibility option essentially describes the development of a full-blown access center. Again, salary requirements aside, an additional $15,000 to $17,000 probably will be needed to purchase the equipment included in the high-end accessibility option.

Maintaining Access: Staffing Considerations

Any discussion of accessibility must include the identification of staff who will be responsible for equipment maintenance and end-user support. This latter function is critical in providing access to new users in particular. The issue of staffing, of course, brings up many questions:

- When will staff be available?
- Who will be involved?
- What level of expertise with adaptive equipment should staff have?
- How will they be trained?
- How much will this impact the budget?

At least one trained staff person should be available during all regular business hours to ensure equal access to the facility for those with disabilities. This does not mean that an expert in all phases of technology must be available at all times but, rather, that someone with the ability to answer basic questions and offer minimal hands-on assistance should be on call whenever the facility is open. This means a sufficient number of staff must be trained to cover all open hours as well as to cover backup situations such as vacations, sick days, and other absences. It is understood that all facilities will not be able to offer full-blown assistance during every hour of operation. Although this situation may not be ideal, it is understandable that specialized services such as braille hard-copy production and sign-language interpretation, for example, may be available on a limited basis. In this circumstance, it is incumbent upon the staff to identify users with unique requirements and to inform them of hours when the service will be available, or to schedule appointments for those services. In the day-to-day operations of an accessible workstation, several levels of staff may be involved. First, someone from the MIS department, or the contractor who maintains your system, must be able to set up specialized system requirements such as menuing options and annotated help files. Access developers can often assist in this process. Be aware, however, that the degree of help available varies widely from company to company.

Second, staff must be trained to maintain system integrity. It has been the authors' experience that in academic computing environments, after the initial hardware and software are purchased and set up, often no one is assigned the day-to-day responsibility for ensuring that the system and its peripherals are operational. At the beginning of each day, the assigned staff member should verify that the adapted workstation is fully functioning and that needed supplies are in place (e.g., printers restocked with paper, ink cartridges changed, fresh batteries installed in low-tech devices, replacement bulbs available for use in CCTVs, etc.). A call for assistance or service should be made as soon as a problem is identified. In addition, this staff member must be responsible for registering all new software, ordering upgrades, and renewing service contracts.

It is essential that more than one staff member be trained to assist patrons in using the accessible workstation. Staff may be trained to offer technical assistance at varying levels, but all staff, regardless of their level of expertise with adaptive technology, should receive sensitivity training where disability is concerned. Such training is generally offered free of charge by local rehabilitation agencies.

Regarding technical expertise, staff should be able to offer assistance on three levels: basic help desk, mid-level support, and high-end support. Note that these levels of end-user support coincide with the three levels of accessibility defined above. Each higher level naturally incorporates those skills offered at the lower levels. All levels presuppose a fairly sophisticated working knowledge of both the operating system and applications in use. The degree of technical support provided vis-à-vis the adaptive configuration will vary according to the degree of system accessibility the facility offers.

Where basic accessibility is offered, staff will have knowledge of the procedures involved in getting the adaptive equipment and its peripherals up and running. Beyond that, staff should be able to answer simple questions by accessing cheat sheets or user manuals and by knowing whom to contact when more complex questions arise. Staff should also have a working knowledge of the low-tech components of the workstation, such as CCTVs and cassette recorders. Mid-level support staff should be able to offer basic orientation and training on the adaptive equipment, helping to get new users up and running. At this level, staff also should be able to do some light troubleshooting, such as adjusting magnification levels or restoring loss of synthetic speech capability. The mid-level person should also be able to produce system support materials such as audiocassette tutorials and reference cards. This individual will also be able to train her or his colleagues in basic help desk techniques.

High-end support should come from a full-time staff person who is trained in all aspects of assistive technology and applications. This staff member should be able to assist users who may have little or no prior experience with PC access. He or she will have expert knowledge of accessible hard-copy production, with an emphasis on Grade 2 braille. Training both end users and other staff will be a major responsibility of this staff member. High-end support staff also should be conversant with Web accessibility issues and potentially with Web site development. Although most access developers provide training manuals with their equipment, these manuals are often difficult for the user to understand. If the staff is like many computer users, a little hands-on training goes a long way. Product vendors usually offer some training free of charge with an initial equipment purchase; staff are well advised to take advantage of any training that may be offered. Should additional training be required, it may be possible to purchase the services of a qualified adaptive technology instructor through a local rehabilitation services agency or from the product vendor. After the initial training group is adept at using the equipment, it will be easy to identify individuals from this group who can train additional staff.

Staffing costs will vary according to the level of support to be provided and how staff time is allocated to other functions. Where only minimal support is involved, staff time, and therefore cost, will also be minimal. Where support levels are higher, a portion of the staff person's day will be allocated to equipment maintenance and end-user support. Therefore, these functions should be specifically identified in the job descriptions of all such staff. At the highest level, the staff person's time may be fully dedicated to maintenance and support of the accessible workstation and its users. Here, salary will be determined by the skill set required of that staff person. Some facilities have successfully used volunteers as support staff. Rochelle Wyatt and Charles Hamilton of the Washington Library for the Blind and Physically Handicapped used volunteers as technology mentors for an accessible CD-ROM workstation.[1] The volunteers were required to have experience with IBM-compatible computers and were asked to commit to at least one four-hour shift per week for six months. They assisted with CD-ROM searches and information reproduction, trained patrons in the uses of the station, and recorded comments and suggestions. In academic and research communities, qualified volunteers could certainly fill at least the basic and mid-level support positions, strengthen the program, and keep staffing costs to a minimum.

A Note about Users with Learning Disabilities

This chapter would not be complete without mention of print access for people with learning disabilities. The means to accessibility are as rich and varied for those with learning disabilities as they are for those with visual impairments. And, indeed, there is an intersection of access systems as well. Many of the devices used by blind and partially sighted users, in particular, will also be applicable to those with learning disabilities. Of course, at the lowest (and least expensive) level of access to print, it is always possible to begin with audiotaped books, many of which are available free through local or regional libraries. Special recorders to play these tapes are also available at no charge. Textbooks can be taped, often free of charge or for a nominal fee, at various locations throughout the country. Synthetic speech is a gold mine for this group as well, because they will frequently do better with aural rather than visual information processing. In selecting equipment that will be useful to those with learning disabilities, it is important to identify reading machines and OCR programs that offer word-by-word reading, speed control, and/or highlighting of words as they are read. Reading machine manufacturers continue to move forward in offering equipment that "does it all." Today's reading machines can move throughout a publication easily, reading headlines and captions separately from text, jumping from column to column to maintain the integrity of an article, and offering features such as dictionary definitions, editing, and selective printing of information. A wealth of information on assistive technology and learning disabilities is available on the Internet, and we refer readers to the selective list of resources at the end of this book. ■

Notes

1. Rochelle Wyatt and Charles Hamilton, "Building an Accessible CD-ROM Reference Station," *Information Technology and Disabilities* 1, no. 1 (Jan., 1994). Also available at: http://www.rit.edu/~easi/itd/itdv01n1/contents.html.

services for patrons with hearing loss or deafness:

New Technologies/New Attitudes

Susan Gilbert Beck

Introduction

Create a picture in your mind. Envision a panel of five persons with deafness or hearing loss signing to an interpreter who is sitting with her back to a class of nineteen people. The interpreter is talking to the panel with her hands and all the while vocalizing what her hands are saying for the benefit of the hearing audience of nineteen. She is also signing the audience's questions for the benefit of the panel. Observe the laptop note taker sitting behind the panel, fingers moving quickly over the keyboard, transcribing all that is said onto a large-screen monitor so that people who might not hear or be able to see the signer may read the conversation.

That is what happened when, in the summer of 1998, intern student visitors from the Kresge Institute for Hearing Loss visited the University of Michigan's (UM) School of Information Course 605. SI605 was a toolkit, or short course, that addressed assistive/adaptive technologies, access to information for persons with disabilities, and policy-making issues.

Until that remarkable meeting for all of the class members, to be deaf meant that a certain sameness of personal approach prevailed. The five young people in their twenties who comprised the panel made it clear that nothing could be further from the truth. Just by their personal descriptions, they were obviously different from each other.

Melissa Herzig, a recent graduate of Gallaudet, comes from an immediate family in which sign language is the first language used for communication. She had her hearing loss/deafness at birth and has always attended schools for the deaf.

Sindile Kevin Mhlanga, from the Rochester Institute of Technology (RIT), is from Zimbabwe. He lost his hearing at age 12 when he contracted meningitis. Kevin, a System Tester for the XEROX Corporation, hopes to pursue graduate studies in special education.

Dawn Denny, a junior in biomedical computing from RIT, is from the United States. She went deaf slowly and says, with humor, that her family forgets that she is without hearing. They still expect that she will hear things

The author would like to thank Debbie Passalacqua of the North Regional/BCC Library in Coconut Creek, Florida, whose LSCA-supported program serves people with disabilities. Debbie provided the library's brochure of equipment, which proved most useful as an overview of equipment available; Tom McNulty, the very patient editor of this volume; and Ed Wall, editor of *Library Hi Tech*, for his support.

she cannot. Dawn wears bilateral hearing aids, although she is not fond of them. She lip-reads well, a skill that allows her to take off her aids when she is in the company of familiar people.

Respicius (Res) Batamula, from Gallaudet, does not know what caused his hearing loss. His family, in Tanzania, thought he was being disobedient during his teen years before they realized he had lost his hearing. The only panel member who has worked in a library, Res is interested in working in the field of distance learning.

Jimmie Dixon, from the United States, is a recent graduate of Gallaudet. Like Dawn, he wears hearing aids. Jimmie attends the University of Michigan as an undergraduate special student where he takes a few advanced science classes in preparation for graduate school.

All of the panelists sign, but Melissa, who has done it from birth, is the most proficient and graceful. The other four panel members admire her skill as a native signer. With the exception of Sindile Kevin, all of the panelists have voices of varying strength.

The students were on the UM campus for the summer to work on research projects at the Kresge Institute for the Deaf. Jimmie, for example, created a 3-D model of part of the ear to be made accessible via the Web. The other panel members were working with recording data on projects.

When asked about "deaf culture," the panelists protested, stating essentially that each of them is different from the other. They would like to be recognized for the people they are rather than for the culture by which they are sometimes defined. This statement from the five astonished the class, who had previously maintained stereotypical views of a closed deaf community.

Certainly, the five personalities are neither closed nor the same. Each vibrant member of the panel captured the interest of the class because of his or her unique, friendly persona. When the ninety-plus minutes of the panel were over, the class enthusiastically asked the panel members to leave their e-mail addresses, and some have maintained contact into the fall. They are delighted to talk about all aspects of hearing loss and their personal observations and experiences.[1]

At the end of the panel discussion, the nationally certified interpreter, Paula Berwanger, and the laptop note taker, Martha Chen, who did fantastic jobs of facilitating communication, were visibly tired. Both had an obvious need for a break but continued to work throughout the energetic discussion that ensued. This provided a valuable lesson on the etiquette of deaf communication for the moderator (author of this chapter) and for the class; we came away with an understanding of why UM classes are usually team interpreted.

The university is prepared to provide two interpreters but, according to Joni Smith, the UM interpreter, "often, people get upset when we recommend two interpreters."[2] Possibly, those who are bothered by the idea of two interpreters fear that momentum will be lost or that the quality of interpretation will change noticeably. From the interpreter's or note taker's view, it is difficult to interpret or to take notes for periods of time exceeding twenty minutes without becoming exhausted. Interpreting calls on the total person; it demands skills in language, knowledge on a broad scale, and physical endurance, and it spends emotion.

A gratifying note came from the session. For students learning how to find, promote, and share information using assistive technology, the panel discussion emphasized one very important fact: students with deafness or who are hard of hearing feel, in general, that library services are and have been good. Computers make collections and information easy to access. The one-on-one human service is somewhat unique in the education process. Professionals in the information field are friendly and helpful to students. (Perhaps one thing to remember is that the panel members are excellent communicators, regardless of the medium, and this probably has an affect on their experiences in the library.) The students emphasized the importance of friendly communication in the business and education worlds from librarians and information specialists. One wonders if deaf library users in nonacademic settings feel as positively about libraries and library service. [3]

Historical Perspective

Since 1990, with the advent of the Americans with Disabilities Act (ADA), librarians' awareness of services and technology for deaf or hard-of-hearing library users has grown significantly. The growing number of deaf users makes it important for library staff members to understand the disability. Telecommunication devices for the deaf (TDDs and TTYs) and assistive listening devices (ALDs) are evolving at a fast rate. Emerging technologies, as this chapter shows, will become increasingly sophisticated and provide greater value-added features.

Approximately 22 million people comprise the population with hearing loss in the United States.[4,5] Of these, two million cannot understand speech or hear at all; others are hearing impaired, or hard of hearing.

> Research has shown that at least ten million Americans suffer from noise-induced hearing loss. Irreversible damage may be caused by an isolated gunshot or by exposure to sounds above 85 decibels, the level of noise generated by a typical lawnmower. Though such hearing loss is preventable, appropriate research has been underfunded and legislation poorly enforced.[6]

In the realm of library service, this information is important because the ADA demands that a reasonable effort be made to serve all users with disabilities. Certainly, as the baby boomer generation ages, it is likely that the deaf and hard-of-hearing population will grow exponentially, and so will the need for library and information services using appropriate technologies and other means of communication. Note also that in 1999, it is inappropriate, or politically incorrect, to assume and say that people "suffer" from a hearing loss.

For the population with hearing loss, the challenge to demand the library service to which they are legally entitled holds at least two age-old obstacles:

- Hearing loss is the unseen disability, an invisible barrier to communication.[7] There are no white canes, no Seeing Eye dogs,[8] no wheelchairs, or sometimes, perhaps, no hearing aids.[9]
- Deaf persons seeking information and library services come from diverse backgrounds, which lead to differing modes of communication. If a person is deaf from birth or before speech skills are learned, the difficulty in communication may be greater than that experienced by someone postlingual who lost hearing after speech skills were attained.

Naturally, people learn to speak by hearing and imitating others. So, although American Sign Language is widely accepted in the United States, it is only one of many sign and body languages used by people with deafness. Sign language has its own Tower of Babel. Further, it is often the first language for someone hearing disabled, whereas written/spoken fluency is second or nearly nonexistent.

Because competent communication is basic to adequate library service, librarians and other information professionals should be aware of, if not accomplished at, all possible methods of interacting with deaf users. Other methods besides signing include writing, finger spelling, speech and lip-reading, Tadoma for the blind, cued speech, gestures, taction (touch) and kinesthesis (body movement), interpreters (sign language or oral), computer-assisted note taking (CAN), real-time captioning, devices to enhance listening in rooms and other large group facilities, alerting systems (flashers), telecaption systems, various methods of using the telephone (computer bulletin boards, relay services, text telephones), and finally hearing ear dogs.[10] Many of the latter technologies have been around for many years, but there are newer technologies in the research and development stage that hold great promise in the areas of signing and telecommunications. So far, none of these technologies is specifically directed to library and information tasks; however, the general technology meant to meet the needs of those with hearing loss is of obvious benefit in the library setting.

In order to fulfill their role and responsibility to provide information to their deaf patrons, librarians face three basic challenges:

- They must be knowledgeable about available technology, or at least know how and where to find information about technology, in order to plan and use it effectively.
- They must interact with persons with hearing loss to create a usable service profile (i.e., to address the specific needs of that community).
- They must elicit feedback from persons with hearing loss after a service is in place and make changes if they are needed.

In return, deaf and hard-of-hearing persons must make their needs known and interact with librarians to find workable solutions. Planning service is a two-way street, requiring a willingness to experiment, to accept failure, and to applaud and build on success. Users should be as specific as possible and assertive in identifying their needs and requesting appropriate assistive/adaptive services.

Getting to Know the Community with Hearing Loss

It is important that librarians identify client groups in order to provide optimum service and, in the case of the disabled in general, to espouse fair hiring practices. Alice Hagemeyer, a librarian from the Maryland/District of Columbia area, who has served the population with hearing loss for many years and who has profound hearing loss herself, believes that librarians must take a person-first stance on services, considering the disability as just a part of the whole person. Hagemeyer, who is working with her associates on how the nation's public libraries can provide cost-effective and efficient library and information services to the public concerned with hearing loss and American Sign Language, describes eight groups:

- **American Sign Language (ASL) Users**: Persons who communicate fluently in ASL as their primary language.
- **Bilingual Users**: Persons who communicate fluently in both ASL and English.
- **Oralists or hearing-impaired individuals**: Persons with a hearing impairment who communicate primarily through speech.
- **Deafened adults**: Persons who became deaf after having had the experience of hearing normally and, particularly, after having acquired speech.
- **Hearing-impaired elderly adults**: Persons who have a hearing impairment as a result of the aging process.
- **Minimal language users**: Persons who do not know either ASL or English. They may use gestures, homemade signs, and mime for communicating with others.
- **Hard-of-hearing individuals**: Persons who have a "defective but functional sense of hearing" (*Webster's Ninth New Collegiate Dictionary*, 1991).
- **Family members**: Persons from any of the earlier seven groups who have hearing parents, children, siblings and spouses.[11]

Through her recent research, Hagemeyer has removed deaf-blind as a separate category because in each of the above categories are some individuals who are blind or have other disabilities and who have similar needs for communication. They do not, according to their interviews with Hagemeyer, wish to be included among the original definitions. The eight categories might apply to them, but Hagemeyer, who is currently working on a new book, is developing clearer insights for the library community through an examination of definitions and types of hearing loss. Her examination and the results are based on the reactions of persons with hearing loss and their actual communication needs. She is looking at three main groups: the deaf community, persons with hearing loss, and persons who communicate in American Sign Language.[12]

Although identification of the components of the deaf community will help improve library service, it is also important to recognize common myths that inhibit proper communication and deserved service:

Myth 1: Good speech is an indication that someone can hear well. People who are postlingual—who lose their hearing later in life—will usually be able to speak well. The late-deafened may lose some ability to monitor this speech, which results in deterioration.

Myth 2: All deaf persons can lip or speech read. Lipreading is difficult, and there are varying abilities to read lips among the deaf. It is not likely that lip- or speech reading is the primary mode of communication for most people.

Myth 3: Wearing a hearing aid means that the person can understand or hear everything well. A hearing aid may only alert the wearer to environmental sounds, which are in themselves unintelligible.[13] Under some circumstances, an aid may simply admit all sound, allowing background noise to obliterate speech.

Given the foregoing misunderstandings, the invisible nature of deafness is easy to understand. And because it is difficult to justify service to an unseen, unrecognized condition, relatively few libraries offer programs and technologies for the deaf user.

To locate libraries that do offer services and facilities for deaf patrons, the *American Library Directory* is a good starting point. Prefacing its list of libraries is a statement that underscores the nation's shadowlike recognition of need:

> Although no federal agency provides material for deaf and hearing impaired patrons, as the National Library Service for the Blind and Physically Handicapped does for the blind, libraries are doing so on their own. Many offer TTY or TDD reference service, whereby a deaf patron can call the library and key in a request; have available staff who know sign language; and provide books and periodicals of special interest to the deaf as well as captioned videos and projects.
>
> What follows is an index to those libraries which have available TTY or TDD reference service or other services available for the deaf and hearing impaired. This index is a clear indicator that libraries are concerned with serving deaf patrons and that they are letting the *American Library Directory* know of their services.

For the TTY or TDD number of a specific library, as well as information on the other services available for the deaf and hearing impaired, see the "Special Services for the Deaf" paragraph in each individual entry in the library section.[14]

In the 1997–98 edition, forty-seven states and seven Canadian provinces are included. Some states list just one library that offers service to those with hearing loss; others list more, including public, school, special, and academic libraries. In Canada, the coverage is not so broad in either numbers or types of libraries, but the number of provinces listed has grown from five to seven since 1993.[15] In the 1998–1999 edition of the *Directory*, forty-seven states and six provinces are listed; Newfoundland, included in previous years' editions, with its HUB Specialized Information Centre, Information Services Library, is missing.[16]

The annual list, in any case, is a good idea. It is useful because it offers information contacts for libraries wishing to build services. Then, too, users with hearing loss can identify libraries where they may find the technology they need for information seeking. According to the *Directory*, the fact that not all fifty states or all of the Canadian provinces offer information services for persons with deafness is something of a sad commentary. It is particularly unfortunate because the original resources and technologies are improving and some new tools are emerging.

Technology for Library Users with Hearing Loss

Since 1992, services and technologies for persons with deafness have been growing, but slowly. Vendors are adding pages to catalogs, including some items specifically intended for service to persons with disabilities. Some meet the needs of the deaf population. On the other hand, one vendor of videos reports that because the company had not received any requests for captioned videos, they were not offered for sale. This is indicative of the vicious cycle of noncommunication that eliminates service. In reality, a good number of products are available to serve the deaf, and more are in research and development. A discussion of some available products, along with the laws and guidelines supporting the need to provide them, follows.

Telephone Technology
TDDs AND TTYs

Information services rely increasingly on a variety of telecommunications devices and media. Among those applications, telecommunication devices for the deaf (TDDs) and teletype writers (TTYs) allow users to type messages, which are sent over telephone lines, back and forth to one another. Messages are transmitted from a typewriter-like keyboard, and responses appear on a small screen above the keyboard. They may also be printed out in hard copy. If a hearing person wishes to speak with a deaf person who owns a text telephone (TDD or TTY), it is easy enough to call one of the relay services available throughout the country.

For example, to call someone in Maryland, one dials the 800 number for the Washington, D.C.-based relay service. The relay teletypist, upon receiving the call, asks for the phone number to be called. After the connection is made, everything is typed to the individual called as the person initiating the call says it. When the person has finished a thought, he or she informs the person on the other end by saying "Go ahead." The person with hearing loss then types his or her response as the relay intermediary reads that text to the hearing person. On finishing a statement, the person with hearing loss types "Go ahead," and the cycle continues until "goodbyes" are exchanged.

According to Donna DeMarco, the standard TTY costs between $185 and $600, depending on the machine's features. However, Maryland Relay does offer some of the equipment free of charge. Between March 1997 and spring of 1998, 370 pieces of equipment had been distributed by Maryland Relay, which has grown to mediating 200,000 calls per month. In peak business hours, it handles 6,000 to 7,000 calls. Sprint's Relay Center has 200 employees; of those, 100 to 150 are relay operators. [17]

Relay Texas offers several TDD services. In one, the communications agent types what the caller says, and the person with deafness may speak rather than type back. This is called a voice carryover, or VCO. (There are VCO telephones that display the conversation from the other person on a small screen, but allow a voice response.) In another application, the communications agent may listen to both parties who have difficulty with speech and who are also deaf, and types both conversations.

Another Texas project investigated the interpretation of sign language by the communications agent who typed the meaning of signs to another party. Sometimes the communications agent merely needs to rewrite sign language text into standard English (or another language's) usage. Sign language uses a very different grammar than standard English.[18] It is an "efficient" language that may omit, for example, articles or prepositions, in addition to rearranging sentence structure.

As of July 16, 1993, the ADA, Title IV, required that all telephone companies provide intra- and interstate relay services across the United States. This is in addition to an earlier ruling (October 28, 1988), the Telecommunications Accessibility Enhancement Act, which expanded the (separate) federal relay system. To encourage use, federal TDD numbers are printed in a government-wide directory. Further, in support of the act, each house of Congress has been directed to develop a policy with respect to TDDs in members' offices.[19]

U.S.C. Title 40—Public Buildings, Property, and Works
Chapter 16—General Services Administration
762d. TDD Installation by Congress

As soon as practicable, each House of the Congress shall establish a policy under which Members of the House of Representatives and the Senate, as the case may be, may obtain TDDs for use in communicating with hearing-impaired and speech-impaired individuals, and for the use of hearing-impaired and speech-impaired employees.

The government relay list has a Web address at http://www.gsa.gov/et/fic-firs/firs.htm.

Fortunately, in an effort to serve individuals, many states have begun to absorb the prohibitive price of TDDs and other hearing-assistive devices. Some states place the equipment based on the economic standing of the person; in other states, one simply has to prove deafness. In Michigan, the relay service offers free materials and presentations to help people find the best route to communication.

For those concerned with the cost of subsidy programs, a study on providing assistive phone services to frail elders in the Buffalo, New York, area showed that the average cost of equipment was $ 70.45. Personnel costs were much higher, but this was a beginning project.[20] As a result of the study, one may order a booklet and a video from the University at Buffalo Rehabilitation Engineering Research Center (1-800-628-2281) about phones and related equipment. In any case, the researchers narrowed the most likely telephone needs of the study subjects; the majority of interventions required phones with special features and/or new wiring and jacks.[21]

Unfortunately, some equipment supplied to those with hearing loss operates on the old Baudot code, which is, most often, noninteractive. Newer ASCII TDDs can interact with computers. These TDDs' speed, flexibility in the equipment with which they may communicate, and lower cost to operate make them the desirable option.[22] In addition, there are modems available that promise to turn a PC into a TDD that will read either ASCII or Baudot code. A variation on the latter technology, the IBM Phone Communicator, uses a PC and software that receive messages spelled on the keypads of Touch-Tone telephones. The deaf person keys messages on the computer that are translated through a synthesizer which voices the responses over the phone. If someone telephones the deaf person while he or she is working on the computer, a flasher signals the call. The Phone Communicator will also work if someone calls from or to an ASCII- or Baudot-compatible TDD.[23]

An alternative to the TTY/TDD devices is the telefacsimile. Although it does not allow the communication afforded by the ASCII TDD, it is a way for the deaf person to send and receive print messages. Another way to communicate, of course, is by electronic mail on the Internet, using personal accounts, listservs, and bulletin boards.

Coin-operated or card-operated telephones that include TDDs, or will accommodate them, must be in place in libraries under the new law. Also, if the library has a security entrance requiring that a person telephone into the building for admittance, some provision must be made via a TDD or other device outside the building so that the deaf can gain entry.[24]

One kind of TDD is housed in a motorized drawer, which only opens when the telephone recognizes that it has called another TDD. This protects security, according to one salesperson at Ultra Tech. Both AT&T and Ameritech (Michigan Bell) recommended Ultra Tech TDD phones in 1993.[25] In 1998, AT&T's Accessible Communications agents (1-800-872-3883) report that Lucent Technologies has taken over home equipment sales and installation. AT&T discounts the calls. Ameriphone and Ultratech were listed as suppliers of telecommunications equipment for those with hearing loss.

An Ultratech agent revealed that commercial and home TDDs may cost from $200 to $750; at the lower end of the scale is a nonprinting TTY with no memory. Pay text telephones cost $995, with a full-spec outdoor model (Model M240 with a two-line display) running higher at $1,495.

There are even more accommodating, unusual adaptive/assistive telephone technologies for librarians to consider. They meet the needs of those with multiple disabilities. Ameriphone, for instance, offers a model that is equipped with a notification system. It uses six icons to indicate what is happening in the telephoning process. Ameriphone's prices range from $229 to $489. The most expensive TDD has an answering machine that stores fifty numbers and offers three-way calling. Ameriphone also offers several switches, including a sip-and-puff switch. Other features include large keyboards and room on the keyboard for photographs so that numbers may be keyed, for example, to a picture of the user's Aunt Mary.

MCI brought a helpful change to assistive telecommunication when it introduced the first Text Telephone (TT) calling card. It also introduced teletext operator service for deaf and hearing-impaired users. Text calling cards are identical to other long-distance cards with one exception: Text "prompts" on TT replace traditional audio-prompted instructions on how to place a call. Until this was initiated, those with hearing loss often relied on finesse and guesswork when using a text telephone. Using MCI's Teletext Operator Service, any TT user needing operator assistance may dial 1-800-688-4486 to receive all service available to voice callers. The service is available 24 hours a day.[26]

The State of Maryland is another leader in this assistive service. Recently, with Sprint, it kicked off a $250,000 marketing campaign aimed at raising awareness of the little-known relay service and at allowing businesses to make contact with the 500,000 Maryland residents with hearing loss. One difficulty has been that businesses sometimes think the relay calls are solicitation rather than informational. Also, because conversations via TDD are somewhat delayed, businesses sometimes hang up in impatience. However, the new logo, television commercials, print ads, and more than two million fliers included in Baltimore Gas & Electric Co. bills should place the positive message of the untapped market of those with hearing loss firmly before the business public and society in general.[27]

Problems with Communicating via Relay or Telefax

Either communicating from telefax to telefax or through the relay service is easy. It can be a fine way to offer library reference service; however, not all users can afford TDDs (although some libraries lend them to users) nor can they afford fax machines, which would be another way to send written requests by telephone to the library reference desk. Some people may either dislike typing, or lack typing skills.

Even though relay services may emphasize confidentiality, persons with personal business to conduct may feel that their privacy is reduced or eliminated. Another problem is audiotext; relay operators have discovered that keeping up with the speed of voice mail is sometimes difficult.[28] Also, relay calls take extra time; one positive point here is that most relay calls are offered at some reduced price—for example, 35 percent for daytime and 60 percent for evening. Late night and evening calls are priced the same as voice calls.[29]

> *The ADA and ADA Guidelines advise as follows:*
> Part III, 28CFR, Section 36:303 A public accommodation that offers a customer, client, or participant the opportunity to make outgoing telephone calls on more than an incidental convenience basis shall make available, upon request, a TDD for the use of an individual who has impaired hearing or a communication disorder.[30]

> Appendix A of Part 36: Section 4.30.7 (3) Text Telephones required by 4.1.3(17)(c) shall be identified by the international TDD symbol. In addition, if a facility has a public text telephone, directional signage indicating the location of the nearest text telephone shall be placed adjacent to all banks of telephones which do not contain a text telephone. Such directional signage shall include the international TDD symbol. If a facility has no banks of telephones, the directional signage shall be provided at the entrance (e.g., in a building directory).[31]

> Section 4.31.9 Text Telephones Required by 4.1
> (1) Text telephones used with a pay telephone shall be permanently affixed within, or adjacent to, the telephone enclosure. If an acoustic coupler is used, the telephone cord shall be sufficiently long to allow connection of the text telephone and the telephone receiver.
> (2) Pay telephones designed to accommodate a portable text telephone shall be equipped with a shelf and an electrical outlet within or adjacent to the telephone enclosure. The telephone handset shall be capable of being placed flush on the surface of the shelf. The shelf shall be capable of accommodating a text telephone and shall have 6 in. (152 mm) minimum vertical clearance in the area where the text telephone is to be placed.

(3) Equivalent facilitation may be provided. For example, a portable text telephone may be made available in a hotel at the registration desk if it is available on a 24-hour basis for use with nearby public pay telephones. In this instance, at least one pay telephone shall comply with paragraph 2 of this section. In addition, if an acoustic coupler is used, the telephone handset cord shall be sufficiently long so as to allow connection of the text telephone and the telephone receiver. Directional signage shall be provided and shall comply with 4.30.7.[32]

Section 4.31.6 Controls. Telephones shall have pushbutton controls where service for such equipment is available.[33]

Telephones

For the client whose hearing is assisted by an aid, libraries must provide hearing aid–compatible telephones. Through a series of acts passed from 1982 to 1991, the FCC has created an ever-improving scenario for hearing aid users. After August 16, 1988, the Hearing Aid Compatibility Act required that all telephones manufactured be hearing aid compatible. As of May 1, 1991, all telephones located in common areas of workplaces and all credit card–operated telephones must be hearing aid compatible. These telephones have a switch that allows a user to eliminate electromagnetic excess and to receive the sound meant to be heard: the voice at the other end of the line.[34]

Hard-of-hearing or hearing-impaired users may be helped by telephone amplifiers that raise the possible number of decibels. These amplifiers attach to telephones—either the handsets or the handset cords—and are relatively inexpensive, ranging in price from $20 to $30.

The ADA Guidelines advise as follows:
Appendix A of Part 36, Section 4.31.5 Hearing Aid Compatible and volume Control Telephones Required by 4.1.
(1) Telephones shall be hearing aid compatible.
(2) Volume controls, capable of a minimum of 12 dbA and a maximum of 18 dbA above normal, shall be provided in accordance with 4.1.3. If an automatic reset is provided then 18dbA may be exceeded.

Further, the *Accessibility Checklist* offers the following guidelines for telephone placement:
    A. All Telephones
        1. Floor space is 30 inches by 48 inches minimum, unobstructed by a fixed seat or enclosure.
        2. Cord length is 29 inches minimum.
        3. A volume control is provided.
            a. Phones with volume controls are identified with complying symbols.

4. Telephones are touch-tone if this service is available in the area.
5. TDD Accommodations
   a. Phone is equipped with a Telecommunications Display Device.
   b. An outlet and shelf for a portable TDD device are provided.
   c. TDD telephones are identified by complying signs. Other telephones have directions to a TDD phone location.
B. Side Approach Possible
   1. Heights of coin slot and controls are 54 inches maximum.
   2. Height from the floor to the bottom of the enclosure is 27 inches maximum.
   3. Enclosure does not extend more than 10 inches from the front surface of the telephone.
   4. Telephone books, if provided, are between 9 inches and 54 inches above the floor surface and do not protrude more than 10 inches from the front surface of the telephone.
C. Forward Approach Required (e.g., phone booth or alcove)
   1. Heights of coin slot and controls are 48 inches maximum.
   2. Width of enclosure is at least 30 inches (36 inches if the sides of the enclosure extend more than 24 inches past the front surface of the telephone).
   3. Shelves or other amenities do not extend more than 20 inches past the front surface of the telephone.
   4. Height from the floor to the bottom of the enclosure is 27 inches maximum.
   5. Telephone books, if provided, are between 15 inches and 48 inches above the floor surface and do not encroach upon knee space.[35]

Assistive Listening Devices (ALD) or Systems (ALS)

AMPLIFIERS

Providing pocket amplifiers may help people with partial hearing loss to participate in story hours and hear movie tracks, audio recordings, and other presentations unobtrusively. The amplifiers screen out unpleasant noises, the ads promise, and they can be used with or without hearing aids. The price tag for one of these small, light pieces of equipment may range from around $11.95 to $140.

Of course, one participant on an Internet conference told the story of going to Radio Shack and being outfitted with a stripped-down (except for the condenser microphone) cassette tape recorder, which the dealer marketed as a hearing aid device. Told that Radio Shack was going to phase the model out, the person bought an extra for $29. The participant said that it is used to watch/listen to television and to listen to lectures; further, it is nearly as good as a Telex model, which would cost about $1,200. Conference participants commented that each hearing need is different, so customized applications are often needed.[36] There are, of course, other ways to enhance hearing.

Audio Loop Systems

Enhanced hearing is permitted by the audio loop, which allows people carrying portable receivers or wearing hearing aids with telecoil switches (T-switches) to receive sound from a public address system using a transducer.[37] The PA system broadcasts through a loop of wire (induction loop) placed around an identified audience area. For small meetings (e.g., classroom size), this is a cost-effective approach. It is low maintenance, and it may be integrated into an existing public address system. The disadvantages to this system are that signals may spill over into adjacent rooms, it is not very portable, and it is susceptible to electrical interference. Also, a user's head position may affect the strength of the signal received. In addition, there are no standards for induction coil performance.[38]

Infrared Systems

Moderately priced, but more expensive than an audio loop system, the infrared system (see figure 1) uses a part of the light spectrum for the transmission of sound. This system requires that nothing interfere with the infrared signal sent by the emitter plugged into the PA; a line of sight is necessary between the emitter and the receiver.[39] With Phonic Ear's Starsound infrared systems, the System 400 is meant to be used in multiplex cinemas, conference centers, live theaters, and courtrooms. Its range covers 12,000 feet. The receiver is a single-channel receiver. The StarSound 600 has a typical range over a 4,000

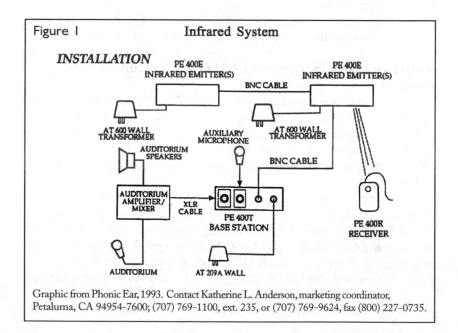

Figure I — Infrared System

Graphic from Phonic Ear, 1993. Contact Katherine L. Anderson, marketing coordinator, Petaluma, CA 94954-7600; (707) 769-1100, ext. 235, or (707) 769-9624, fax (800) 227-0735.

foot area. It has stereo reception. Also, the advertising claims that it prevents interference from ballast lighting.[40] An important value of the two systems is that they do not penetrate walls; therefore, they are secure and may be installed in several rooms.

Problems with infrared include the line of sight needed for transmission, limited portability (Phonic Ear's empty carrying case weighs 4.1 pounds and can accommodate 12 body-worn receivers), and the installation required. Outdoor use is not possible because daylight interferes with transmission. Also, incandescent light in a room may cause interference.[41]

FM SYSTEMS

Narrow band FM systems send out radio signals and allow users to tune into one of what may be several programs going on in the library—or within the same room. Users wear or hold receivers to pick up the programs from a large area transmitter.[42] Actually, Phonic Ear offers a personal FM system for use in classrooms, live tours, senior centers, conference rooms, banks, hospitals, or in the home—small situations.[43]

For example, the average classroom is offered as a most challenging acoustical situation for any student. A Phonic Ear brochure reports that studies have shown that the typical classroom has approximately a 60 dB (decibel) noise level—like an office full of noisy typewriters. So if the teacher wishes the student with a hearing loss to understand, speech must be 15 dB to 20 dB higher than the background noise. Audiologists call this a 15 dB to 20 dB signal-to-noise ratio. In a normal setting, the teacher's voice is five decibels higher than the background noise. The difference between the decibels of the normal teacher's voice and the 15 to 20 additional dBs required make sound systems necessary.

Reverberation (echo) is another problem. It can be handled by wall, floor, and ceiling materials that absorb noise; however, it has been discovered that monitoring the student's distance from the teacher is more effective as a control. Because this latter is not always a practical possibility, FM systems are the answer.[44] In addition, Phonic Ear promises with its Solaris Binaural System to allow a child to go from class to class, changing channels among forty channels available, to hear comfortably in each class. Of course, the system may be used by any age group. Users wear or hold receivers, as they do with the other systems, to pick up the programs from a large area transmitter.

Phonic Ear's Easy Listener FM Wireless Hearing Assistance System is portable. It may draw power from a wall outlet, or it may use an optional portable power supply connected to a PA system or microphone. Depending on the antenna used (standard or large), the area covered ranges from 300 to 1,000 feet.[45] The receiver on Phonic Ear's Easy Listener may attach to a teleloop, a Silhouette coil, a headset, a stetoclip, binaural earbuds, or monaural earbud (see figure 2).

AM Systems

AM systems are similar to FM systems. Receivers, which may be AM radios in some cases, pick up the signal broadcast from an AM radio transmitter coupled to a microphone or PA system. Again, users need to have the appropriate listening attachments (neckloops, earbuds, or headphones) on the receivers to meet the user's needs.

This technology is both simple and inexpensive. Users have the freedom to choose where they want to sit. They can supply their own personal AM radio and attachments and fine-tune the broadcast. On the other hand, AM systems have relatively poor sound quality (they are subject to the same sources of interference that often disrupt AM radios) and they do not perform well in buildings with large amounts of structural steel. They are rarely used now and suppliers may be hard to find.[46]

DAI

Although DAIs (direct audio input) still are used, the technology seems more and more directed toward wireless applications. In any case, individual listening devices may be used with personal hearing aids via DAI or induction neck-loop and telecoil. DAI means there is a direct wire connection between, for example, the hearing aid and the receiver. The rechargeable receivers may also be self-contained in earphones.[47] DAI systems are available in six-channel and single-channel models, and their typical range is 100 feet at 72 MegaHerz. The speaker wears the transmitter with microphone while the person with hearing loss wears the receiver with earphones.[48]

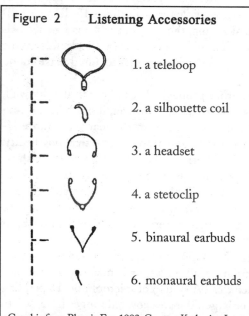

Figure 2	Listening Accessories
	1. a teleloop
	2. a silhouette coil
	3. a headset
	4. a stetoclip
	5. binaural earbuds
	6. monaural earbuds

Graphic from Phonic Ear, 1993. Contact Katherine L. Anderson, marketing coordinator, Petaluma, CA 94954-7600; (707) 769-1100, ext. 235, or (707) 769-9624, fax (800) 227-0735.

TMX

Another application from Phonic Ear is the telepin system with TMX for use with the Solaris personal hearing system. This is intended for users who want DAI performance but who also dislike DAI cords. The receiver attaches to the behind-the-ear (BTE) hearing aid shoe. The TMX loop is worn loosely around the neck, over or under clothing. It fits children or adults, and works with numerous hearing aid brands: Bernafon, Danavox, Oticon, Unitron, and Widex BTE aids and audio shoes.[49]

A relatively new type of FM receiver is now available that combines the hearing aid and FM system in a single behind-the-ear unit (BTE/FM). This new BTE/FM system eliminates the body-worn case as well as all loops and cords for the listener. The unit can function as a hearing aid alone, an FM system alone, or a hearing aid/FM system simultaneously. These FM systems were produced first by Phonic Ear, whose product is called Free Ear and by AVR Sonnovation in Israel which introduced its version, the Extend Ear. They come in a variety of power and frequency combinations to cover a wide range of hearing loss configurations, from mild to profound. Telex has recently introduced its own FM/BTE unit called the SELECT 2-40. All of these FM/BTE units have an antenna on the end. The devices are becoming more sophisticated in channel changeability—Sonnovation attaches a boot to the unit and Telex has two channels built into its system.[50]

FM Technology is continually expanding. Two exciting new developments that are just being introduced include a "boot" attachment called the UNICOM, developed by Unitron, which will change one of their over-the-ear hearing aids—the US80— into a FM/BTE. This is designed for individuals with severe to profound hearing loss who need to communicate in noisy environments. This product is the result of a collaborative effort by Unitron and Sonnovation. The second major new development in the FM arena is the Microlink, produced by Phonak; this is the world's smallest FM chip at 1/3 inch. It attaches to a boot that slips over the BTE and has an antenna that does not protrude. This is considered to be the most up-to-date technology, but it is recognized that improvements are needed in FM.[51] Other companies that produce FM systems include Telex, Comtex, and Earmark.

CONFERENCE MICROPHONES

Phonic Ear's conference microphone is decorative as well as useful. It may be placed in the center of a table or on any hard surface. It differs from the usual microphone in that it is multidirectional. Since 1995, the radius it covers is reported to have increased from 20 to 75 square feet. In a demonstration of the microphone in the spring of 1998, it was noted that the acoustics of the room may affect reception and broadcasting. Also, equipment used to complement the microphone may have an effect.[52]

An advantage of the microphone is that it need not be passed from person to person. If an unidirectional mic is used, people must at least turn the microphone to catch sounds. The cost of the Phonic Ear microphone is $500 or more.[53]

Guidance in Technical Assistance

It is clear that making choices among assistive listening devices and systems might require more than a little experience. To help institutions and businesses facing these expenditures, the Architectural and Transportation Barriers Compliance Board (Access Board) has published a pamphlet on assistive listening systems. It may be found on the Web at <www.faa.gov/arp/C1.HTM>. The pamphlet lists demonstration centers across the country where technical assistance may be obtained in selecting and installing appropriate systems.[54] To obtain a paper copy of the pamphlet, contact: United States Architectural and Transportation Barriers Compliance Board, 1331 F Street, NW, Suite 1000, Washington, D.C. 20004-1111, or phone 1-800-USA-ABLE.

The pamphlet says:

Specifications for assistive listening systems in the current federal accessibility requirements under the Architectural Barriers Act are prescribed in sections 4.1.2, 4.33.6, 4.33.7 and A4.33.7 of the Uniform Federal Accessibility Standards (49 *Fed. Reg.* 31528) issued August 7, 1984. 4.1.2 Accessible Buildings:

New Construction (18) Assembly Areas: (b) Assembly areas with audio-amplification systems shall have a listening system complying with 4.33 to assist a reasonable number of people, but no fewer than two, with severe hearing loss. For assembly areas without amplification systems and for spaces used primarily as meeting and conference rooms, a permanently installed or portable system shall be provided. If portable systems are used for conference or meeting rooms, the system may serve more than one room.

4.33.6 Placement of Listening Systems - If the listening system provided serves individual fixed seats, then such seats shall be located within 50 ft. (15 m) viewing distance of the stage or playing area.

4.33.7 Types of Listening Systems - Audio loops and radio frequency systems are two acceptable types of listening systems. 4.33.7 Types of Listening Systems - A listening system that can be used from any seat in a seating area is the most flexible way to meet this specification. Earphone jacks with variable volume controls can benefit only people who have slight hearing losses and do not help people with hearing aids. At the present time, audio loops are the most feasible type of listening system for people who use hearing aids, but people without hearing aids or those with hearing aids not equipped with inductive pickups cannot use them. Loops can be portable and moved to various locations within a room. Moreover, for little cost, they can serve a large area within a seating area. Radio frequency systems can be extremely effective and inexpensive. People without hearing aids can use them but people with hearing aids need custom-designed equipment to use them as they are presently designed. If hearing aids had a jack to allow a by-pass of microphones, then radio frequency systems would be suitable for people with and without hearing. Some listening systems may be subject to interference from other equipment and feedback from hearing aids of people who are using the systems. Such interference can be controlled by careful engineering design that anticipates feedback and sources of interference in the surrounding area.

Information about assistive listening systems is available from several sources. Three national organizations are listed below and other local information sources are listed in the appendix. The Access Board does not endorse these organizations or any information they may provide.

Self-Help for Hard-of-Hearing People (SHHH), 7800 Wisconsin Avenue, Bethesda, Maryland 20814 - A nonprofit educational organization of hearing impaired people with chapters in 48 states and a national demonstration center where assistive listening devices and systems are shown. SHHH publishes a bimonthly journal and disseminates information on a variety of topics including technical information on assistive listening systems.

National Association of the Deaf (NAD), 814 Thayer Avenue Silver Spring, Maryland 20910 - A nonprofit organization of deaf people, NAD has an assistive devices center where assistive listening systems are demonstrated.

National Information Center on Deafness, Gallaudet University Washington, DC 20002 - The Center offers listings of assistive devices demonstration centers across the nation and technical assistance on installing assistive listening systems.[55]

Simply by virtue of the quality of the three organizations listed, the Access Board pamphlet will keep persons interested up to date on the technology. Also, the *ADA Guidelines* and the Access Board promise to update information as the technology changes.[56] The flexibility of language in the pamphlet and the *ADA Guidelines* must be noted, as well as the firm demands for accessibility. The pamphlet's language is a bit stronger than that of the *Guidelines* insofar as "reasonable" access is presented.

In parallel to the Access Board pamphlet, the *ADA Guidelines* advise as follows:

Part III, 28CFR, Part 36.303 Auxiliary aids and services:
(a) General. A public accommodation shall take those steps that may be necessary to ensure that no individual with a disability is excluded,

denied services, segregated or otherwise treated differently than other individuals because of the absence of auxiliary aids and services, unless the public accommodation can demonstrate that taking those steps would fundamentally alter the nature of the goods, services, facilities, privileges, advantages, or accommodations being offered or would result in an undue burden, i.e., significant difficulty or expense.

(b) Examples. The term "auxiliary aids and services" includes— (1) Qualified interpreters, notetakers, computer-aided transcription services, written materials, telephone handset amplifiers, assistive listening devices, assistive listening systems, telephones compatible with hearing aids, closed caption decoders, telecommunications devices for deaf persons (TDDs), videotext displays, or other effective methods of making aurally delivered materials available to individuals with hearing impairments.

(3) Acquisition or modification of equipment or devices; and (4) Other similar services and actions.

> (c) Effective communication. A public accommodation shall furnish appropriate auxiliary aids and services where necessary to ensure effective communication with individuals with disabilities.

> (f) Alternatives. If provision of a particular auxiliary aid or service by a fundamental alteration in the nature of the goods, services, facilities, privileges, advantages, or accommodations being offered are an undue burden, i.e., significant difficulty or expense, the public accommodation shall provide an alternative auxiliary aid or service, if one exists, that would not result in an alteration or such burden but would nevertheless ensure that, to the maximum extent possible, individuals with disabilities receive the goods, services, facilities, privileges, advantages, or accommodations offered by the public accommodation.

Appendix A of Part 36
A7.2(3) Assistive Listening Devices. At all sales and service counters, teller windows, box offices, and information kiosks where a physical barrier separates service personnel and customers, it is recommended that at least one permanently installed assistive listening device complying with 4.33 be provided at each location or series. Where assistive listening devices are installed, signage should be provided identifying those stations which are so equipped.[57]

Captioning
THE LAW
More stringent rules for the captioning of television programs have evolved since the adoption of the ADA. The mandates came from the Telecommuni-

cations Act of 1996 which charged the Federal Communications Commission (FCC) to examine the accessibility of television programs. As a result, the FCC has established a schedule, not just for the captioning of programs in English, but also in Spanish. Separate schedules were set for "new" and "old" programs. A major target date for the majority of programming is January 1, 2006.[58] Dates in between have been, and most likely will be, affected by lobbyists from organizations such as the National Association for the Deaf. One way to stay on top of the captioning calendar is to check Boston's WGBH Web page on captioning.

This information might be of particular interest to libraries operating their own cable stations. On the other hand, as providers of information, librarians in general could serve the community with hearing loss by making this news available to them. Responsibilities for providing captioned television take in, not just broadcasters, but also cable operators, direct-to-home providers, home satellite dish providers, and open video system operators, among several agencies. As with other disability laws, providers may claim reasonable restrictions based on their budgets and resources. However, the literature shows that if the changes in the laws continue to follow the same pattern as they have in the past few years, the captioning laws will become tougher.

DEFINITIONS OF CAPTIONING

Captioning is an intricate, evolving part of services to persons with hearing losses. It is important, in this transitional state, to understand the changes in the technology and the definitions that have been important to date. There are four basic kinds of captioning. The fifth listed here impacts the basic four:

1) Open captions appear superimposed over the picture on the screen, are visible to all viewers, and require no special equipment for viewing.

2) Closed captions are transmitted to the television receiver. This method uses the vertical blanking interval (the black bar that is seen when the television picture rolls). It is known as the Line 21 System. PBS began working on the technology in 1972, and WGBH in Boston led the way in developing new technologies for closed captioning of television programs. The National Captioning Institute began to caption television programs on major networks in 1980. A decoder may be used to "open up" Line 21.

3) Prerecorded captions are used for programs on videotape. A captioner views the film or program, cuts extraneous material, and then the program is played on one machine and the captions on another, with the two being integrated into one tape that also contains audio.

4) Real-time captioning is for live programs for which no script exists. Captions are typed into an electric stenotype machine, similar to those used in courtrooms. A computer reads the steno-captioner's shorthand and translates the words into captions, which are then projected on the screen.

5) Instructional captioning modifies the reading level to that of the intended audience.[59]

ATTITUDES

Two librarians who work intensively with services to persons with disabilities and, in particular, people with hearing loss, as well as with public librarians, had positive, hopeful comments about librarians' attitudes toward captioned videos. One, Mary Kirby, executive director of the Library Media Project,[60] says her organization deals with 13,000 libraries, 10,000 of which are actively involved with the project. The project also curates collections gathered from 130 different distributors.

Kirby reports that independent film makers cannot afford to caption. (This fact is supported by the results of a short survey done by Gilbert Beck of video producers and video projects listed in *The Librarian's Yellow Pages*. The most frequent response was that captioning is expensive. One or two producers volunteered that if people come to them wanting to raise grant funds to caption, the producers are quite willing to work on the projects.[61]) Kirby also reports that public librarians would like to have captioned films. Unfortunately, she estimates that only 20 percent of the videos her project handles are captioned.

One wonderful exception, Kirby notes, is entitled *In the Land of the Deaf*. This video includes signing in French and in English as well as closed captions in English. Whether all that captioning is gracefully embedded in the video may be a matter of the viewer's taste. On the other hand, whatever the final product might be, it is an acknowledgment of need and a harbinger of possibilities.

There are areas where help exists to offset the financial demands of captioning:

> Is this wonderful ASL (American Sign Language) world real? Imagine standing in your local library looking at shelves filled with ASL videos! More than 140 ASL videos stand proud, ready to show off their heroes and their history, theater, storytelling, sign lessons, and more, all put there by ASL Access and YOU. ASL Access is not a business that makes or sells videos. Rather, ASL Access is a non profit organization assisting public libraries in finding and funding ASL resources for communities. Qualified evaluators have chosen a "core collection" or "ASL Bookshelf." Your local library system can

acquire this excellent collection when area businesses, groups, and individuals contribute toward the cost of the set. For now, you can check out the Web site (<http://www.aslaccess.org>), where you will find ASL video reviews, information on the collection, articles, and a listing of more than forty catalogs and other sources of ASL videos. You can help by telling your local librarian that you would like to see these videos added to the library and by giving the librarian information on ASL Access.[62]

Some of the ASL videos are the sign equivalent of text-captioned videos. The same challenge applies to both kinds of captioning: finding the funding to caption in any way is difficult. However, another line of thought comes from Mike Gunde, associate director of the Florida Department of Education Division of Blind Services.[63] In talking with Gunde, one hears that vendors say captioning is not expensive.

If one travels onto the Web, one finds myriad pages on captioning, and in the light of worries about costs, the following Web site offers a simple, inexpensive solution. Its author has created freeware, stating that he believes that everything should be captioned. He advocates open captioning and lists the technology necessary to use his software at <http://members.aol.com/Andy8080/SimpleCaption.html>.

Another Web site recounts how one teacher had her elementary class caption a film. Not only did the class accomplish the project, but the teacher comments that their language skills improved as well as their skills of observation. That site may be found on the Web at: <www2.edc.org/NCIP/library/v&c/Reingold.htm>. It, too, offers a list of the technology needed to do the job.

A basic captioning workstation consists of a personal computer, two VCRs (one for playback and one for record), and a character generator that allows text to be superimposed onto video. A computer monitor, a video monitor, and a printer are also needed. Some systems require a time-code reader.

Of course, these are simple solutions; however, they are signs that society is taking more notice of what must be done and that accessibility can be thought through, accomplished, and perhaps be useful to all.

Gunde notes that libraries have not made much progress in listing whether a video is captioned in the bibliographic record. He did state that he has noticed that the video vendors who come to the ALA meeting do note captioning. This is a positive change from the early years of ADA. In 1994, vendors were not likely to carry that information in their catalogs or on their order sheets. Gunde hopes that the new listing comes in response to a demand from librarians. Also, practically, it may be a response to the ADA.

Gunde recommends that libraries buy only videos with captioning.[64] Also, he suggests that librarians always preview videos to check for captioning and mark them as open or closed captioned. This marking should also be included in the bibliographic record. In his newsletter (editorship since assumed by Ruth O'Donnell, consultant), *Focus: Library Service to Older Adults, People with Disabilities,* Gunde recommends Stuart Gopen's *Gopen's Guide to Closed Captioned Video.*[65]   In the process of previewing more than 9,000 videocassettes, Gopen and his staff found 150 that were captioned, but not marked as such.

The Laws

As the ADA indicates, public accommodations must make assistive devices available so that users' needs are met. Title IV of the ADA also requires all television public service announcements that are produced or funded by the federal government to include closed captioning. As a result, televised information on general health and consumer issues will be available to the community of those with hearing losses.[66] Libraries offering cable television are affected by this measure.

Theaters need not show captioned films for entertainment, but public agencies concerned with education—and this includes hotels—must consider the needs of those with hearing losses. One deaf person in an audience is reason, according to the law, to use a captioned video or film if the purpose is educational. For entertainment purposes, six people from the deaf community must be in the audience before captioning is required.[67]

THE TELEVISION DECODER CIRCUITRY ACT

The Television Decoder Circuitry Act of 1990 states that since July 1, 1993, all television sets with screens 13 inches or larger manufactured for sale in the U.S. must contain built-in, closed-caption decoders. In addition to serving as a lifeline for deaf and hard-of-hearing viewers, captioning benefits people learning English as a second language and children and adults learning to read. The Caption Center is extremely proud to have played a prominent role in its passage—drafting language for the bill, testifying on its behalf before both the U.S. Senate and the House of Representatives, and assisting in the development of standards for decoder features.

All decoder-equipped TV sets must now meet the standards issued by the FCC. Television manufacturers may also incorporate optional features, such as Text Mode and changeable character colors (see below).

Display Standards for Decoder-Equipped Televisions

• **Placement:** New decoder designs permit captions to appear anywhere on the screen, resulting in more precise positioning of text. (Previously, captions could appear only in the upper- and lower-third of the picture.) This will more clearly indicate who is speaking, and important parts of the picture will be covered less often.

• **Italics:** Caption-capable televisions must display italicized characters using either a true italics or slanted letters. (Caption agencies often use italics to indicate vital information such as sound effects, narrators, and offscreen voices.) Manufacturers may offer other options to denote italics, such as color reversal.

• **Background:** The FCC requires the use of a black background (as used in some set-top decoders) to guarantee the legibility of caption characters. Manufacturers may offer other background colors as long as black is available at the user's option.

• **Upper- and lowercase letters:** Beginning January 1996, new caption-capable TV sets will be required to display both lower- and uppercase letters. Until 1996, certain televisions were only required to display uppercase letters. However, it is anticipated that most televisions will utilize the upper- and lowercase feature.

• **Labeling:** Manufacturers must specifically label packing boxes and owners' manuals to inform consumers if the set does not support the options of Text Mode (see below), color characters, or lowercase characters.

Optional Features for Decoder-Equipped Televisions
• **Text Mode:** Text Mode is used to provide information services. Currently, C-SPAN uses Text Mode to publish program listings and information for teachers. ABC-TV also uses it to list their captioned programs. In a few agricultural states, Text Mode delivers information to farmers.

• **Changeable character colors:** The FCC strongly encourages, but does not require, manufacturers to include the ability to display color characters. Because color capability will cost practically nothing in newer TV designs, it is anticipated that most televisions will incorporate this feature.

Display Capabilities of Current Set-Top Decoders
• **Pacific Lotus:** FCC compliant, incorporates all new FCC-mandated caption display features.

• **Teknova:** FCC compliant, incorporates all new FCC-mandated caption display features.

• **NCI TeleCaption II, TeleCaption 3000, Telecaption 4000, VR-100:** Will continue to work correctly until about 2002, then may malfunction with some captioned programs.

Telecaption Adaptors began experiencing minor problems (extra characters, slash marks) in the summer of 1994. In 1995, the original Telecaption Adapter began to miss some captions.[68]

In addition to the technical problems, captions that truly meet the needs of the people who rely on them are not always available. The placement of captions on the screen or the picture is under study. It has been found, for example, that many captions appear and disappear too quickly for the people to read and comprehend them. It is important that librarians, as part of the community of educators and communicators, keep a positive attitude toward the progress in captioning though it is not yet perfect.

Technology to Serve Persons with Hearing Loss:
In Transition and in the Future

Though the technology for those with hearing loss and the economy of the technology are not perfect, there is wonderful research in progress. Also, the patent database holds many new inventions that offer hope. One of the latest breakthroughs is the cochlear implant.[69]

> The cochlear implant is a prosthetic replacement for the inner ear (cochlea) and is only appropriate for people who receive minimal or no benefit from a conventional hearing aid.

> The cochlear implant bypasses damaged parts of the inner ear and electronically stimulates the nerve of hearing. Part of the device is surgically implanted in the skull behind the ear and tiny wires are inserted into the cochlea. The other part of the device is external and has a microphone, a speech processor (that converts sound into electrical impulses), and connecting cables. It is battery powered, adjustable, and expensive.[70]

A cochlear implant is considerably more expensive than a hearing aid.[71] Total costs (evaluation, surgery, device, rehabilitation) may range from about $15,000 to more than $25,000. If the FDA approves the cochlear implant device, many insurance companies will provide benefits that cover some or much of the cost.[72] Though the new digital hearing aids are quite expensive for some budgets, their inclusion in benefits is slow arriving.

The importance for librarians in regard to either solution is that both change the service community's needs. Vinton Cerf said, in a speech to the Marshall Symposium at the University of Michigan in spring 1998, that his wife who had a profound hearing loss all of her life is suddenly like a teenager having had the cochlear implant. She is always on the telephone! That is a major life change. One wonders, as a person who helps people to pursue information, what the new hearing ability means in terms of changes in communication. If the person used sign language before the operation, how will the new mode of communication feel to both the person newly able to hear and to the person communicating with that person? What should both parties remember to observe in the transition? Certainly, at the global, universal level of technologies, society is in transition.

Other remarkable steps toward better service involve microphones to be implanted in the ear via a cochlear implant or a hearing aid.[73] The microphones work to eliminate noise and to refine sound. The parts of the hearing aid are placed specifically in the patient's anatomy:

> The housing has at least two legs which are oriented at an angle relative to one another, one leg holding the microphone capsule and

being provided with a sound inlet membrane, and the other leg containing the electrical lead-in wire connector. As a result of the two-legged geometry of the microphone housing, the microphone can be implanted after a mastoidectomy in the mastoid cavity such that the leg which has the sound inlet membrane lies in a hole in the posterior wall of the auditory canal wall, an acoustic signal incident in the external auditory canal is acoustically received, while the leg of the microphone housing containing the electrical lead-in wire connector is in the area of the mastoid tip … on the implant side, a battery arrangement for power supply which can be recharged transcutaneously via an external charging device. The audiological implant functions can, likewise, be transcutaneously controlled via a remote control.[74]

Another set of inventions, perhaps easier to understand, but difficult in their challenge, are the new approaches to facilitating captions for the movies.[75] Three technologies were tested by researchers at the National Center for Accessible Media (NCAM), at WGBH, the Boston public broadcasting station:

- **Virtual vision glasses:** These are oversized eyeglasses with a small crystal display that sits at the top of the glasses. Captions come from a computer and are sent through cables.

- **A seatback display:** A vacuum-fluorescent display is attached to the back of the seat in front of the viewer. It can be adjusted to be within the viewer's sight along with the film. Print is bright green dot-matrix.

- **A rearview display:** A large light-emitting diode (LED) display located at the rear of the theater, it displays captions in mirror image. The user sees the display reflected in a clear plexiglass panel mounted on an adjustable stalk attached to the arm of the seat while simultaneously watching the movie through the glass.[76]

When these three methods were researched, each offered difficulties. The glasses were tiring to wear. The dot-matrix green did not show up well. The rear view model had the viewer straining to follow the pictures and the captions. Experimentation continues with the latter designs. The designs in the following list offer a different hope for better communication. Some interesting patent titles to consider from the U.S. Patent database on the World Wide Web in late 1998 were:

- Audible Environment Awareness Restoring Device (bone conduction speaker mounts against the sternum, allowing the person to

perceive, through the sense of touch, sounds corresponding to the human voice). Filed 18 March 1997.
• Echo Canceller for Non-linear Circuits Filed 24 July 1996
• Directional Hearing System (directs video camera to follow the source of sound). Filed 22 April 1996.
• System and Method for Providing Videoconferencing Services (directional microphones included). Filed 1 November 1996.
• Digital Hearing Aid. Filed 6 December 1996.
• Electro-magnetic Interference Shield for a Telephone Handset (used with hearing aids). Filed 31 July 1996.
• Protective Cover Assembly Having Enhanced Acoustical Characteristics (for telephones). Filed 28 May 1997.[77]

Finally, if people are not creating the technology, they may be using it creatively. Sometimes creative thinking takes the person to a sensory realm that no one else would imagine. The *DEAFDIGEST* carried this story of a man wanting to advertise his business:

A DEAF CEO USING THE RADIO TO ADVERTISE!
Just because the deaf cannot hear the radio does not mean they cannot place ads on the air. Jamie Clark, the former CEO of Clark Internet Services and now the Vice President of Development for Verio Mid-Atlantic, said his marketing director urged him to place ads on the radio. Naturally Jamie was skeptical but decided to give it a try. Said Jamie, "It turned out that radio is the best media to place ads."[78]

Conclusion

Upon searching the HyperAbleData database or any other listing of assistive/adaptive technology, one notes the enormous range of assistive/adaptive equipment and software that are available to the deaf community. Costs are sometimes prohibitive, and anyone who wears a hearing aid or, now, who receives a cochlear implant or hearing aid implant, knows the expense of being deaf. One is told that it is not the bit of plastic and wire itself, but the research and development that make aids expensive. Moreover, in the United States, health insurance is just beginning to change to absorb the costs. Also, as in the CostCo example, some businesses are working to decrease the expense.

Although administrators in libraries may be fully aware of the "reasonable" financial clauses in the disability laws, they must also consider ways to offer excellent services and to meet guidelines. Given the information shared here, the following guidelines might be helpful to librarians as they evaluate needs, purchase technology, and introduce their communities to new and improved services.

GUIDELINES FOR SERVING THE DEAF COMMUNITY THROUGH TECHNOLOGY

1. Include services to persons with disabilities in your plan to provide universal access to the library. Incorporate universal design into any architectural plans.[79] (For example, when volume amplification is built into the original design of a telephone, the cost is inconsequential. As a specialized device, incorporated after the fact, it costs about $40—an additional expense for people who are hard of hearing. The benefits for this particular application are that it is useful for persons with hearing loss, and also for anyone using a telephone in noisy environments such as airports, hotels, offices, or public phone booths.[80])

2. Make your system user-driven. Get to know the community of persons with hearing loss or deafness served by your library. Hold meetings directed to their interests (e.g., invite them in to discuss their needs and what the library already has that may be of use to them). Be ready to share selection policies and to receive their opinions on items needed in the library.

3. Maintain a staff position with responsibility for knowing and understanding assistive/adaptive technology. If your staff is too small, network with other agencies and libraries for understanding and sharing information on equipment and software. Join a listserv such as EASI Inform, the conference on concerns of those with disabilities—technology, etc.

4. Know the disabilities laws and guidelines, especially including changes. Share the information with your governing body, users, and staff for discussion and possible policy and procedural changes.

5. Start a foundation or a fund for services to the disabled, including assistive/adaptive equipment and software.

6. Keep aware of grant possibilities and involve your governing body, users, and staff in grant-writing projects.

7. Offer workshops to increase staff and community understanding. Include persons with disabilities in the workshops as presenters and participants.

8. When the library receives a grant or a new technology, celebrate visibly.

9. Make sure to try the equipment and encourage the staff to try the equipment. Hands-on experience is the best way to become familiar with technology.

10. Ask for feedback from your community about the technology your library is offering.

11. Let vendors know how you feel about their products and their approaches to serving your institution.

12. Contribute to research on services to those with disabilities, by either conducting studies or participating in surveys and allowing researchers access to the library. ∎

Notes

1. E-mail communication with Melissa Herzig, Jimmie Dixon, Sindile Kevin Mhlanga, Respicious Batamula, and Dawn Denny, Nov. 98.
2. E-mail communication with Joni Smith, UM Interpreter, Nov. 15, 1998.
3. SI605: Assistive Adaptive Technology, Disabilities, and Policy Making in Information Institutions, July 20, 1998, taught by Susan Gilbert Beck.
4. Roberta L. Null, with Kenneth F. Cherry, What Is the Americans with Disabilities Act? Universal Design (Belmont, Calif.: Professional Publications, Inc., 1996), 2.
5. Alice Hagemeyer, April 1, 1992. Hagemeyer refers to the nine groups within the deaf community. In a letter to Susan Gilbert Beck, dated October 9, 1992, Hagemeyer suggested that "hearing impaired" does not describe all conditions and that "deaf community," in fact, is a better subject heading for catalog and computer access. "Librarians and public servants should not focus on hearing problem(s) (or any other disability) when serving people who have a range of loss of hearing from mild to profound. They must be treated as people first. Everyone has different communication needs." Further, "Should you use 'deaf and hearing impaired,' this phrase can be misleading to many people who will assume that all deaf people know sign language and hearing impaired don't."
6. "A Quiet Investment," *Technology Review* (Feb./Mar. 1993): 17.
7. Alice Hagemeyer, "Deaf Awareness in the Library," in *DEAF: Communicating with Hearing People* (The Red Notebook)(Silver Springs, Md: Library and Information for Deaf Action, 1980).
8. But there are hearing ear dogs.
9. Julie Ann McDaniel, "They Can't Hear Us Does Not Mean We Can't Serve Them," *Journal of Library Administration* 14, no. 4 (1992): 131.
10. Alice Hagemeyer, "We Have Come a Long Way," *Library Trends* 41, no. 1 (summer 1992):11.
11. Ibid.
12. E-mail exchange and TDD relay conversation between Hagemeyer and Gilbert Beck, Nov. 14, 1998.
13. Warren R. Goldman and James M. Mallory, "Overcoming Communications Barriers: Communicating with Deaf People," *Library Trends* 41, no. 1 (summer 1992): 24.
14. "Libraries Serving the Deaf and Hearing-Impaired," *American Library Directory*, 1997–1998 (New Providence, N.J.: R.R. Bowker, 1997), 2,559–64.
15. Comparison between statistics report in *American Library Directory, 1993* (New York: H.W. Wilson, 1993): 2,359 and *American Library Directory, 1997–1998* (New Providence, N.J.: R.R. Bowker):2,564.
16. "Libraries Serving the Deaf and Hearing-Impaired," 2567–72.
17. Donna DeMarco, "Agency Touting Deaf Market (State Administered Telephone Service Provider Maryland Relay)," *Baltimore Business Journal* May 22, 1998, p. 1.
18. Relay Texas <http://www.puc.texas.gov/relaytx/index.htm> Nov. 15, 1998.
19. Sy Dubow, "Telephone Service," in *Legal Rights: The Guide for Deaf and Hard of Hearing People*, 4th ed. (Washington, D.C.: Gallaudet Univ. Pr., 1992), 11.
20. William C. Mann, et al, "The Use of Phones by Elders with Disabilities: Problems, Interventions, Costs," in *Assistive Technology* , no. 1 (1996):23.

21. Ibid., 33.
22. Dubow, "Telephone Service," in *Legal Rights,* 206.
23. From an IBM sales video on the Phone Communicator. Viewed at the Learning Living Resources Center in Lansing, Mich. Available at: <http://www.nethead.com/~dr-bill/sibmscom/html>.
24. Dubow, "Telephone Service," in *Legal Rights,* 210.
25. Interviews with Ameritech, AT&T, and Ultra Tech representatives, Dec. 1993.
26. "MCI Broke New Ground Wed., Introducing First Text Telephone (TT) Calling Card and Teletext Operator Services for Deaf and Hearing-Impaired Users," *Communications Daily,* July 7, 1994, p.7.
27. DeMarco, "Agency Touting Deaf Market," 1.
28. Dubow, "Telephone Service," in *Legal Rights,* 214.
29. Ibid., 31.
30. "Rules and Regulations: Nondiscrimination on the Basis of Disability by Public Accommodations and in Commercial Facilities; Final Rule," *Federal Register* 56:144 (Friday, 26 July 1991): 35,597.
31. Ibid., 35,660.
32. Ibid., 35,662.
33. Ibid., 35,661.
34. Dubow, "Telephone Service," 212.
35. Susan M. Goltsman, Timothy A. Gilbert, and Steven D. Wohlford, "15. Telephone," in *Survey Forms: The Accessibility Checklist: An Evaluation System for Buildings and Outdoor Settings,* 2nd ed. (Berkeley, Calif.:MIG Communications, 1993).
36. From EASI Inform, EASI Project List <easi@sjuvm.stjohns.edu>, 1993.
37. A transducer is "a device that is actuated by power from one system and supplies power usually in another form to a second system (as a telephone receiver that is actuated by electric power and supplies acoustic power to the surrounding air)." *Webster's Ninth Collegiate Dictionary,* (Springfield, Mass.: Merriam Webster, 1991), 1,252.
38. "Rules and Regulations, 35,661.
39. "Specifications: StarSound Infrared System 400," (Phonic Ear, 1998),1.
40. Ibid.
41. Ruth O'Donnell, "Helping Those with Hearing Loss," *Library Journal* 117, no. 12 (July 1992): 54.
42. "Specifications: Easy Listener Large Area FM System," (Phonic Ear, 1998), 1.
43. Ibid.
44. "All About FM: Technology for Improving Speech Understanding," (Phonic Ear, 1998).
45. Easy Listener brochures (Phonic Ear, 1993 and 1998).
46. <www.faa.gov/arp/C1.HTM>.
47. "Rules and Regulations," 35,689.
48. "Specifications: Easy Listener Personal FM System."
49. "TMX Telepin System with TMX for Use with the Solaris Personal Hearing System (PE572R/575R)" (Phonic Ear, 1998).
50. Barbara Franklin, "FM Systems with Children Who are Deaf-Blind," available at: <http://www.educ.kent.edu/deafed/970410y.htm>. Department of Special Edu-

cation, San Francisco State University, 1600 Holloway Avenue, San Francisco, Calif. 94132.

51. Ibid.

52. University of Michigan, spring 1998.

53. O'Donnell, "Helping Those with Hearing Loss," 54.

54. "Rules and Regulations," 35,690.

55. <www.faa.gov/arp/C1.HTM>.

56. Ibid.

57. "Rules and Regulations," 35,690.

58. "Federal Captioning Mandates: What They Are and What They Mean to You," *Caption Center Online* (WGBH/Caption Center/Consumer Information, 1998).

59. Gail L. Kovalik, "Silent Films Revisited: Captioned Films for the Deaf," *Library Trends* 41, no. 1 (Summer 1992): 103.

60. Formerly known as the MacArthur Foundation Library Video Project and based in Chicago. Telephone conversation with Mary Kirby, Dec. 3, 1998.

61. Interviews with vendors listed under "Video Producers," *Librarian's Yellow Pages* (Garance, Inc., 1998): 57–59.

62. *BLUE SECTION DEAFDIGEST: a free, weekly e-mail newsletter for anyone interested in the deaf* 3, no. 14 (For DEAFDIGEST subscription requests, mail to: barry@clark.net.)

63. Telephone conversation with Michael Gunde, Nov. 4, 1998.

64. Ibid.

65. "Video Access Guide," *Focus: Library Service to Older Adults, People with Disabilities*, no. 9 (1993). Unpublished.

66. Dubow, "Introduction," in *Legal Rights*, 44.

67. McDaniel, "They Can't Hear Us Does Not Mean We Can't Serve Them," 136.

68. <http://www.boston.com> (WGBH).

69. The cochlear implant is not necessarily favored by the culture of those with deafness.

70. "Cochlear Implants," from The Voice Center at Eastern Virginia Medical School <http://www.voice-center.com/cochlear_implants.html>.

71. The author recently discovered that CostCo, a discount store, offers hearing aids for one-third the cost of major suppliers of hearing aids. A top of the line digital aid costs $3,100 from a well-known dealer; the same aid was $1,300 at CostCo.

72. <www.hope4hearing.org/implant.htm>.

73. Muller, et al. "Implantable Microphone and Implantable Hearing Aids Utilizing Same," filed March 13, 1997 (U.S. Patent 5,814,095).

74. Ibid.

75. Joe Clark. "Reading the Silver Screen," *Technology Review* 97, no. 5 (July 1994): 18.

76. Ibid., 19.

77. <http://patent.uspto.com>.

78. *BLUE SECTION DEAFDIGEST.*

79. See chapter on "Wayfinding."

80. "Advisory Groups' Recommendations and Pacific Bell's Response," June 1994. <http://trace.wisc.edu/docs/pacbell_ud/agpd.htm?Pacific+Bell>.

accommodating the hand-disabled library user

Greg Shaw

Introduction

Compared to other groups of people with disabilities, those with hand, arm, and upper body musculoskeletal problems (for simplicity, I will use "hand-disabled" here) have received relatively little consideration for accommodation efforts. This is probably because the hand-disabled population has lagged behind other disability groups in organizational efforts, and so there has been less pressure for accommodation. But another reason might be that, until recently, not much *could* be done or the possibilities were few and relatively simple. In academic libraries, although many accommodations can be made for hand-disabled patrons, these have not until recently involved archi tectural modification, special collections, equipment investment, or highly specialized knowledge, as have accommodations for wheelchair users, the visually impaired, and the deaf.

Recent and rapid improvements in voice-recognition technology have largely changed this situation. In the space of a few years, voice recognition has developed from a very expensive, slow, and unreliable technology into a very fast, accurate, mass-marketed software product often priced lower than a single, new art book. Although voice input technology still requires a significant investment in equipment and technical expertise, suddenly there is an important tool that opens the world of computing and electronic information to hand-disabled users. Because it is now available, increasingly reliable and inexpensive, voice-recognition software is nearly as necessary a component of ADA compliance as provision of ramps for wheelchair users.

Many libraries and academic computing centers have not yet responded to these rapid changes, nor do they have comprehensive programs in place for accommodating hand-disabled users. This chapter, discusses computer-based access solutions as well as more traditional accommodations for the hand-disabled. Although computer-based accommodations that do not involve voice recognition are discussed to some extent, the bulk of this chapter focuses on the technical and organizational aspects of a program to provide access to computers equipped with the latest voice-recognition technology.

The exact legal requirements of the Americans with Disabilities Act and other disability laws are beyond the scope of this chapter. Although many of the elements of a good hand-disability access program may in fact be legal necessities, it is assumed here that the intention of an accessibility program is to provide equality of service for all patrons, rather than to meet the minimum requirements of the law.

The Hand-Disabled Population

In this chapter, the term hand-disabled encompasses those with injuries to hands, arms, and shoulders, and some who technically do not have hand injuries at all. The chapter takes a functional approach and groups together those people requiring similar accommodation solutions. Those with "hand disabilities" can be divided into those with "mobility limits" and those with "hand budgets." Although the needs of individuals with learning disabilities are touched on minimally, the focus here is access for individuals whose primary obstacle to full computer use is physical, rather than cognitive, in nature.

MOBILITY LIMITS

For those not familiar with disabled populations, the term hand-disabled may first bring to mind people with upper extremity mobility loss or paralysis, or amputees. As with other disabilities (e.g., the visually impaired population which is composed more of low-vision than blind individuals) the hand-disabled population is largely composed of people with only partial loss of hand use and movement. People with upper body limitations frequently have lower body mobility limitations as well. Paralysis from spinal injuries tends to mean immobility everywhere below the injury; strokes may paralyze a whole side of the body. Such patrons may have significant hand-accommodation needs, but these may be submerged behind other needs, such as the need for wheelchair ramps. Also, those with overlapping disabilities may be more likely to use assistants, who will in many cases serve as the person's hands. Others with hand limitations (e.g., those with a single absent or immobile limb) may have fewer accommodation needs because writing, keyboard entry, and retrieval can all be done, if awkwardly, with their healthy hand.

HAND BUDGET LIMITS

The larger group of hand-disabled patrons may have no mobility loss whatsoever and little, or no, obvious disability. For this group of hand-disabled, instead of having missing limbs or paralysis, disability consists of a particularly low "budget" for use of the hands. If they overuse an extremity and exceed their budgets, this group might then lose mobility from fatigue, might experience high levels of pain, or their injuries might be exacerbated. The largest group of hand-budgeted disabled patrons in any library will probably have repetitive strain injuries (RSI), chronic and long-term (if not permanent) injuries to hands, arms, and shoulders as a result of overuse; the most commonly known type of RSI is carpal tunnel syndrome. In the past, these types of injuries were common only to sweatshop workers and manual laborers. Now, as a result of extensive keyboard use and the ergonomically incorrect practices they frequently and unwittingly employ, students and other serious computer users are increasingly entering the ranks of the hand-disabled.

RSI is an extremely widespread form of disability, occurring in frequency just behind back injuries in workers' compensation claims. In 1994, the U.S.

Bureau of Labor Statistics "logged 332,000 cases of repetitive strain injuries (RSI), quadruple the number reported just three years earlier.[1] BLS further estimates that the total annual costs (related to RSI) to businesses at $10.8 billion in 1994, with carpal tunnel syndrome carrying an average price tag of $12,700–$12,900 per affected worker.[2] Although not always accorded the status of "serious injury" or "real disability" in popular opinion, people with RSI have longer return-to-work times than amputees, and, unlike amputees, the serious injuries are very frequently bilateral.

People with RSI generally strive to maintain their pain levels within limits. To avoid extreme fatigue, partial loss of mobility, and nerve damage, as well as to prevent further degeneration, those with RSI must maintain extremely low hand-use budgets, which might permit, for example, as little as ten minutes of typing per day and no lifting anything that exceeds five pounds—simple tasks that place serious limits on day-to-day life.

Overuse injuries are not the only disabilities that impose hand-use budgets. Lupus, MS, and Fibromyalgia, systemic disorders rather than injuries, often precisely mimic the symptoms of RSI, particularly in their early stages. One can view the effects of these diseases as overuse injuries caused by the lowering of limits through systemic weakness rather than through excessive use; again, the problem is not paralysis, but a "budget," although this budget may extend to walking and other tasks unrelated to hand use. Also, arthritis-like conditions may engender a need for similar adaptations, because movement can cause pain and therefore place limits on use, even though mobility might not be limited and there is no strict necessity to ration use.

These different groups of "hand-disabled" people may require different kinds of sensitivity on the part of staff members. Where those with obvious hand-mobility limits may be most sensitive to discrimination or patronizing behavior stemming from their disability, a common experience for those with budget limitations on their hand use is that they are frequently questioned by those who are not accustomed to dealing with disabled populations. Sensitivity training on these issues for professional and support staff may be a big part of a hand disability accommodation effort.

Traditional Accommodation for Hand Disabilities

Although voice-recognition technology is the latest and most promising development, it will not, by itself, make the library fully accessible to hand-disabled patrons. Noncomputer library tasks offer substantial accessibility obstacles. These hurdles essentially revolve around the fact that books are heavy and may not be easy for patrons to lift off the shelves, carry home, return, or position on a photocopier.

To deal with these obstacles, the following accommodations should be considered:

Book retrieval: For patrons who are unable to retrieve books independently, speedy book retrieval service should be made available.

Checkout and renewal: If library renewal policies require bringing books physically back to the library for renewal, these policies can be waived for those with disability status.

Lockers: A major challenge for hand-disabled library users is carrying personal belongings—especially heavy textbooks and library materials—that are needed to get through a day of classes or research. Lockers and other safe places to leave personal belongings let hand-limited users "stage" this carrying, leaving off anything unnecessary while saving upper extremity use for essential tasks.

Reprographic services: Most academic libraries offer full-service photocopying. These services should be provided to disabled patrons at rates charged for self-service copying. In the absence of such services, staff time will have to be devoted to making copies for disabled students, because many academic curricula and research tasks require photocopying and disabled students may be unable to take notes from materials that must be kept in the library.

Carts: Students may be able to retrieve books from shelves but might not be able to carry them to the circulation desk or other areas of the building. Providing handcarts or book trucks will have the added benefit of reducing users' reliance on book retrieval services.

Good working order of manual machines: The hand-limited may be able to use equipment if kept in repair. Is the knob on the microfilm viewer hard to turn? Is the automatic drive broken? Does coin operation require endless feeds of small denomination coins? Simply keeping machines in good working order improves accessibility.

Research assistants: If access issues cannot be otherwise solved, research assistants can be employed to assist patrons. However, this is costly for the library and inconvenient for patrons, who must coordinate library use with times when assistants are available.

Voice Recognition and Accommodating Computer Access

Libraries rely heavily upon computers and keyboard input for access to catalogs, research databases, and the Internet. These computerized information resources might also overlap with university-wide services including e-mail, access to word processing, desktop publishing, and specialty software. Researchers also have a need to write, a fact so obvious it almost goes without saying; taking notes, recording citations, and summarizing texts are just a few of the tasks that must be possible and comfortable for all users, regardless of their disability status.

How can the hand-disabled user gain full access to the library? Voice recognition, an access solution really only practical within the past two to three years, holds the promise of being the all-in-one solution to computing obstacles. Patrons with the ability to type ten words per minute, or for no more than fifteen minutes per day with conventional keyboards, or who are unable to use either pen or keyboard, can dictate at speeds of approximately one hundred words per minute, with endurance comparable to those of their nondisabled counterparts. This technology can open the world of writing to people with hand-related disabilities who, in the not-so-distant past, had to rely on work-around solutions for this vital task.

However, voice-recognition access programs are still full of pitfalls. It is very easy to make large investments for equipment that is never used because the appropriate software and hardware products were not purchased, because no one knows the program is available, because staff and students have not received training, or because machines have crashed and no one knows how to fix them. But with the proper research in purchasing appropriate software and hardware, a suitable location, support staff, proper training for users, and coordination with university-wide access efforts, voice recognition is an option that can really work for library and/or computing center accommodation.

HISTORY OF VOICE RECOGNITION

Practical voice recognition is a very recent development. Voice recognition has existed for decades as a research subject with code run on mainframes, but it did not appear as a desktop computer product until the early 1980s, and then only with the capacity to recognize a very small vocabulary. The first commercially available, large-vocabulary, general-purpose dictation system for PCs was released in 1990 with the first version of DragonDictate, soon followed by other competitors. But the early products were nothing like those of today in terms of quality, speed, and cost. Some very determined and computer-literate users with money to pay costs on the order of $20,000 were able to use these products. But, at best, they remained poor substitutes for pen and keyboard. As the advocate for a voice-recognition program for your library or computing facility, you might encounter negativity on the part of those who saw voice recognition demonstrated in this era.

The real breakthroughs have been the result of gradual improvements in recognition algorithms and the vast improvements in computing speed. By 1995, discrete voice recognition quietly achieved an order of magnitude improvement: dictation speed reached sixty words per minute, accuracy rates exceeded 95 percent, the software became easier to use, and bottom-of-the-line new computers became fast enough to run it. A more abrupt order-of-magnitude improvement came as recently as late 1997 with the first desktop real-time continuous voice-recognition software, which now has launched frantic competition among software vendors to try to produce a product that can replace the keyboard for the nondisabled market. Despite the claims in software vendors' advertising, there are still problems with the technology from the perspective of nondisabled users, most of whom will still want to use keyboards, especially if they can type and do not do all their work in sound-insulated offices. But for disabled clients, these limitations will be unimportant, because voice-recognition should allow productivity similar to nondisabled users, with reasonable cost and moderate inconvenience. For the hand-disabled, voice recognition is now an essential life tool.

Voice-Recognition Basics

Before discussing specific voice-recognition products, it is important to get a feel for their quality and general characteristics. Voice recognition works, but it is not effortless. Recognition is astonishingly accurate and quick—in the range of 95 percent or greater accuracy and 100+ words per minute dictation speed. Some voice-recognition products allow users to speak at their normal conversational speed, and will recognize almost all words. The technology is at the point that, even taking a much more skeptical view than the sales literature, it can be argued that certain nondisabled users might want to use it instead of keyboards. But it is not effortless, like the voice recognition on *Star Trek* or speaking into a tape recorder, mainly because it does not understand every word correctly. A great deal of effort is spent on correcting mistakes. Using voice recognition requires a set of skills and mental concentration perhaps not much harder than typing, but that requires adaptation and a reasonable amount of computer literacy or training on the part of the user.

Continuous versus discrete voice recognition: There are two basic kinds of voice recognition. The first, discrete recognition, requires the user to ... speak ... with ... pauses ... between ... each ... word. The second, continuous recognition, lets the user speak without pauses between words. Continuous recognition allows for much, much faster recognition, in the range of 100+ words per minute, versus the 40–60 wpm for discrete dictation. It is, however, the newer technology, and discrete recognition, as a more mature technology, can be used more flexibly with a wider range of applications and is a bit more reliable.

Controlling applications versus large-vocabulary text entry: Another basic distinction in voice-recognition products is the difference between command and control recognition and programs designed to dictate sentences of text in a full range of English words. A few years ago, many of the products available were command and control, that is, products designed to recognize only a small range of words in order to use the operating system or record certain data. For example, such voice recognition comes bundled in the Macintosh operating system, and UPS uses this kind of recognition to allow voice entry of tracking numbers. All of the products described here, by contrast, can recognize a large vocabulary of conventional English words, from 20,000 to 60,000, and words not in the vocabulary sets can be added as they are used. These products also perform, with varying degrees of difficulty, functions provided by the older command and control products.

Software, not hardware: Voice recognition does not rely on special machines but, rather, is simply software running on conventional computers. Voice-recognition software may run in the background of other programs, allowing input into these programs the same way that keyboards do, or it may use special word-processing programs for entering text.

One of the challenges for the institutional application of voice input technology is that each user must create her or his own voice file; the totally public voice-recognition computer is not here yet. The voice-recognition products available today vary in their ability to recognize words on the first day of use, but the major products all require an initial training period during which the user reads in a script or list of words before the product works properly. All of the currently available programs create files for individual users. The voice input computer that can be located in a public place, where unregistered users simply sit down and begin dictating, has not been developed yet; some software is available for recognizing a simple range of words in such settings, but for anything more advanced, the system must be trained to understand the individual user's voice.

The programs keep individual information in "voice files," which over time adapt to the speaker's voice and, if correctly maintained, gradually reduce error rates. Most of the effort in using voice recognition is in correcting misrecognitions. Compared to the products of several years ago, recognition accuracy is extremely high: 95 percent recognition rates can be expected, lower when introducing new or complex words or dictating in new subject areas. But any product will require that the user be fluent in correcting the errors that are made. In some products, if the errors are not immediately corrected, recognition will get worse because the software is "learning" mistakes. For example, when the user dictates the word *dog* but the computer hears *frog*, if this mistake is not corrected the computer will try to use *frog* for each instance of the word *dog*. Even for the newer products, such as NaturallySpeaking, that permit the user to postpone correcting misrecognitions, correction is still necessary. Unlike keyboard typos, voice-recognition errors are difficult to understand if left uncorrected. For example, the historian who dictates "the sans-cullote incendiaries" might see "the signs could lot instant areas" appear on the monitor—a misunderstanding that would be very difficult to correct after the fact.

Moreover, programs rely on corrections to improve working accuracy. Users must learn how to make these corrections using special commands and correction alphabets and must become comfortable enough with the process to be able to write without being distracted by it. Software dealers may try to argue that voice recognition does not require special skill, but even in the newest products, this correction process requires a good bit of practice, reasonable computer literacy, and possibly training to learn, especially for hand-disabled users who cannot resort to the keyboard for simpler correction as most abled users of voice recognition do.

Context recognition: The major voice-recognition products claim the ability to distinguish between homonyms such as " to" and "two" using context clues. However, because computers are not really intelligent, this context recognition may be a mixed blessing. Context recognition works well for simple business or newspaper-like writing and complete sentences but may actually lower recognition rates where grammatical style is not so predictable. Context recognition will tend to recognize more common words at the expense of difficult ones. For these reasons, context recognition is not at all perfect, and although future software versions will probably improve recognition rates with better context recognition for certain kinds of writing, it may not help at all with other uses.

Although voice recognition is not trivial to learn and may require special training, this difficulty should be put in perspective. It is no more difficult to master than other tasks expected of college-level students. It also is easier than learning to read braille or learning sign language. Although software is changing quickly, many of the essential skills needed by users will remain the same: mental comfort writing with the voice, and fluency in using the international correction alphabet and other correction procedures.

Ultimately, to get a feel for voice recognition, the consumer should experiment with the software. Although vendors will demonstrate the software, they will generally use simple words they have used before or read from the kinds of text that do well in voice recognition (such as newspaper writing) in order to ensure better-than-average recognition rates. Although this gives you a feel for the software, ideally, you should find a way to try out the software yourself. Try to find a disinterested organization that allows hands-on use of voice-recognition products, such as the Center for Assistive Technology in Berkeley, California.

Current State of Voice Recognition

When it comes to describing specific products, anything described here might very well be superseded by the time you read this. The products and players are changing exceedingly quickly, and the products described as this book goes to press may be entirely different in six months. It is absolutely essential to conduct a little product research at the time of purchase. The best way to begin is by referencing vendors' Web sites. Vendors have released different versions and packages, bundling together different vocabularies, vocabulary sizes, and discrete and continuous products, and additional features, varying the packages almost from month to month. Because prices vary so much depending on the source, the following can give only a general sense of the prices, and these will likely change. Finally, at this writing new versions are expected to be released within weeks.

CURRENT SOFTWARE PRODUCTS

With these caveats in mind, the principal companies producing voice-recognition software for the Windows platforms are Dragon, IBM, and Kurzweil. All three offer both continuous and discrete voice-recognition products, and all are usable products with broadly similar features (though with some important differences for disabled users). The cheapest versions of the discrete recognition products are running in the range of $100 or less, and the most advanced continuous recognition versions go for up to $800, although sometimes for much less.

Having once produced a product roughly equivalent to the IBM and Dragon products, Kurzweil has fallen behind in development but will release a continuous voice-recognition product in the near future. Kurzweil's discrete recognition product does extremely well with out-of-the-box recognition rates. It is nearly user independent but sacrifices some long-term accuracy for it. Kurzweil also offers a trial downloadable version of its discrete recognition product, which provides a good opportunity to try voice recognition before committing to it.

IBM offers a discrete recognition product called SimplySpeaking, while the company's continuous recognition product is ViaVoice. Each of these comes in a "Gold" version with a larger vocabulary size and some extra command and control features for ViaVoice Gold.

Dragon's discrete voice recognition product, DragonDictate, is very good for hands-free use and the only one that seems to have been designed with disabled users in mind, perhaps because Dragon has been selling to this market for a longer period of time. DragonDictate is sold in two versions, differing only in the size of vocabulary files, and also comes bundled with the continuous voice recognition product. NaturallySpeaking, Dragon's continuous voice recognition product, is also of high quality, although, it is difficult to use completely hands free. As of now, NaturallySpeaking is being sold in Individual, Deluxe, and Preferred editions, which differ in vocabulary size, ability to dictate into more than Dragon's word-processing program (Deluxe and Preferred support Word 97), ability to support multiple users (Deluxe and Preferred), and certain advance features (support for multiple vocabulary topics and macro scripting ability).

For a reason not obvious from sales literature, the disability access products of choice should be Dragon NaturallySpeaking and DragonDictate. Only Dragon allows full hands-free correction of misrecognitions, an absolutely essential feature for disabled users. IBM products require the user to type in its correction window and therefore are difficult for the hand-budgeted to use and nearly impossible for those with no use of their hands. The library or university will almost certainly want to purchase the higher-end NaturallySpeaking Deluxe, which comes bundled with DragonDictate and allows for multiple users. For either IBM or Dragon, it will be necessary to purchase a discrete recognition product if you do not purchase it bundled with a continuous one. All of the continuous products have limited ability to dictate into programs other than the special word processor that comes with the program, making a discrete recognition product essential for many uses. IBM and Dragon products are also available in most European languages. Both come with text-to-speech capabilities, but these are designed more for enhanced ability to correct misrecognitions than for use by the visually impaired.

Voice recognition for the Macintosh is problematic, but not impossible. The only product currently available for free-form dictation is

PowerSecretary, a product now owned by Dragon. PowerSecretary is roughly equivalent to the DragonDictate of three or four years ago—it is discrete recognition only. It is extremely awkward to use for command and control. Beyond a few commands (e.g., File Save and Mouse Click), users must be able to write AppleScript macros to be able to access menus, desktop icons, and other features of the operating system using their voice. Nevertheless, the software is sold for as much or more than the best PC products. Nor do there seem to be any plans to update this software (Dragon seems to be intentionally sitting on its hands in this regard). An advanced voice-recognition program for the Macintosh is reportedly under development by another company, but there is no indication yet when this will be available. PowerSecretary is usable (The author got through his first six months of graduate school papers with this product), but, if at all possible, make the transition to the PC. The Macintosh will no longer seem user-friendly if you have to access it through PowerSecretary.

As noted above, when you are ready to purchase, the products available may be completely different. Expect continued improvement in recognition quality and especially better integration of discrete and continuous products into a single version. On the other hand, given the marketing thrust of voice recognition developers, new products may not be "improved" from the perspective of disabled users. All these companies are now primarily focused on abled markets and are beginning to neglect hands-free features and advanced features that require more skill to learn but allow better dictation for those who use the program as their primary mode of data entry. Heavy competition among vendors means that the consumer will probably continue to have to look skeptically at sales literature and search for critical reviews of these products that are oriented toward the needs of disabled users.

Hardware Requirements

Hardware requirements, once prohibitive, are now relatively minimal; a new desktop or slightly better than bottom-of-the-line portable PC will certainly suffice. At this time, one cannot use a dumb terminal or run voice recognition on a server, but there is no problem using the software on a machine that networks with a server—the issue is the local machine.

Clock speed: DragonDictate (discrete recognition) can be run on a 486/66 processor, but a 100 MHz Pentium machine is preferable. Continuous recognition requires at least 133 MHz clock speed for Dragon NaturallySpeaking or 166 MHz for IBM ViaVoice. More speed does not hurt, and the fastest computers can make continuous recognition much more comfortable to use. Also, new releases tend to require faster clock speeds, so purchasing a top-of-the-line computer may be economical in the long run. However, in contrast to the situation of just a few years ago, computers running at the minimum clock speeds suggested by software vendors for continuous products will work well for users.

Depending on the software product, anywhere from 16 to 32 MB of RAM is required. More RAM will greatly improve voice recognition quality and help to avoid system crashes. RAM is currently quite inexpensive, so it is advisable to purchase as much as possible for optimum use of voice input software.

Operating system: DragonDictate runs on Windows 3.1 (Dragon has discontinued its DOS-only version). Most programs, however, are designed for Windows 95, and Windows 95 is a bit easier to use by voice. Before upgrading to Windows 98, be sure that your voice-recognition software is compatible.

Sound card: The trickiest part of hardware purchase is getting the sound card right. Vendors are trying to avoid advertising that their products work better on certain sound cards and that there are incompatibilities with others. Over-the-counter purchasers will not see this important information displayed prominently (if at all) on the packaging; rather, it is usually hidden in back Web pages or known only by technical support staff. A premium sound card (in the range of $300–400) will make a big difference in recognition quality for continuous voice recognition. When ordering, watch out for sound cards that boast 100 percent compatibility with a sound card on the compatibility list—this may not be good enough for voice recognition. In general, discrete recognition will be more tolerant of poor sound cards than continuous recognition. Be especially careful with portables—their compact arrangements may increase "noise." Several portables are being advertised as NaturallySpeaking-ready or may even come bundled with NaturallySpeaking, so such portables may be the best option.

Drive requirements: A CD-ROM drive is required (for installation only) and 50–100 MB hard-drive space for the continuous recognition products. In review, voice recognition now demands hardware no better than one would expect in any new (low-end) PC. Factoring in extra RAM and sound cards, one should be able to acquire the requisite hardware for a voice-recognition computer for less than $1,500. Librarians who do not have the technical expertise, or access to staff members who do, should consider acquiring their voice recognition PC from a reseller.

Macintosh hardware: PowerSecretary theoretically runs on any PowerPC, but it is advisable to have as much power behind it as possible, including a minimum 180 MHz and 32 MB RAM. PowerSecretary does not require an extra sound card, but in exchange you have to deal with the ambiguities of finding out which machines PowerSecretary will run on. Sound is implemented differently on different PowerPCs, and as noted earlier, PowerSecretary is only nominally supporting this software so that compatibility lists have not been updated for a few years. To be safe, buy from a reseller or get a money-back guarantee that your hardware and software will work together.

Architectural Modifications

If voice recognition is so good, why is it that abled users are not already using it? A big reason, and one the voice-recognition developers seem almost oblivious to, is that voice recognition requires sound privacy for optimal effectiveness. Sound insulated spaces for voice-recognition PCs are necessary for the same reasons that quiet is enforced in most library areas: it is hard for people to study or concentrate with other people talking near them. Many libraries provide group study rooms that are acoustically isolated from the rest of the library; for the same reason, spaces for voice recognition need to be isolated from other library areas.

Besides the obvious need for quiet in the library, voice recognition is also very sensitive to environmental noise (despite some vendor claims). Nearby conversation will make voice recognition very difficult, if not impossible. Discrete voice recognition is a bit less sensitive to environmental noise than continuous, but it still requires relative quiet. Voice recognition can be trained to ignore predictable noises (e.g., a cough or door slam) but is sensitive even to distant conversation, traffic noises from an open window, or moderately loud white noise. In a pinch, voice recognition can be accomplished in moderately noisy areas, but this is not ideal.

Privacy is also important from the user's point of view. To get an idea of why this is so, try walking into a computer lab and reciting your e-mail. For even more laughs, try dictating in the varying-pitch singing voice that is good ergonomic practice for voice recognition. Writing and reading have evolved as methods of communicating partly because they can be done silently and therefore privately. With voice input, there is essentially no privacy anywhere within earshot. Using voice recognition in a public place would be similar to typing on a computer that projects words on a screen that everyone in a room can see, hardly a comfortable way for most people to write.

The ideal space for voice recognition, therefore, is not a spacious room with lots of computers but, rather, a small, individual room with a single computer, with walls and ceilings professionally sound insulated. Professional sound insulation may cost upward of $1,000 for materials and labor.

Administrators may balk at the necessity of private rooms that use valuable space and sound insulation that costs as much as voice-recognition hardware and software. But without acoustically isolated spaces for voice recognition, expect to have equipment that is only used by disabled students in desperation, that works badly, that discourages proper ergonomic habits, and that causes a constant barrage of complaints from other patrons. Finally, because disabilities frequently overlap, when selecting locations for voice computing, be sure to take into consideration the needs of wheelchair users.

Specific Library Applications

Word processing: Word processing is normally provided for students in computer labs. But disabled students unable to use pen and paper need the capacity to take notes from library materials, and "computer lab" functions requiring free-text entry such as e-mail are often provided in libraries, raising an obligation to provide equal access. Word-processing-like dictation, that is, dictation consisting of English words used in sentences, is what voice recognition does best. As mentioned, as of this date, hands-free corrected continuous voice recognition essentially only works in word-processing programs or in special versions bundled with common software products. As this book goes to press, a plug-in available free, but not sold with NaturallySpeaking, allows dictation into applications other than the word processor provided with the program, but hands-free correction is not possible with this plug-in. Presumably this feature will be enhanced in forthcoming releases, but beware vendor claims—sales literature already claims the ability to dictate into any word-processing program. It actually does so but does not allow the disabled user to correct mistakes.

Any text-based program can easily work with continuous voice recognition. For example, to dictate into an e-mail program, dictation and correction can be done in the voice recognition word processor and cut and pasted (by a voice macro if necessary) to the e-mail program. The discrete recognition products are also good at basic command and control (e.g., opening and closing programs or selecting a font from a menu). Voice users may actually be quicker at menu selection than abled mouse users. The continuous voice recognition products all advertise ability to control programs by voice but actually require users to script macros to accomplish many functions and are primarily designed for word processing, not command and control.

Command lines and data strings, as with library catalogs: For many library applications—online catalogs, research databases, and so on—instead of complete sentences with common English words, one needs to use strings of special commands, letters and numbers, and less-common proper names and English words (e.g., f su = grasshopper & au = Jiminy).

Such entry is harder for voice recognition because each keystroke has to be entered as a single "word." Also, voice recognition is not as good with less-common words and proper names, and such words may have to be spelled letter by letter, or at least have to be corrected after dictation. Letters must usually be dictated using an international alphabet (alpha, bravo, charlie, etc). For example, the above would have to be dictated "foxtrot space bar sierra uniform equals sign grasshopper [possible need for correction] ampersand" (etc).

The more an interface requires streams of gibberish versus words (ax4_3 rather than auxiliary 4 3), the slower it will be in voice recognition. If a discrete recognition program allows a dictation rate of 60 words per minute it will only dictate 60 characters per minute of a data string. This problem still makes it hard for the hand-disabled to use the more obtuse command line interfaces (such as Dialog). Continuous voice recognition is much faster (at best, 130 words per minute and therefore 130 characters per minute) and so may be more comfortable to use with data string interfaces. As mentioned above, at the current time, continuous voice recognition is hard for disabled users to use outside the special word-processing programs that come off the software, although this is likely to change with future products. Still, even 60 characters per minute may be far better than what the user can do without voice recognition. Also, by training special words in a program and writing macros, speed can be increased. In fact, with proper use of macros, the voice-input-proficient disabled users can probably beat their nondisabled counterparts in speed of use, but this takes some computer literacy on the part of the user or careful planning on the part of a librarian or computer administrator.

Graphic interfaces: Many library computer systems are switching to graphical interfaces, including the graphical Web browsers. If a user does not have trouble moving a mouse, voice recognition in a graphic environment will be simple. Even clicking the mouse can be easily accomplished by voice. DragonDictate and other discrete voice-recognition programs provide a full set of commands for clicking the mouse, for example, "Left Click."

Moving the mouse by voice is a bit more awkward. The discrete recognition programs provide a variety of ways to move the mouse by voice. The best of these, in DragonDictate, uses a command (the user simply says "mouse grid") that divides the screen into a tic-tac-toe board of nine numbered squares. The user selects a number, and the grid then focuses in on that square, and by continuing to select grid numbers the user can zero in on any point on the screen. An experienced user can get quite fast with this process, but it is inherently more awkward and slower than using the mouse to perform the same function. But again, if the mouse is not an alternative, slow access is better than no access.

When possible, provide alternatives with command-line operation. Offer text-only browsers such as Lynx. However, given trends in Web design, text-only browsers will not be able to access many features on the Web, although universities should already be designing their pages to work via Lynx for a variety of accessibility reasons.

Products under development, and probably new versions of the Netscape browser, should make it easier to use the Web by allowing voice selection of hyperlinks and form entry, which would make the mouse unnecessary for the Web. A stand-alone product, SurfTalk, exists for the Macintosh for voice browsing.

USE IN ARCHIVES AND SPECIAL COLLECTIONS

Most archives restrict access to materials to use in the archival area, and it will probably not be feasible to have a voice-recognition lab in each archival location. One approach is to dictate to tape recorders and transcribe the material elsewhere. High-quality digital tape recorders can be purchased for about $400, which can then be input to a computer for processing by NaturallySpeaking. The text can then be played back and corrections made by listening to the original tape. This system may not work well for dictation rich in the less-common words and proper names that NaturallySpeaking has trouble with—it is difficult to correct voice material in which there is a high error rate—but this approach may be preferable to using a tape recorder and having to wait for transcription by typing services. Another solution is to put voice-recognition software on portable computers (some libraries already provide portable computers for patrons to borrow). In any of these cases, it is necessary to have space set aside for use of sound input devices where other patrons will not be bothered. Yet another way to solve the problem of access in archives and other special collections may be to create procedures for disabled users to remove materials to voice-recognition computer labs that serve the whole library or university, while maintaining sufficient control over materials.

APPLICATION TO DIFFERENT POPULATIONS

One hundred percent hand mobility-limited: Those with complete or near-complete hand impairment can use voice recognition with little assistance, although careful planning may be required. Only DragonDictate has really been designed to be 100 percent hands free, though the other products could be used with someone around who could assist from time to time or by careful setup of the operating system (to bring up programs automatically) and writing of macros (to extend the command and control functions). The user has to be able to get a microphone on his her head (a desktop microphone could be used but would not get good recognition). Also, the program occasionally crashes or suffers minor glitches that require hand use to get out of or to restart the program, so that it would be best to have an attendant or computer support person available. Still, as discussed above, a user with zero hand use can get very close to 100 percent of computer tasks accomplished with voice recognition, hands free.

Hand-budgeted: Those with hand budgets who can do little keyboarding are really the ideal users of voice recognition, though it does make it a great deal easier if the user can occasionally resort to the keyboard to get out of trouble. Those with even more tolerance for typing on the keyboard can use the keyboard and mouse to correct misrecognitions, which will make learning the program a little easier but also greatly increase the ergonomic use of the hands. Manual correction of mistakes would require hitting the keyboard once every 15 or 20 seconds at best. Most hand-budgeted users should make the time investment and learn complete hands-free correction, including international alphabet.

However, hand-budget users may need to take special care to protect their voice, because vocal strain injuries are common, and they may suffer from systemic conditions that make them susceptible to such injuries.

Those with some hand use will want to use the mouse, because voice replacement of these functions is awkward and slow, although this use may stress the hand budgets of many users. Voice-recognition workstations for such users should be designed with some of the non-voice-recognition ergo-nomic solutions described below, with special attention to mouse use.

Learning disabilities: Another very large and important group of users of voice-recognition software are those with learning disabilities. Voice recognition is not a catchall solution for those who need accommodation for reading and writing: voice recognition requires visual selection skills (spotting mistakes, choosing correct words quickly from a choice list) that may be harder, not easier, than writing and keyboarding for those with certain learning disabilities. Although learning disabilities are complex, in most cases it is appropriate to introduce the student to voice recognition—either hands-on or by demonstration. Many, if not most, students will be able to judge their own capabilities, and most who take the time to go through training will become serious users.

Vocal disabilities: Voice recognition requires reasonably consistent speech patterns. People with cerebral palsy or other conditions that prevent consistent speech may require non-voice-recognition solutions.

TECHNICAL SUPPORT

The modern trend in software engineering is to release to market products with a lot of bugs. Voice recognition is no exception: the products are new, and the competition between IBM and Dragon has resulted in rushed development. It is absolutely essential that the voice-recognition program have someone on staff who is capable of dealing not only with problems that ordinarily arise with conventional software but also with voice-recognition-specific problems.

As just one example of what can go wrong, the author has found that running versions of NaturallySpeaking and DragonDictate simultaneously will occasionally lead to a disastrous conflict. If both microphones are turned on at once, the DragonDictate voice files will be completely disabled. There is a way to recover the old files, by doing initial training on a new file and copying the old voice files to the appropriate directory, but on the first call, Dragon technical support was not aware of this problem, and solving these kinds of problems takes specific knowledge of the programs.

Although this and other specific problems will doubtless be corrected, the pattern of "bugginess" is common to all the voice-recognition products. The library or computing center will not necessarily need to employ a voice-recognition expert (although large campuses might consider this), but it is extremely important to have at least one person who is capable of trouble-shooting these sometimes frustrating systems. Without this kind of expertise, problems are likely to occur that will keep the software from being used at all. Reliability will doubtless increase with new versions, but one cannot assume that these problems will disappear.

Voice-Recognition Training

As stated earlier, voice-recognition programs are not effortless. Users must master correction commands and alphabets in order to use the program. To ensure maximum use of your voice input system, it is essential that your patrons have access to some sort of training program, whether conducted by the library, academic computing staff, or outside trainers, to assist them in gaining these skills.

The trick is not in the dictating but, instead, in knowing how to make corrections and properly maintain the voice file. Technically sophisticated users can learn this process without formal training, but even they will benefit from it. The software is, in general, poorly documented (DragonDictate is an exception). But the majority of users will probably not be able to use the product seriously without help from an expert trainer. Also, training serves a "gatekeeping" function: untrained users can cause damage to other users' files, and because learning the program takes a fair amount of self-motivation, users who will not commit to this learning process should be screened out before taking up valuable resource time.

The average college student will need between four and sixteen hours of training. In addition, the user must have a moderate degree of computer literacy and must be familiar with traditional word-processing programs as well as basic use of the operating system. Although most university students have this knowledge, those who have not been able to use computers because of disabilities may have to acquire this basic knowledge first. In addition to the knowledge needed to operate the software, learning voice recognition takes a bit of transition time, mostly self-taught, simply to get used to the new modality of writing.

Most university-level students will be able to learn and successfully use the program with sufficient motivation. But users should not be led to expect that they will complete training and dictate graduate-level papers the next day. Several weeks should be allowed to become comfortable with the process. Voice-recognition software resellers usually offer training but typically charge from $60 to $100 per hour. It is usually much cheaper to develop the expertise in-house. Use outside trainers to bring someone in the library up to speed, who then can become the student trainer; ideally, the in-house trainer should be an actual user of the program.

MODEL TRAINING CURRICULUM

The training outline that follows can be used for either continuous or discrete voice-recognition programs. An experienced trainer can adjust the speed of the curriculum to the client's level of computer literacy. The continuous recognition products will be a little quicker to learn than the discrete, but most disabled users should learn both, as mentioned earlier.

Background: At the beginning of the lesson, the trainer should get an idea of the user's computer literacy level, specific programs, and potential uses of the program. Users can be introduced to any bureaucratic requirements (e.g., obtaining an account, reserving particular equipment, etc.) for using software and other computing facilities at this time.

Initial training required by program: Before users can begin dictating in voice recognition, they need to go through a preliminary training of their voice file, reading from a script or list of words so that the voice file can adapt to their voice. This process takes no more than about ten minutes for DragonDictate, but NaturallySpeaking requires the user to read an excerpt that can take up to two hours. A reasonably computer-literate user can be left alone to go through this registration, but some users may need the trainer to remain with them during this process.

Ergonomics: At the very beginning of the lesson, the trainer should give an introduction to proper voice dictation ergonomics. Repetitive strain injury clients and others with "budgets" will likely be very receptive to admonitions to protect their voice, perhaps even overly fearful of using it, but those with other disabilities may be hard to convince. The case for proper voice ergonomics should be made strongly: vocal strain is very common among people who use their voice regularly, such as singers and teachers, and substituting the voice for hands can provide a similar strain on individuals who use voice input software on a regular basis. It is possible to completely lose the voice as a result of vocal strain. Those with systemic weaknesses that have led to hand overuse may also be prone to voice overuse.

General rules for healthy dictation are:
- Rest frequently. Take longer breaks if you start to get hoarse.
- Drink large amounts of water.
- Vary the pitch at which you dictate; do not dictate in a monotone.
- Breathe from the abdomen and do not dictate in staccato bursts.
- Stretch the voice. Singers use warm-up exercises to stretch the vocal cords.
- Singing is much easier on the voice than speaking and is a natural way to vary the pitch. You are in a sound-insulated room, right? Forward into the bold new future of data entry!

First-day dictation (getting correction working, with "alpha-bravo" words): Begin by learning basic dictation (bring something to read so the client does not have to focus on thinking what to say). The idea is to get the user quickly and properly using the commands to correct mistakes by voice. In DragonDictate and NaturallySpeaking, this means learning the two simplest commands:

1. "Scratch That," which commands the system to erase the last thing said and also erases any record of this from the voice file.
2. "Spell Mode" in DragonDictate, or "Correct" in NaturallySpeaking, which allows one to correct a mistake and instruct the voice file what should have been recognized. Disabled users should begin by learning to spell into the correction window with the international alphabet. NaturallySpeaking allows using regular letter names to enter letters, but this is not as accurate as the international alphabet—disabled users will benefit from the extra accuracy. Also, DragonDictate requires

the international alphabet. Some users with mild disabilities can be taught to use the keyboard for corrections, but ideally, hands-free skills should be developed from the beginning. The ultimate goal should be to dictate the international alphabet as fast as an auctioneer, and this will only come with practice. On the first day of training, the user should dictate slowly using a cheat sheet with the international alphabet and basic commands written on it. The trainer may have to guide the user through other problems that may occur in first dictation, for example, misrecognitions in correction windows or handling the many small bugs that appear in all these programs.

Basic operation of the program: Although not difficult to learn, the trainer should make absolutely clear the basic operation of getting into and out of the program and saving voice files. It is not difficult for inexperienced users to destroy not only their own voice files but other people's as well, undoing perhaps years of work. Users also should be taught how to back up their voice files.

This point in the curriculum can often be reached in one sitting and provides a good place to break so that users can become comfortable in basic dictation on their own without danger, and can come to the next session knowing the international alphabet and with questions about more advanced use.

Text entry in discrete dictation program, second-order correction, and command and control: The goal of the second, and possibly third, session should be to teach the more advanced commands available and to teach the skills necessary to maintain voice files that cannot be dealt with by the basic commands (e.g., Scratch That and Spell Mode/Correct [word]). You should teach:

- the full range of correction commands (e.g., the commands that allow correction of words several words back or that allow correction of mistakes made in the correction window);
- the full range of style commands: for setting font style, moving around in the dictation program, etc.;
- basic command and control (selecting menu items, moving around in the operating system, clicking and moving the mouse by voice).

Macro writing and customizing the program: For a final session, users who are interested and sufficiently computer literate should be taught the use of the macro scripting capabilities that are included with both DragonDictate and NaturallySpeaking. For other users, this time can be used as a problem-solving session. You may want to write macros for actions that will be repeated frequently, for example, to copy material from a research database into a word-processing program.

This is the time to work out how to use command-line programs such as library catalogs or graphic interface programs such as Netscape, and to create commands and macros that make use of these programs comfortable. An advanced lesson is also the point at which to discuss conflicts and bugs the trainer is aware of, so that users can handle problems on their own. If training a staff voice-recognition support person, this subject should be dealt with extensively.

Alternatives to Voice Recognition

Accessibility can be increased without voice recognition. Voice recognition is not going to work for everyone with hand limits, and traditional approaches to working around disabilities for data entry on keyboards may work better for many users. Also, many users will want to combine voice recognition with traditional data entry but will still need the assistance of non-voice-recognition technology to keep hand use within budgets.

Products are available for dealing with specific patterns of mobility loss. Quadriplegics may be able to use a variety of methods for communicating with computers, including head pointers, eye position tracking, and mouth sticks.

Those with difficulty controlling hands can use special guides and braces that keep hands on mice or large-keyed keyboards that are easier to strike. One-handed users can use special single-handed keyboards, some of which work about as quickly as the conventional QWERTY. Such products include BAT Personal Keyboards (about $200), Right and Left-Handed Maltron Keyboards ($700), or the HandyKey Twiddler (about $200). Mice designed to be operated by the feet are available, for example, the NoHands Mouse. However, solutions that offload to other extremities should be strongly discouraged for those with unilateral RSI or other budget problems because simply transferring excessive use to other extremities can cause new injuries.

Ergonomics

There are also many products available that fall into the category of ergonomic devices. These might be used by abled users to increase the safety of computer use, and also might provide accessibility. Ergonomic adjustments, if they accomplish what they purport to, reduce the total stress on the user to do a given task by working with the natural function of the body or reducing effort needed to accomplish a given task. For the hand-disabled with budgets rather than mobility loss, these improvements may be essential for accomplishing tasks within budgets.

A great deal of literature describes good ergonomic practice in setting up workstations and using computers. See, for example the especially good Harvard RSI Action Web page at http://www.eecs.harvard.edu/rsi/, or any of the many books on RSI. The basic idea is to allow keyboarding with forearms parallel to the ground, upper arms vertical, and monitors at eye level, and as much adjustability as possible.

A cornucopia of ergonomic devices is available—arm supports, alternative keyboards, mice, etc.—with varying degrees of usefulness. The claims of vendors of ergonomic equipment should be viewed skeptically because there is no regulatory body to enforce accuracy in ergonomic claims and many vendors take advantage of this. For example, the ubiquitous pads in front of keyboards, advertised as preventing "carpal tunnel syndrome," do not actually do anything at all except provide a place to rest one's hands when not typing. If one were to rest hands on the pads while typing, this would be poor ergonomic positioning.

The author's own opinion as to what is useful, albeit based not on scientific research but as a hand-limited computer user and service provider to other disabled users, is that the following products are good investments, perhaps for a single workstation also including voice recognition:

- Arm supports that take the physical load of arms held up to keyboard off the shoulders (such as the ErgoRest Articulating Arm Rests).
- A mouse with an extra button or two to eliminate clicking and dragging and double clicking, for example, Kensington mice. Track balls or drawing tablets may be useful for some patterns of injuries.
- Macro programs that allow multiple keystrokes to be replaced by a single keystroke such as QuicKeys, or programs that reduce keystrokes by attempting to finish words from one or two letters may be useful to reduce typing but will probably require special training for most users.
- Alternative keyboards are generally more expensive than voice recognition, but if you must use them, perhaps because you do not have a suitable location for voice recognition or have users who cannot use their voice for data entry, you should purchase a product such as a Kinesis keyboards or the DataHand that dramatically reduces the distance fingers have to move to reach keys. However, these keyboards can be difficult to learn, rather than using keyboards that simply place the slope of the keyboard at different angles and positions.

The wealth of possibilities makes for complicated choices. A good place to get feedback on an individual product is the RSI listserv, Sorehand (see http://206.109.1.6/internet/paml/groups.S/sorehand.html).

Organizational Aspects of a Successful Voice-Recognition Program

You should not make the mistake of focusing only on the technological aspects of the access program. The following subsections discuss other aspects to consider in organizing a successful voice-recognition program.

TRAINING STAFF

As mentioned above, a classic problem with accessibility technology is that it sits on a shelf somewhere because the person who was responsible for its purchase and learning how to use it has now left the institution. Set up formal procedures for training appropriate staff members. If you do not have someone who knows how to train and troubleshoot the inevitable technical problems that will arise, someone should know how to hire outside help to provide training or repair.

ADVERTISING

If no one knows about the program, no one will be able to use it. Advertise the availability of access resources. Just as signs (should) direct wheelchair users to ramps and elevators, it should be easy to find voice recognition resources and for a new disabled student to find out about the process for getting training and using equipment. Make sure that disabled students groups know about the program, as well as staff in university-wide student disability offices and in the library, especially those at information and reference desks.

ELICIT FEEDBACK FROM DISABLED STUDENTS

Disabled students who regularly use the library are the real experts on access. Actively solicit feedback on what obstacles keep them from using the library, from using voice recognition equipment, and that interfere with their daily tasks. I found out that one patron I was charged with training with lupus was not using the equipment because she could not afford the risk to her immune system of using a microphone shared by others, but could not afford her own microphone. Such problems, perhaps unique to one individual, can be solved, if you know about them.

GENERAL SUPPORT FROM STAFF

In one major academic university, network connections necessary for connecting voice recognition to library catalogs were under the bureaucratic control of a particular computer administrator who felt that accessibility staff and student users were encroaching on his administrative turf and so were a kind of threat. The point is that even though accessibility may seem the right thing to do—most librarians are quite sympathetic to the needs of their various user groups—do not underestimate the opposition because not everyone shares this viewpoint. In addition to general hostility toward and/or fear of disabled people, a program for hand-disability access may run into misunderstandings about what constitutes a disability. Many people may try to judge the level of disability by sight, expecting a wheelchair or obvious mobility problem, and may not feel that those with budget limits are "really disabled" and so refuse to provide services for such patrons.

COORDINATION WITH OTHER ACCESS EFFORTS

A common mistake is to try to create one machine or one lab that is accessible to people with any kind of disability, from quadriplegia to hearing loss to the hand-disabled. This kind of all-in-one approach can waste resources and create serious problems by:

- making access solutions unnecessarily complicated (would it be simpler to provide access in separate locations?);
- solving problems before they occur (should you invest in the equipment for deaf and blind and hand-disabled users before having such a patron?);

- creating compatibility conflicts (does the text-to-braille software conflict with voice recognition software?);
- unnecessarily limiting the access of some users (software for some disabled user groups may run on more machines than voice recognition software);
- creating conflicts among users (if it is all on one machine, will the users be waiting in line?).

UNIVERSITY-WIDE COMPUTER FACILITIES

An access effort in the library should be coordinated with a university-wide approach to access. Although the access measures discussed above may be necessary for the library, they do not have to be done completely in the library and by library staff, and are probably not ideally done so. The combined costs of staff and student training, architectural modifications, and computer software and hardware may best be shared by those organizational groups responsible for university-wide disability access and for maintaining computer facilities. For example, a library may not be able to afford a devoted technology access staff member, but the campus as a whole should have such a person.

Some library access needs may be met with computer services outside the library because library catalogs can usually be accessed over networks or the Internet. The university could even purchase access equipment for the student in his or her home, for access over phone lines. On the other hand, just as able users need access to catalogs in the library so that they can go back and forth from stacks to looking up references, disabled users should ideally not be required to commute back to their home or across campus every time they want to check a book or take some notes.

Conclusion

To recapitulate, a hand disability program for an academic library or computing facility should include:

- support for the physical tasks of moving, retrieving, and using books and other materials
- continuous and discrete voice recognition, with working and compatible hardware, in acoustically isolated spaces
- a training program for users and staff
- special non-voice recognition data entry equipment as a complement to voice recognition and for those who cannot use voice recognition
- integration into a campuswide disability program, with advertising, student involvement, technical support, and wholehearted backing by key staff. ■

Notes

1. David Anderson, "RSI Can Strain the Bottom Line," *Business & Health* v16, no. 1 (Jan 1998): 44.
2. Ibid.

creating a web for all:

Access for Blind and Visually Impaired Users

Judith M. Dixon

Introduction

In April 1993, the Library of Congress connected to the Internet with MAR-VEL, (Machine-Assisted Realization of the Virtual Electronic Library). This event symbolized a major step forward for everyone attempting to gain access to the wealth of printed materials that exists today. A text-based gopher, MARVEL was the beginning of a massive effort that eventually found the library placing millions of documents online so that users who were located in far-flung areas could connect to the information with computers and have instant access to a library that most people would never see.

For blind and visually impaired computer users, the availability of electronic information presents an even greater opportunity than it does for those who are able to read standard printed material. Now, those who cannot read print in the normal fashion can connect to online resources with computers and use assistive technology to translate the visual text into speech, braille, or enlarged print.

Prior to the development of Internet access, only a very limited amount of reading material had been available in a braille, recorded, or large-print format. In fact, many texts, such as large reference works, have never been accessible to visually impaired users. For this reason, blind people soon found the burgeoning online services of numerous public and specialized libraries to be of great interest. As a result, librarians should expect that a growing number of people who have heretofore not been part of their patron population will seek to avail themselves of the library's online offerings.

At the time that MARVEL went online, the Internet was a much smaller, slower, simpler electronic environment than it is today. In 1993, text documents were displayed as ASCII text, and the use of highly formatted displays was limited because connections were often too slow to transmit complex graphical information. Access for blind persons was straightforward and unimpeded.

Now, as we head into the next millennium, Internet technology is changing rapidly. The single most striking change from a nontechnical observer's point of view has been in the elements introduced to enhance visual "interest." The Internet is now a highly formatted graphical environment where text can be displayed as a true likeness of the printed page.

Although this evolution may be seen as progress for those without a print disability, the obvious question remains: What effect is all this technological progress having on Internet access for those who rely on assistive technology?

To answer this question, it is necessary to describe briefly how a blind or visually impaired person accesses electronic information. To read material in electronic form, including material found on the Internet, a person with a visual disability uses a computer equipped with all the usual hardware and software that anyone would need to use floppy disks, CD-ROMs, or online services. In addition, such persons also need some type of interface hardware and software. This adaptive equipment can take many forms depending on the severity of the individual's impairment and the extent of the his or her skills.

Generally, however, interface with a computer system for a person who is visually impaired is via output devices for braille, synthetic speech, or large print. If a refreshable braille display or speech synthesizer is used for output, accompanying screen-reading software also is required. Numerous software and hardware options are available for reading the screen in large print.

Because all computers operate in more or less the same way, digital information can be easily transferred from one machine to another. Thus, text stored in digital form can be read by a sighted person using a color monitor or a blind person using a braille display, magnification system, or speech output device.

All this having been said, the short answer to the question of how technological progress is affecting Internet access for blind and visually impaired users is that people unable to read the printed word are continuing to enjoy their tenuous grip on their new-found ability to access the Internet. But the "enhancements" to Web environments are constantly throwing up new roadblocks that stymie even the most experienced user. It may seem that modifications to the screen reader, the browsers, the authoring tools, or the Web pages would just take care of things. The screen reader developers are having to update their software on a regular basis; advocacy efforts to continue trying to persuade the browser and authoring tool developers to consider the needs of blind and visually impaired persons in developing their products are ongoing. But by far the easiest, fastest road to access is a well-designed Web page. Web content creators should be aware of the fact that what they do to create their pages may have a negative impact on some users.

Some Specific Issues

Factors that can cause accessibility problems for print-disabled readers can be classified into two broad categories: bad practices and problematic practices. Bad practices cover those attempts by Web page authors to create documents with inappropriate codes. HTML (hypertext markup language) is the set of codes used to create Web pages. All Internet browsers are designed to interpret the HTML codes and display the Web page on the screen according to the instructions contained in those codes. Some authors use certain codes to create a formatting effect that may "look" pleasing, but when interpreted by a screen reader, chaos occurs. A prime example is the use of an HTML code that tells a browser to display the following material as a table. But in reality, there is no table of data. Screen-reading software tries to read the paragraphs after the table code as a table. Extensive use of the "precode" can also cause difficulty and imprecise page reading. This command tells browsers that the following text is preformatted and not to look for HTML codes. In short, when a Web page author breaks the rules of page coding, the Internet browser, and especially the screen-reading software, can not predict what effect the author is trying to accomplish.

The second category—problematic practices—includes several Web page–authoring practices that are not only technically correct but often require advanced authoring skills. Some of these practices are highlighted below. When these elements are used, it is usually necessary to provide an alternative for the text-based user, such as a non-Java page or a no-frames display. More information on the latest guidelines for creating accessible Web pages can be found on the Web sites of the organizations listed at the end of this chapter.

Java

Web developers seem to love it, blind computer users fear it. Java is a specialized way of putting miniature computer programs on the Internet. When a person connects to a site that uses Java, the little program starts running and can do very simple tasks such as running a marquee across the screen as well as complex jobs such as displaying and processing highly formatted forms. The creator of the Java programming language, Sun Microsystems, is working diligently to make Java scripts more compatible with assistive technology, but at present, a site that requires the use of Java script to access its content may pose serious access problems for blind users. To make a Java-dependent site accessible can be difficult, especially where the Java script is the active component testing for passwords and other Web security features.

Portable Document Format (PDF)

It looks so good that many people have trouble understanding why it is considered a less-than-ideal format. PDF files look great because they are pictures of printed pages—images created to make the display look like a true photograph of the print document. From the author's and publisher's point of view, PDF allows them to deliver to the reader, in electronic form, a printed document that has all of its formatting preserved. For the person relying on assistive technology to access the computer, trying to have a screen reader decipher a page in PDF is about the same as asking a screen reader to describe a photograph.

Adobe has made efforts to provide access to its PDF files. At the present time, PDF files are "accessible" in two ways: with the Acrobat plug-in for Windows, and with an HTML converter. The intention of these processes is to extract the text of the document in an approximate reading order and then to format the resulting document as a single column. HTML versions of

PDF files on the Internet can be created in three ways: through an Adobe proxy server, through the submission of a URL to a Web-based form, or by sending a URL by e-mail. In the latter case, an HTML or ASCII file will be returned. Although these efforts are encouraging, the experience of many blind people suggests that conversion of all but the simplest PDF documents yields results that can be more than a little confusing.

The best practice to follow for those who wish to offer documents in PDF is to also offer an alternative format, such as a plain vanilla text version. In reality, the PDF file is the alternative format because documents are converted to, and not created in, PDF.

Images, Frames, and Animation

The key word for accessibility with any of these techniques is "label." HTML has an "alt=" attribute that allows authors to assign text labels to images. Screen readers used by blind and visually impaired people cannot interpret the pictures on a screen, so it is left up to the author to provide in text form any essential information he or she is trying to convey with an image.

The use of frames to enhance the screen layout does not by itself preclude easy access to a page. However, often the labeling of these frames is imprecise. HTML tags for labeling frame names should be used routinely. Because the blind user cannot see inside the frame with a screen reader until the frame is actually opened, imprecise labeling of frames forces the screen reader user to randomly search each frame until the sought-after text is found. Labels such as "top," "bottom," "left," and "right" have little meaning. More accurate and useful labels might be "text of page," "navigation bar," or "order form."

Authoring Tools

Most Web page creators these days use one or another of the popular authoring tools, such as HTML Assistant, Front Page, Netscape Composer, and HotMetal Pro. Many of these software packages provide opportunities to add "alternative text" when creating images that will be useful for text-based users. The only authoring tool that has been specifically designed with accessibility in mind is HotMetal Pro.

Accessibility Checkers

It is possible to submit a URL to an accessibility checker and receive a report on the accessibility of the page. One of the most popular of these is Bobby (http://www.cast.org/bobby), which tests Web page accessibility. Bobby will redisplay the requested Web page, appending an accessibility report to the bottom of the page. The accessibility report consists of, at most, six sections: accessibility errors, accessibility recommendations, accessibility questions, accessibility tips, browser compatibility, and download time.

The accessibility errors section lists problems that seriously affect the page's usability by people with disabilities. Accessibility recommendations are access problems that should be fixed, if possible. They are not completely necessary to guarantee access but are important to correct. The accessibility questions are all those places where Bobby thinks there might be an access error but has no way of telling. The accessibility tips section is a list of tips that can be applied to improve the overall accessibility of a site. All of these access sections are important. The browser compatibility section lists those HTML elements and element attributes that are used on the page that are not valid for particular browsers. The download time section provides a summary of how long the Web page and images would take to download on a slow modem line. Clicking on any of the problems that Bobby reports will produce a more detailed description of how to fix them.

Choices for Providing Access

Libraries that provide Internet access to patrons are certainly going to be expected to provide equal access to print-disabled individuals. Can this be done? Fortunately, the answer is yes. Libraries can provide Internet access to visually impaired and blind patrons without a large outlay of money for specialized equipment.

For a public access system the focus is on speech output. This is the least expensive alternative output and the most durable from the standpoint of requiring little ongoing maintenance. It can be used by almost all blind and visually impaired library patrons. If the library has active braille readers and is able to purchase braille output equipment, braille access to the Internet can be a very useful and meaningful tool for users of braille.

There are three components to any speech output system that are in addition to the normal software that anyone would run on a computer. First, there is the voice—the hardware that actually makes the sounds. Second, there is software that gives the hardware voice some intelligence so that its output sounds like English, French, or any other language. Third, there is the screen reader, which tells the "voice" when and what to speak.

If a library wishes to provide access for print-disabled people to a computer, including all its word-processing and other program functions, a complete speech output system, including hardware and screen reader, will have to be added to the computer. Fortunately, most computers today already have a sound card installed, and this hardware can serve as the voice of the speech system.

If Internet-only access is desired, libraries have a couple of alternatives. At this writing, at least two self-voicing browsers are available in the U.S. and more may be coming from overseas. These browsers, which include their own speech software, are designed to work with existing sound cards. They operate by examining the HTML code of Internet pages and sending text to the sound card in the order deemed appropriate by the page coding.

The two self-voicing browsers currently available are WebSpeak from Productivity Works Inc. (http://www.prodworks.com) and Home Page Reader from IBM (www.austin.ibm.com/sns/hpr.html). Both programs allow Web browsing without viewing the visual screen.

A major difference between these two systems is, Home Page Reader runs as an overlay to Netscape. This means Netscape must be installed on the computer. Because Netscape is a popular browser for sighted Internet users, this addition generally poses no problems.

WebSpeak, on the other hand, requires no additional browser and has one other important feature: WebSpeak allows a person with low vision to enlarge screen characters and change foreground and background colors. A library interested in providing an accessible system should review both of these systems and, if possible, get patron comments before settling on a specific system.

Resources for Information on Web Accessibility

Because the Internet is constantly changing, so is access to it. For this reason, it is very important to acquire the most up-to-date information and review it on a periodic basis. The following Web sites are good resources for finding the most practical and useful Web accessibility guidelines.

WWW Consortium: Web Accessibility Initiative (http://www.w3.org/WAI)

Trace R&D Center, University of Wisconsin (http://trace.wisc.edu/)

Starling: Accessible Web Page Design (http://www.starlingweb.com/acc/index.htm)

Adaptive Technology Resource Centre, University of Toronto (http://www.utoronto.ca/atrc/)

CPB/WGBH National Center for Accessible Media (NCAM) (http://www.wgbh.org/nca)

making a web page more accessible with bobby:

A Case Study of NYU's Bobst Library

Tom McNulty and Eric Stedfeld

Introduction

By now, most colleges and universities have a presence on the Web. The vast majority offer a Web version of their institution's catalog, including course offerings, for current and prospective students. In terms of the latter, the Web page represents an important marketing tool, and its accessibility can be the prospective user's first indication of the institution's commitment to individuals with disabilities.

Most libraries' pages provide links to Web-based databases, subject-specific pages, local and national online catalogs, and other invaluable research tools. Finally, the Web page, like any other of the college's offerings, is subject to the principles of inclusion set forth in the Americans with Disabilities Act.

In the preceding chapter, Judith Dixon describes some of the obstacles encountered by visually impaired net surfers and identifies Bobby, a diagnostic tool available free of charge on the Web, as an invaluable resource for gauging the accessibility of Web pages. In this brief chapter, the authors explore the realities of making a Web site accessible to the library's target audience, using Bobst Library's "front page" as an example.

Legal Basis for Accessible Web Pages

Just as the college or university might be expected to provide alternative format (e.g., large-print or audio-recorded) versions of its printed materials, so is it under a legal and ethical obligation to make its electronic resources as accessible as possible to users with disabilities. For the most part, visually impaired and learning-disabled users face the greatest obstacles to Web pages which continue to have a large graphical component. This is not to underestimate the proliferation of sound and video on the Web but, rather, to take a pragmatic look at the still-ubiquitous textual Web pages produced by colleges and universities everywhere. Given what they are, and the relative ease with which they can be "fixed" in ways that are invisible to those users who do not rely upon any specialized technologies, the majority of Web pages should, by now, be accessible to users of most screen access technologies.

The Office of Civil Rights has already presented some rulings that directly affect Internet-based communications. In an article describing the noteworthy program of Web accessibility instituted by the City of San Jose, ADA Coordinator Cynthia D. Waddell summarizes an OCR Settlement Letter of 1996:

Not surprisingly, web accessibility issues are now being faced by educational institutions. Library reference services are being transformed by the efficiency of Internet access to information systems and search engines. Professors are teaching long distance learning courses over the Internet and even if a student is physically in class, homework assignments and resources are being posted on class homepages. Yet, even if a library terminal has assistive computer technology installed for students with disabilities, Internet research by students with disabilities is not possible with inaccessible web page design.

In a complaint by a student that a university had failed to provide access to the Internet, the Office of Civil Rights, United States Department of Education (OCR) discussed what was meant to provide effective communication. In a nutshell, the issue is not whether the student with the disability is merely provided access, but the issue is rather the extent to which the communication is actually as effective as that provided to others. Title II [of the Americans with Disabilities Act of 1990] also strongly affirms the important role that computer technology is expected to play as an auxiliary aid by which communication is made effective for persons with disabilities.

In addition, we should all be forewarned that the acquisition of equipment or software which is not adaptable to our target population can be analogous to retrofitting a building renovation project that is not up to code and that "the subsequent substantial expense of providing access is not generally regarded as an undue burden when such cost could have been significantly reduced by considering the issue of accessibility at the time of the initial selection."[2]

Many Web designers are probably working under the assumption that making their pages accessible will result in a boring, graphics-free look. In an attempt to debunk this myth, the remainder of this chapter describes the diagnostic tool Bobby and takes a look at a page that was made accessible to those who use screen readers, without changing the original page's look in the least.

The Center for Assistive Technology (CAST) and Bobby

Founded in 1984, CAST is a not-for-profit organization whose mission is to expand opportunities for people with disabilities through innovative uses of computer technology. One of CAST's many projects is Bobby, an online tool for the evaluation of Web page accessibility.

To check your page's conformity to access standards, simply enter the URL on the Bobby form, which can be found at: **www.cast.org/bobby** Bobby will quickly return an Accessibility Report (see figure 1) composed of several sections including:

Figure I

Copyright © 1996-1999 CAST Center for Applied Special Technology

URL: http://www.nyu.edu/library/bobst/, June 11, 1999 2:54:29 PM EDT
Bobby Core v3.1.1 build 6, Guidelines Version: W3C WAI GL 99/05/05 (2), Bobby Server v3.1.1 build 6
Browser Compatibility: HTML4.0, AccEval

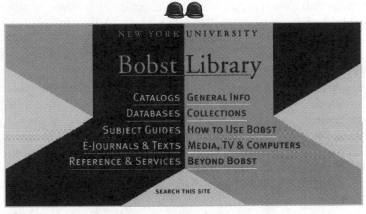

Bobst Library | NYU Libraries | NYU Home Page
Catalogs | Databases | Subject Guides | E-Journals & Texts | Reference & Services
General Info | Collections | How to Use Bobst | Media, TV & Computers
Beyond Bobst | Search This Site | Comments

Priority 1 Accessibility | Priority 2 Accessibility | Priority 3 Accessibility | Browser Compatibility Errors |
Download Time

Priority 1 Accessibility

This page does not yet meet the requirements for Bobby Approved status. Below is a list of 1 accessibility problems that should be fixed in order to make this page accessible to people with disabilities.

1. Provide alternative text for all image map hot-spots. *(12 instances)*
   Line 69: <area shape="rect" coords=185,5,428,29 href="http://www.nyu.edu/"><!-- NYU HOMEPAGE -->
   Line 71: <area shape="rect" coords=207,113,298,136 href="http://www.nyu.edu/library/bobst/cat.htm"><!-- CATALOGS -->
   Line 72: <area shape="rect" coords=198,137,298,163 href="http://www.nyu.edu/library/bobst/database.htm"><!-- DATABASES -->
   Line 73: <area shape="rect" coords=155,164,298,188 href="http://www.nyu.edu/library/bobst/subguide.htm"><!-- SUBJECT GUIDES -->

Priority 1 lists problems that seriously affect the page's usability by people with disabilities. To use the "Bobby Approved" icon, all errors at this level must be removed on all pages.

Priority 2 identifies those problems that one should try to fix, but which are not as prohibitive to the user with disabilities as those in Priority 1.

Priority 3 consists of third-tier access problems that also should be considered.

A browser compatibility section identifies those HTML code elements that are not valid for particular browsers.

Before discussing the specifics of Bobby's diagnosis of the authors' home page example, the following section discusses the basic philosophy governing the design and maintenance of Bobst Library's Web pages.

Basic Principles

All of the library's Web page development begins with the underlying goal of making information as accessible as possible to its patrons. This means that the "market pressure" is toward increasing the library's user base, as opposed to utilizing cutting-edge technologies or demonstrating state-of-the-art capabilities. Limited budgets further require that Web development be dispersed across a broader staff base with varying levels of expertise, as opposed to highly skilled specialists. This requires the use of simpler tools and simpler solutions.

This general direction toward increased access and simpler Web development is pitted against any restrictions that vendors might place on access to proprietary materials, as well as the "common" expectations within the broader user community. Specialized requirements for certain Web applications might call for specialized solutions, which necessarily limit the ability of a broader base of patrons to access that application or resource. A good example of this is the recent live Webcast of our commencement activities, which required the user to download a free Real Networks plug-in application.

Finally, theoretical goals and abstract expectations must necessarily meet the realities of production schedules, available resources, and sustainable production methods and procedures. Benchmarks and standards must be established with the goal of meeting most of the needs of most of the patrons most of the time.

The general approach to library Web page development, therefore, follows the following guidelines:

- Most of the pages currently conform to the HTML 3.2 specification. This standard has been in existence for approximately three years and is compatible with the version 3 level of Netscape or Internet Explorer.
- Most of the pages do not use frames, and although tables are used extensively for formatting, most of the new and updated pages contain the bulk of the page information in a single table cell. The use of formatting tricks also is minimized, such as <PRE> format text graphics (making letters and their spacing look like pictures), using invisible

graphics with WIDTH and HEIGHT attributes to push the elements around, or using specialized fonts. An exception is the footer, inherited from the library's previous page design firm, which specifies font sizes and faces in its navigation area.

- No applets, special plug-ins, or special scripting are used.
- All images on the pages are accompanied by ALT attributes, which provide a text descriptor of the element.

Despite these general guidelines, however, exceptions do exist. The pages for the TV Center, which, although organizationally under the library has a somewhat different mission, use specialized scripting and graphics to provide a livelier look. Some technical pages that have long lists of information use frames to keep the captions on the page while the user scrolls through content. The library's emerging Intranet, which will post official documents, will undoubtedly warrant consideration of Acrobat portable Document File (PDF) format. In addition, the emergence of XML-compliant browsers in the very near future will allow extended searching of online finding aids and will put pressure on the library to provide these resources in a way that will render them viewable only with the most recent browsers. In each of these cases the library requires a rationale and justification for the use of the technology that enhances or enriches capability or content, although it risks limiting accessibility to those resources utilizing that technology. Where possible, an alternative version of the information that is more accessible is also provided. Because the library's development resources are limited, we must restrict the number of pages that require such double-duty production efforts. Therefore such technology is not used unless there is a strong justification to do so.

The consideration of the accessibility of the Bobst Library home page began with the use of Bobby, the Web-based diagnostic tool. (A portion of the Bobby printout is reproduced in figure 1.) Although Bobby expressed some caution in the use of tables or resource files such as PDF files, its main concern was with the large-image map graphic that is used by the visitor for navigating the Bobst Web site. Bobby specified the need for ALT attributes for the <AREA> tags, which define where one would link when clicking on that area of the map. Although the page already has a text version of the navigation choices at the bottom of the page, the authors explored how to put these ALT attributes into the <AREA> tags.

At this point, the authors came across an interesting issue that is typical of what may occur when attempting to make pages more accessible. Although in the interest of maximizing accessibility one of the general guidelines is to make pages HTML 3.2 compliant, the ALT attribute for the <AREA> tag is actually in the HTML 4.0 specification! Now the authors were faced with the choice of making the page compliant to a more recent standard, resulting in a page that is more accessible to disabled users, but potentially less accessible to those using earlier versions of Web browsers, or keeping the page HTML 3.2 compliant and less accessible to visually impaired users.

In this situation, it was decided to make this particular page HTML 4.0 compliant. Although this choice is marginally better, neither approach is clearly right or wrong.

In setting out to make your Web site as accessible as possible:

- To the greatest extent possible, consider the needs of your audience as well as the range of technology (browser versions, etc.) they might have at their disposal for gaining access to the Web.
- Consider what resources you have at your disposal to establish and maintain a sustainable level of development. Remember that if you decide to provide alternative "text-only" versions of your library's pages, a significant amount of staff time may need to be allocated to dual development and updating.
- Stay informed of your implementation choices and aware of the implications and effects of those choices. Keeping accessibility high on your list of priorities will help to make your Web pages accessible to the greatest potential number of users.

Finally, control over accessibility of online resources can only go so far. Page designers will certainly want to provide pointers to resources that are less accessible than one would hope. Finally, and perhaps most important, library Web designers can fulfill a very important advocacy role by sharing information on Web page accessibility not only with others in the library and around campus, but also with the many commercial vendors with whom they have considerable financial clout. ◼

Notes

1. Cynthia D. Waddell, "Applying the ADA to the Internet: A Web Accessibility Standard" (http://www.rit.edu/~easi/law/weblaw1.htm).
2. Ibid.

training professional and support staff members

Courtney Deines-Jones

Introduction

To work effectively with students, faculty, and employees with disabilities, library staff members must be provided with the tools they need to be proactive service providers. This means not only learning how to use assistive technology or how to access the Internet via nongraphical interfaces, but also how to approach patrons who have disabilities and how to ensure all patrons are receiving excellent library services regardless of disability status. A supported, ongoing training program is key to ensuring that staff develop and maintain technical and interpersonal skills. It also is vital to demonstrating the administration's commitment to universal service access throughout the library.

Fulfilling the ADA Promise

Some administrators may put a training plan in place solely for the purpose of fulfilling requirements of the Americans with Disabilities Act (ADA). Indeed, many ADA compliance training modules are on the market explaining how to meet the letter of the law in employment and public services. But meeting the letter of the law does not address how comfortable a patron feels in the library, to what extent a student believes her or his needs are being met, or how willing a faculty member is to approach a librarian.

More important than the letter of the law is the spirit of the ADA. This law was enacted to ensure that all people have the best possible access to programs, facilities, and services, whether or not those people are among the 20.6 percent of Americans who have a disability (U.S. Census bureau 1994 survey of disability status, http://www.census.gov). An excellent training program addresses this spirit, encouraging library staff members to develop a toolbox of appropriate strategies for meeting service goals.

One size does not fit all in the training world. Each academic library has its own profile of training needs and resources. Librarians can help ensure they are developing appropriate training strategies by:
- assessing the training need as driven by patrons;
- considering the unique needs of different training groups;
- exploring each type of training;
- evaluating the resources at hand;
- planning an ongoing training strategy;
- providing appropriate policy supports.

147

Evaluating the need for training

It seems superfluous to say that training must be driven by need. But in practice, training needs often are determined without consulting staff members or patrons to find out not only what staff members *do not* know, but also what they *should* know. When training needs are defined and staff members know why the training is important, they will be more willing participants and more likely to retain and use information.

In keeping with a philosophy of promoting consumer-driven service access, the first source of training needs assessment should be the disability community within your college or university. Student groups as well as the disability services center should be consulted to learn about student and employee demographics; these groups also can help vitalize a presentation by providing training resources, audiovisual materials, or guest speakers. Contacting consumer groups within the academic community demonstrates to the university and to staff members that the library is serious about its commitment to providing excellent service to all patrons. Of course, not all patrons with disabilities belong to campus groups. Ongoing in-house surveys such as the one provided in figure 1 will augment the information you receive from organized groups with ideas gleaned directly from individual library users. The library Web site is also a good place to solicit feedback and ideas.

Pretraining needs assessments also should be collected from staff members. Anonymous forms may promote a more honest critique of library services and training needs but are likely to reduce the response rate. Staff needs assessments should be more specific and comprehensive, as illustrated by the skeletal employee needs assessment form shown in figure 2. Department and job title information is important because it can help in targeting training and also in identifying resources. For example, if most people were moderately comfortable assisting deaf patrons, but all the student workers said they were very comfortable, training to reach patrons with hearing impairments might be a lower priority for this group. It also would be reasonable to assume the students were working with someone in the library who is deaf. This person might agree to be a resource when designing training for other groups within the library.

Finally, use the training self-assessment as a guide to potential trouble spots within training groups, some of which may be anticipated. It is likely, for example, that people in technical services departments may not see the need to learn to use adaptive equipment or may not understand the point of awareness training for staff members who do not generally provide direct public services. But even these behind-the-scenes players are crucial to ensuring the overall success of a disability services training program, whether by helping catalogers understand why some Library of Congress terms may be offensive to patrons or giving acquisitions specialists a personal and immediate understanding of selection criteria for disability-related material. Explaining the need and benefits of training will give staff members a reason for attending other than that they were told to, and drawing training programs directly from staff members and patrons will further emphasize the programs as a means of improving service.

Figure I

Sample Training Needs Assessment for Consumers

Please help us develop our training sessions so that we may better serve you! Complete this form and bring it to any service desk. Thank you!

The library's strongest resources for people with disabilities are:

_____

_____

To improve services to people with disabilities, library staff members could benefit most from training in: _____

_____

Please feel free to recommend a person or an organization as a speaker or source of expertise:

Name: _____

Title/Affiliation: _____

Phone Number: _____

E-mail: _____

Topic or Area of Expertise: _____

If you would like to help the library improve services to people with disabilities, please provide the following:

Your Name: _____

Title/Affiliation: _____

Phone Number: _____

E-Mail: _____

Area of Interest/Expertise: _____

Contact preference: E-mail _____ Phone_____

Thank you for your help!

Figure 2

Employee Training Needs Assessment

In its ongoing effort to improve services to patrons with disabilities, the library is soliciting your ideas for staff member training. Please think about your work with library users who have disabilities—what worked, what didn't, and where you think training would help you and your peers perform your job better.

Please rate how much you agree with the following statements. Use a scale of 1–5, with 5 representing complete agreement and 1 representing complete disagreement.

I am very familiar with the library's adaptive technology.   1 2 3 4 5

I am very comfortable assisting patrons who have   1 2 3 4 5
physical disabilities.

I am very comfortable assisting patrons who have   1 2 3 4 5
mental/learning disabilities.

I am very comfortable assisting patrons who have   1 2 3 4 5
visual impairments or who are blind.

I am very comfortable assisting patrons who have   1 2 3 4 5
hearing impairments or who are deaf.

In my job, it is extremely important that I understand   1 2 3 4 5
assistive technology and concepts of universal design
(design of space, furniture, computers, etc., to be
accessible by all people).

In my job, it is extremely important that I understand   1 2 3 4 5
concepts of service to people with disabilities.

If you could attend two courses to improve your ability to serve people with disabilities, what would they cover?

1. _____

2. _____

What other tools would help you improve services to patrons with disabilities? _____

_____

Please provide the following information about yourself:

Employing Department: _____

Job Category: _____

Thank you for your help!

Audience

In small academic libraries, the training audience may comprise the entire staff. It is more likely, however, that training will be done with smaller groups of targeted audiences. Understanding the various unique needs of each group will help the training facilitator develop the most effective plan possible.

ADMINISTRATORS

Administrators and senior management sometimes need a special touch. Some characteristics and points to watch out for:

- *Administrators may be more interested in the implications of disability training for their management skills than to service provision.* Stressing the positive impact disability awareness and assistive technology training will have on improving staff effectiveness may help managers buy into the training program.
- *Administrators may be more concerned with legal implications of the ADA.* Training should leave management feeling confident about filling their legal obligations, with an additional emphasis on how the ADA can be a springboard to increased library utilization by students and faculty with disabilities.
- *Administrators may be at a level "above" the person responsible for coordinating training.* Strong commitment to the program and its goals is necessary to ensure they will not feel "above" the need for training, too. To emphasize the importance of training, it may be important to include professional trainers or consultants, instead of relying on library staff.

Administrative staff members should be the first to be trained, whenever possible. They set the tone for their departments and are responsible for acting as liaisons to the rest of the academic administration. With training and commitment, administrative staff members will be able to demonstrate the library's awareness, sensitivity, and desire to serve all segments of the academic community.

FRONTLINE PROFESSIONAL AND SUPPORT STAFF MEMBERS

Frontline professional staff members include reference librarians, circulation staff members, special collections librarians, and all others who interact with students and faculty on a daily basis. These staff members may also be responsible for conducting research, teaching classes, and actively participating in library associations. Support staff usually do not have teaching and research duties, although they may assist in these efforts. Training for this group should consider its unique placement.

- *Frontline staff members are most aware of the library's patron base.* Trainers should use feedback from these librarians to determine how the library is serving its patrons with disabilities and to assess which areas produce the greatest discomfort among service providers. If training is being conducted in an area that has been identified by these key staff members as low priority, the trainer must be certain to explain why the training is important.

- *Front line staff members may be wary of having their duties increased.* One of the main anxieties associated with service to people with disabilities is the fear that "extra" service will be required that will take time away from an already-stressed workday. Training coordinators should stress that the goal of training is to make services for people with disabilities a normal part of library routine. When staff members know how to help people and operate equipment as a matter of course, their schedules will not be significantly disrupted by a change.
- *Frontline staff members have diverse responsibilities.* Not all frontline staff members do the same jobs or spend the same amount of time with patrons. The nature of collections is also a major consideration; people who are responsible for the music collection will have different access issues than those in the rare books department, even if both are working at reference desks.

Frontline staff members are the ones who will translate a library's universal access policies into reality for most patrons. Hands-on, pragmatic training is most appropriate for this group.

TECHNICAL STAFFERS

Technical staff present the biggest challenges when doing preliminary legwork for a project. Nonetheless, their participation is essential if the library is to develop a culture of excellent service.

- *Technical staff members may believe they do not need training because they do not have much public contact.* Use creative means to emphasize the importance of training for these staff members. Explain how awareness affects everything from the placement of labels on book spines to the design of the library's Web page.
- *Technical staff members do not use library equipment every day.* All library staff members should understand how the library's assistive technology works, but training for technical services staff members may focus more on awareness and creative innovations for improving the library's interfaces to promote universal access.

STUDENT WORKERS

Student workers pose their own challenges to trainers. Because of high turnover and relatively structured duties, student workers often receive little more than basic training in the job they will be doing. However, they can be remarkable assets to the library if they receive proper training.

- *Student workers may have flexible, irregular schedules.* Training should be easily replicated to accommodate several sessions.

- *Student workers may be less open to formal training.* Training for student workers should be hands-on and should stress how disability awareness and knowledge of assistive technology is both interesting and of service to others. Students should not feel as though they are taking "one more class;" rather, the learning experience should be hands-on and dynamic.
- *Student workers may have high turnover.* Although more formal training may make sense at the start of each semester, self-instructing training modules can be used to guide those students who are hired in midsemester. Having another student help with the module will hone their skills as well.

After the audience is determined and analyzed, the trainer is prepared to select the most appropriate training strategies and to evaluate appropriate resources for conducting the training.

Focus of Training

When developing clear and measurable training goals, clarifying the focus of the training is of paramount importance. Training can be classified into four general categories:

- *Attitudinal* training, designed to improve awareness of and sensitivity to disability-related issues;
- *Facility* training, in which people are trained to use equipment or to make physical facilities accessible;
- *Service* training, aimed at teaching staff how to design programs and services which are accessible to all;
- *Legal* training, that explains the letter and requirements of the law, whether the ADA or other legislation.

ATTITUDINAL TRAINING

Overwhelmingly, people with disabilities report that the most serious barrier to full access to services is attitude. The best "training" to improve attitudes is expanded on-the-job exposure to people with disabilities. Unfortunately, attitudinal barriers prevent many potential library users from visiting the library frequently, and attitudinal training must be used to get the ball rolling.

A recommended approach to attitudinal training is to have people within the academic community who have disabilities visit the library; speak about their experiences, both good and bad; and explain how and why staff members' attitudes had an impact on them. It is important that these speakers be committed to library service and that they illustrate both positive and negative experiences to give staff members examples of behaviors to emulate when working to improve service. When community speakers visit the library, they should have the opportunity to mix informally with staff members so as to exchange information and ideas one-on-one.

Role playing is also used frequently when conducting attitudinal training. If role playing involves having people "assume" a disability by wearing darkened glasses or using a wheelchair or the like, it must be very carefully done so that participants come away with a realistic attitude about the disability. A sighted person who puts on a blindfold for an hour may be able to do very little and must remember that a blind graduate student, for example, has probably developed many strategies to minimize the impact of his or her disabilities.

Role playing can reveal interesting prejudices about people with disabilities. In awareness sessions demonstrating how credible librarians find people with disabilities, students and practicing librarians alike tend to extend more sympathy to and are more likely to believe people who have obvious physical disabilities. Using the examples shown in figure 3 and figure 4 the author has found that with very few exceptions people do not even consider the possibility that the man who uses a wheelchair might be a pervert, but they tend to be extremely distrustful of the young woman who claims to have a learning disability. These role-playing exercises are also useful because they demonstrate that people with disabilities are not all saintly people to be alternately pitied and admired but, rather, are library patrons like all others, with potentially different information access strategies.

Many "canned" resources are available to improve disability awareness and to address attitudes. The ALA's videotape, *People First,* is particularly useful because it specifically addresses disabilities in a library setting. Generic attitudinal surveys can be modified with ease to incorporate academic library issues.

College and university librarians at institutions with a Disability Services office (these go by various names depending on the school) should use it as a resource especially for attitudinal training because awareness is a cross-discipline issue and resources available through Disability Services are almost always appropriate for library use. Depending on its resources, the Disability Services office may even be able to facilitate training for the library and may run periodic university-wide training sessions to accommodate employees new to the institution.

Library staff members who do not interact frequently with patrons may be reluctant to attend attitudinal training. For technical staff members, it may not be necessary to combine attitudinal training with service provision training, which provides day-to-day, hands-on tips such as how to arrange lighting when talking with a deaf patron. But awareness training will help them understand how important it is for catalogers, electronic services designers, acquisitions specialists, and others to consider the needs of patrons with disabilities so that the infrastructure they build will be accessible after it reaches the library floor (or Web).

Whereas attitudinal training is important for technical staff, it is critical for any public service staff, including administrators, professionals, paraprofessionals, and student workers. Most patrons do not distinguish between "real" librarians and other library staff, and regardless of title all workers represent the library and must be committed and ready to service its full patron base.

Figure 3

Role Play 1
HE GRABBED ME!

To use this role play, put each player's information on a separate sheet and distribute each of the roles to the players. Do *not* let them (especially the "patron") share information with one another. The role play begins with the indicated player speaking his or her lines. It continues ad lib until a resolution is reached. Depending on the size of the group, encourage people to make suggestions as you go. At the end of the role play, the players should reveal their information.

Student Worker: You are a female undergraduate working as a library page in the Special Access library, which is used primarily by students with disabilities. You don't have anything against them, really, but you have to admit that some of them give you the creeps. Today, every time you turn around, there seems to be this guy who uses a wheelchair just staring at you. His hands keep jerking, and something about him is really scary. You are shelving some books, not paying attention, and all of a sudden you hear this patron next to you. You turn, and as you do so, his hand jerks up and clutches at your breast. He gasps and says, "Sorry, I was reaching for a book." You are scared, though, and walk as fast as you can back to the information desk to tell the librarian. You walk even faster when you hear him following.

Librarian: You are the Special Access Librarian in charge of the part of the library which coordinates services to people with disabilities. Much of the adaptive equipment and a considerable large-print and braille collection are hosted in the Special Access section, so you employ several student workers to keep the equipment running and to maintain the library collection. Usually, those student workers who do not have disabilities have no problems, but this year you are concerned about one particular worker. She seems extremely nervous around people who have disabilities, especially ones with obvious physical disabilities. You have thought about asking if she wants to transfer to another library section, but you believe that as she becomes more familiar with people with disabilities, she will also be more comfortable. You look up from the counter to see this student worker walking quickly toward you and looking very agitated. Following her is a young man in a wheelchair.

Student: You are a male undergraduate who uses a wheelchair. You are also a pervert and have found out that by faking muscular spasms; you can get away with groping young women. Today you spotted a library page, but when you finally managed to make your move, she spooked. You used your standard excuse—that you were reaching for a book—but she took off to her supervisor. How dare she! You follow, confident that with your disability you will be able to "prove" it was an accident; and the page will be the embarrassed one, not you.

The role play starts when the student worker points at the student, and says to the librarian, "He grabbed me!"

Figure 4

Role Play 2
I LOST MY WALLET

To use this role play, put each player's information on a separate sheet and distribute each of the roles to the players. Do *not* let them (especially the "patron") share information with one another. The role play begins with the indicated player speaking his or her lines. It continues ad lib until a resolution is reached. Depending on the size of the group, encourage people to make suggestions as you go. At the end of the role play, the players should reveal their information.

Student Worker: You are an MLS student who has taken a job in the computer lab. You hate it. The students put off their work until the last minute and then yell at you when all the computers are filled up. This Sunday night has been awful. Everyone seems to have a project due involving the Internet, and the terminals have been backed up for hours. There is an "access" terminal reserved for people with disabilities; you are continually kicking off people who don't have disabilities and so are not authorized to use it. You feel like you have been spending your whole shift mediating fights over terminal time limits. You see a student hovering around some of the terminals, sort of fidgeting. Finally, the student approaches you.

Librarian: You are a supervisory librarian who works every fourth Sunday in the computer lab. Usually you enjoy the frontline service, but tonight has been exasperating. Every student at the school appears to need the computer. Terminals are scheduled full until closing, and "vultures" have signed up on a waiting list to take advantage of no-shows. One of the "access" terminals is free; you have thought about opening this up to all students, but administrative policy dictates that the terminal be available at all times to students and faculty who have disabilities. To use an access terminal, the student must show a school ID, which has a special access sticker issued each semester by the Disability Services office. As you are reviewing sign-up sheets, you notice a student hovering around some of the terminals. Finally, the patron approaches and addresses the student worker.

Student: You are a student with a learning disability. You have a major project due tomorrow, and you need to use the computer. Normally, you would not be too worried about getting a spot because there is rarely a long sign-up list for the access terminals, but last night you lost your wallet. You have looked everywhere and called campus security, but the wallet is gone and with it your student ID, which has a special access sticker on it that qualifies you to use the adaptive terminal. You have no way of replacing it until the Disability Services office opens on Monday, but by that time it will be too late. You would use the regular terminal, but there are half-hour time limits on it and because of your disability it will take you longer to browse the Web for the information you need. You go to the library and look at the long lines; you also notice, though, that one of the "special needs" terminals is empty. After some hesitation, you decide to approach the information desk and explain your situation.

The role play starts when the student says to the student worker: "I need to use the access terminal, but I don't have my ID because I lost my wallet last night."

FACILITY TRAINING

Facility training ensures that library staff members know how to make and keep their departments universally accessible and how to operate all adaptive equipment. Facility training also gives staff members the tools they need to evaluate what facilities or equipment may not be fully accessible so that they can either design measures to increase accessibility or devise work-around strategies.

Simulating disabilities may be most useful in facility training. By navigating the library from curb to stacks to rest rooms using a wheelchair, for instance, staff members can get a feeling for how accessible the library is, why a person who uses a wheelchair may need help browsing for books, or how important an accessible computer workstation is.

Role playing can also be helpful as part of this exercise, with trainers modeling how best to give directions to someone with low vision or how to arrange items on a book truck so that a wheelchair user can browse through them. Again, trainers must remember that there are significant differences between someone who is simulating a disability and someone who really has one. But role playing and simulations can bring home the fact that even if assistive technology is available and facilities are in compliance with the ADA, they may not be accessible to all people.

As with attitudinal training, there are a lot of existing resources that can be used or modified for use in the library. For group training, the DO-IT project's manual, *Universal Access: Electronic Resources in Libraries*, provides a complete module and videotapes to support training on computers and assistive technology. One-on-one training can be obtained through the many courses on assistive technology and library services offered by Equal Access to Software and Information (EASI). Information on EASI can be found at www.rit.edu/~easi/.

For the library facility itself, checklists that can be modified into training tools and handouts can be obtained from *Surveying the Public Libraries for the ADA*. Although items such as parking, children's services areas, or community meeting rooms may not apply in an academic setting, the information on public accommodations, browsable stacks, and reading areas are the same in an academic setting as they are in a public setting.

Again, an institution's Disability Services office is often a useful resource in providing facility training. The office may have equipment such as that used to measure the amount of force necessary to open a door. In addition, it may have staff members familiar with compliance surveys who can show staff members how to measure slope. Disability Services staff members may know of consumers within the community who are expert users of certain types of adaptive equipment or assistive technology, and be able to arrange to have them demonstrate the equipment so that staff members understand how it works when used by the people for whom it was designed.

Facility training is appropriate for everyone within the library who works with the public. Student workers and paraprofessionals may not have the authority to make decisions regarding furniture, fixtures, and equipment, but they should know whether service counters might be a barrier to some patrons and how they can arrange their work flow so that they do not inadvertently block access to patrons. Senior staff and administrators will learn not only how to ensure their libraries comply with facility regulations but, more important, will understand why modifications are important and how they benefit the entire library community. Facility training is also critical for technical services staff members who design electronic library resources and interfaces so that they understand how their products will appear to people using alternate access strategies.

SERVICE TRAINING
Universal design, staff awareness of facility and equipment issues, and positive attitudes will help make an academic library independently accessible to most people with disabilities. But the goal of the library goes beyond this to ensuring that all library services are accessible to its entire user base. Helping staff members prepare for this is the purpose of service training.

Service training shows staff members how to work around access problems. Role-playing exercises are excellent tools for exploring creative service solutions. For example, the exercise given in figure 4 provides the opportunity to discuss how to accommodate someone without a "provable" disability without either denying service to a patron or compromising services to students who do not have disabilities. Role playing can also be a useful tool in exploring how staff members feel about providing "special" services, such as readers or students who will page books for patrons with disabilities. Many times, these are closely related to attitudinal issues.

In-house trainers who are themselves thoroughly trained in access issues and disability law can be invaluable in analyzing service concerns and library policy to both instruct staff members and reassure them. Library policies will address circulation, reference, student assistance, and other areas, and provide the framework under which services to people with disabilities are provided. They will reassure staff members that patrons with disabilities are expected to maintain the same standards as those without and will reiterate the fact that all patrons, regardless of disability, should receive equally excellent service.

Most available training modules address attitudes, facilities, and legal issues, although service is the unspoken, unifying thread. Training developers who wish to use existing manuals should be prepared to cull several for relevant material and add to it information related to the specific policies in place at the library or university.

Once again, the Disability Services office may be a tremendous help. The office coordinates academic and support services to students, and sometimes employees and faculty, who have disabilities and should be able to assist librarians in locating both on- and off-campus resources to make programs and services fully accessible. Their staff members can work with the library's training coordinator to develop a curriculum that will not only address service issues but also give staff members a sense of confidence and support in meeting challenges as they arise.

Service access training is most important for administrators and senior staff members because it addresses how policy can be set and adapted to ensure equal access. Service access may also have budgetary implications (as, for example, when interpreters must be hired), which are of greatest import to senior staff. Junior staff members and student workers will also benefit from service access training, but as part of an overall introduction to the library's policies toward services to people with disabilities or if they will be called on to provide some services, such as paging books, to library patrons.

LEGAL TRAINING

The goal of library training should be to maximize service provision, not simply to meet the letter of some law. But like it or not, much of the impetus for many colleges' and universities' expansion of programs to accommodate students with disabilities has been legal. It is also understandable that most administrators want to be thoroughly aware of what they and their libraries must do to comply with federal, state, and local regulations.

Training in the letter of the law can also be obtained from modules, although most of these are more generic in nature and do not specifically address libraries. To minimize the risk of costly confusion, legal training should almost always be provided by outside professionals with proper credentials. Sometimes these people can be found within the academic community, either through either an ombudsman's office or the institution's Disability Services office. Consultants specializing in disability law are easy to find if off-campus resources are necessary.

Because the disability rights movement, like the civil rights movement, has been driven in large part by court decisions and legislative action, it is important to include basic information about the ADA and the history of disability rights in all awareness training. In-depth legal training, however, is best reserved for administrators and senior management personnel who will be making both employment and library policy decisions and who must bear legal responsibility for the library's actions.

Training: Current and Future

Whoever the audience and whatever the training type, it cannot be conducted as a "one-shot" effort. Training curricula need to combine different methods and must show an ongoing commitment from library management. At minimum, a library should conduct at least one annual large group training session at the beginning of the academic year, after most student workers have come on board. This broad-based, kick-off session should emphasize the library's commitment to service and outline training efforts to follow. Small-group training in facility and equipment access, service issues, attitudes, and general awareness should follow, tailored to each group. Finally, ongoing training should be provided to both hone the skills of existing staff members and prepare new staff members to serve the full library community.

To supplement training, library workers should be encouraged to practice what they know every day. Facilities should be kept neat. People should use the TDD to place test calls to other departments. Service concerns should be discussed at staff meetings and solutions widely distributed. A staff listserv, electronic mail distribution list, or print newsletter can become a vehicle to distribute new information on disabilities, assistive technology, and library services.

Conclusion

A thorough training program can be your best tool in promoting service excellence. Library trainers can develop superior, effective curricula by addressing the needs of specific groups of employees, selecting the most appropriate types of training for each group, and using all available resources. In many cases, Disability Services or a similar office will be able to assist with library training efforts and even may be able to conduct some training efforts. Training programs build employee skills while demonstrating the importance of services to people with disabilities and improving staff members' confidence and morale. Finally, an ongoing training commitment can be used indefinitely as an instrument of continuously improving service to all members of the academic community. ■

Suggested Readings

The Alliance for Technology Access. 1994. *Computer Resources for People with Disabilities: A Guide to Exploring Today's Assistive Technology.* Alameda, Calif.: Hunter House.

Designed for consumers, this book contains a "chart to determine your technology needs," which is an extremely useful awareness tool for staff members. The "Product Descriptions" section, although somewhat dated, also is very readable, practical, and a useful quick reference.

The Annotated Compendium of Assistive Technology Training Resources. 1997. Philadelphia: Pennsylvania's Initiative on Assistive Technology Institute on Disabilities/ University Affiliated Program, Temple University.

This provides a full-page description of AT curricula grouped by subject. It also includes advocacy; accommodations; consumer responsiveness; assistive technology and computer access; education; and fund-raising and grants seeking. Reviews are substantive, and full contact information is included.

Assistive Technology Projects, Easter Seal Society of Utah, and Utah State University Center for Persons with Disabilities. 1994. *An Introduction to AT Information and Referral Services (AT-I&R).* Logan, UT: Utah State University.

This manual provides excellent information on conducting reference interviews to determine what assistive technology is most appropriate for a person and how to refer a person to appropriate AT sources. The manual is also a useful aid for librarians who may be using AT I&R services to locate appropriate library equipment.

Baker, Denise B. and Scott P. Robertson. 1995. *The Potential of Assistive Technology: A Training Guide for Developing an Awareness of the Scope and Benefits of Assistive Technology.* Philadelphia: Pennsylvania's Initiative on Assistive Technology Institute on Disabilities/University Affiliated Program, Temple University.

Training module is very comprehensive and includes direct instructions to the trainer. Many of the devices are specific to daily living activities not commonly found in libraries (e.g., showering), but much of the information is either directly applicable or applicable with slight modification. Poor quality of some handouts may make redesign or retyping necessary.

Black, J.B., Janet Black, Ruth O'Donnell, and Jane Schueuerle. 1992. *Surveying Public Libraries for the ADA.* Tallahassee, Fla: Pinellas Public Library Cooperative.

An extremely pragmatic guide to ADA history and compliance; this book includes historical information, facility checklists, and compliance tips. Although designed for public libraries, much of the information is appropriate to an academic setting. It is available through state libraries or directly from the Florida Bureau of Library Development, Division of Library and Information Services, 500 S. Bronough St., Tallahassee, FL 32399-0250.

Burgstahler, Sheryl, Dan Comden, and Beth Fraser. 1997. *Universal Access: Electronic Resources in Libraries.* Seattle: University of Washington.

This training module was designed specifically for library staff members and includes step-by-step presentation information, reproducible handouts/overheads, and video presentations on Internet access and successful pairing of computers with people who have disabilities. The module is highly recommended for all library trainers.

Cunningham, Carmela, and Norman Coombs. 1997. *Information Access and Adaptive Technology.* Phoenix: Oryx Press.

Part of the American Council on Education's Series on Higher Education, this book includes an appendix of "best practice" campuses and academic library services. Although staff training is not covered explicitly, many of the hints and frontline strategies may be incorporated into training materials.

Deines-Jones, Courtney, and Connie Van Fleet. 1995. *Preparing Staff to Serve Patrons with Disabilities: A How-to-do-it Manual for Librarians.* New York: Neal Schuman.

Although designed primarily for an audience of public librarians, most information is easily adaptable to an academic setting. It contains a chapter on training with advice on selecting appropriate training methods and speakers from the community.

Fifield, Marvin G., and M. Bryce Fifield. 1997. Education and training of individuals involved in delivery of assistive technology devices. *Technology and Disability* 6(1,2):77–88.

This article describes training options and the type of training appropriate for different professionals. This is especially useful as a guide to develop training that is appropriate for frontline workers or consumers.

People First: Serving and Employing People with Disabilities. 1992. 40 min. Library Video Network, Baltimore County Public Library.

This video, available from the ALA, explains how to use the "people first" philosophy to provide service to patrons. It includes interviews with library users and staff who have disabilities, and provides basic etiquette tips.

appendix A

Noteworthy Access Programs and Projects

Queen's University Libraries
Special Readers' Services

Contact: Michele Chittenden, Coordinator for Special Readers' Services
Queen's University Libraries
Douglas Library, Queen's University
Kingston, Ontario, Canada K7L 5C4
Phone: (613) 533-2833
Fax: (613) 533-2584
E-mail: chittend@stauffer.queensu.ca
Institutional URL: www.queensu.ca
Project-related URL: http://stauffer.queensu.ca/inforef/srs/

INSTITUTIONAL PROFILE

Queen's University Libraries serve more than 13,000 students (11,337 undergraduate, 2,264 graduate) and 960 full-time faculty. The library's collections comprise 1,465,735 titles (books and journals). In total, there are more than four million items (including government documents, newspapers, maps and air photos, microforms and audiovisual materials, and electronic data files) in the library collection, which is housed in seven libraries across campus. A total of 305 students with disabilities were registered for service during the 1997–1998 academic year.

TARGET POPULATION

All students who have a disability and are taking courses at Queen's University are eligible to use the services and facilities offered by the Special Readers' Services program. This includes students who have a full- or part-time course load; students who are taking correspondence courses, and students who are registered for specialized programs such as the Queen's Executive Programme.

The Special Readers' Services program meets the needs of students who have a wide range of disabilities, including students who are blind, deaf, learning disabled, and physically disabled and those who have medical or psychiatric disabilities.

PROGRAM FUNDING

The Province of Ontario has funded the project since its inception in 1991 when special funding to develop or enhance current services to students with disabilities was given to all Ontario colleges and universities. The funding envelope is administered by the Ministry of Education and Training, Province of Ontario. Special Readers' Services continues to be funded by this source with contributions from the Queen's University Library system (in 1997 the library began funding a half-time library technician to assist the coordinator for Special Readers' Services); the student government; and donations from alumni.

Of note, in March 1998 the Accessibility Task Force (under the umbrella of the student government, the Alma Mater Society), spearheaded a referendum campaign asking Queen's undergraduates to donate $1.50 of their student interest fees toward purchasing technology for the library's two adaptive technology labs. The referendum was an overwhelming success with more than 75 percent of the student body voting yes. As a result, Special Readers' Services is guaranteed approximately $16,000 annually for the next three years. This money will be used to purchase new computers, adaptive technology, specialized software, and assistive devices. In three years' time, the student body will have the opportunity to renew or terminate the financial arrangement in another referendum.

PROGRAM BACKGROUND

The idea of hiring a librarian whose sole responsibility was to establish and administer an adaptive technology lab and provide library services to students with disabilities was initiated in 1991 by the Office of the Vice-Principal (Human Resources); the coordinator for Disability Services; and the chief librarian. At that time, the position was the first of its kind in Canada. Many librarians had special readers' services as a component to their positions, but library service to students with disabilities was not their full-time responsibility. Currently, the position reports to the associate librarian, Queen's University Libraries and the director of Health, Counselling, and Disability Services. Beginning this academic year (1997–1998), the coordinator's position has been divided between doing library reference work (30%) and providing services to students with disabilities (70%).

DESCRIPTION OF THE ACCESSIBILITY PROJECT

Access to information is the cornerstone of a university education, and academic libraries are central to the learning process. Special Readers' Services is an innovative, award-winning program that provides access to information and teaches library research skills to students with disabilities. Approaches based on this model emphasize the crucial role libraries play in the potential for academic achievement for students with disabilities.

Since its inception in 1991, Special Readers' Services has greatly enhanced library services to a user group whose needs were not adequately being met. Because of this program, previously inaccessible library resources such as the online catalogue, CD-ROMs, print and electronic indexes, research materials, library publications, and textbooks are now available to students with disabilities. Students also have access to state-of-the-art adaptive technology labs located in the two main libraries on campus.

The establishment of an adaptive technology lab or technology center in the library is critical. The main purpose of the lab is to facilitate access to information for students with disabilities. The first adaptive technology lab officially opened on September 30, 1991. What began as a room in the basement of the main library with two workstations, a laser printer, a scanner, and a closed-circuit television (CCTV) has now grown into two state-of-the-art technology labs. One lab is located in Stauffer Library (humanities and social sciences) and the other is in Douglas Library (science and engineering).

Technology alone is not enough. Full accessibility to library resources demands dedicated, ongoing staff support. The success of Special Readers' Services is due largely to employing a librarian dedicated to coordinating and providing special library services. It is the librarian's role to assist students to use the library and its resources effectively to support present and future learning.

The coordinator has developed a number of services and programs designed to meet the information needs of students with disabilities. These programs include bibliographic instruction sessions designed for students with specific types of disabilities; personalized research assistance; and training programs that teach students how to operate the adaptive technology available in the labs. The coordinator for Special Readers' Services works closely with the learning support counsellors and learning disabilities specialists, Health, Counselling, and Disability Services to develop effective library research skill programs for students with learning disabilities and attention deficit disorder. Instructional methods, materials, and communication techniques are adapted to meet the needs of the students.

The coordinator for Special Reader' Services is also responsible for ensuring students receive their textbooks, course readings, and research material in alternate formats (braille, audiocassette, disk, or large print). Materials such as journal articles, book chapters, course packs, and class handouts, which are not available from commercial producers, are read onto tape by volunteer readers. Other material is scanned and converted into electronic format.

Additional services offered by the Special Readers' Services program include retrieval of material from the stacks, extended loan periods for books, and photocopying. The coordinator's office also lends four-track tape recorders to students requiring taped texts.

Each year, the coordinator gives disability awareness sessions to interested librarians, library technicians, and student assistants.

The coordinator is assisted by a half-time library technician, two student assistants (five hours each per week), one office volunteer, and twenty (this number varies from year to year) volunteer readers.

The coordinator for Special Readers' Services is a member of the Disability Services Group on campus. This group meets twice a month to develop university-wide policies on services to students with disabilities; to discuss service issues; and to plan programs for students with disabilities.

The coordinator for Special Readers' Services is also the staff liaison for the student group, Special Needs Voice.

PROGRAM EVALUATION

The Special Readers' Services program is evaluated yearly, both formally and informally. Since 1991, students who use the program have been consulted and involved in such activities as planning adaptive technology purchases. Throughout the years, user groups including the Technology Aids Advisory Committee, the TDD Committee, and Visually Impaired Student Access Committee have been formed. These committees and others have provided an ongoing forum for dialogue between students with disabilities and the coordinator for Special Readers' Services.

In addition, a written survey (distributed once every two years) that queries students about their satisfaction with the adaptive technology labs and equipment needs for the labs gives students an opportunity to express their opinions and influence the program.

In June 1994, the Special Readers' Services program won the Canadian Association of College and University Libraries (CACUL) Innovation Achievement Award. This was formal, national recognition of the program's successes and accomplishments.

The Accessibility Centre at the Dana Porter Library University of Waterloo

Contact: Jane Forgay, Librarian, Services for Persons with Disabilities
Dana Porter Library
University of Waterloo
Waterloo, Ontario, Canada N3L 3G1
Institutional URL: www.uwaterloo.ca
Project-related URL: www.lib.uwaterloo.ca/tour/DP2Access.html

INSTITUTIONAL PROFILE

The University of Waterloo, founded in 1957, is one of Canada's leading comprehensive universities, with undergraduate and graduate programs in applied health sciences, arts, engineering, environmental studies, independent studies, mathematics, and science. UW is North America's largest cooperative education program that operates year-round. Situated on a 900-acre campus in Waterloo, Ontario, some 90 minutes west of Toronto, UW has more than forty buildings. Most of these are accessible, and many are linked by underground tunnels. Campus housing is available for students with disabilities, including facilities that support 24-hour attendant care if required.

THE DANA PORTER LIBRARY

The Dana Porter Library of the University of Waterloo holds 3.4 million items. With a professional library staff of thirty, the library serves the educational/research needs of the university's 16,309 full-time students and 712 full-time faculty members. Founded in 1992, the Accessibility Centre of the Dana Porter Library is intended as a resource for the university's disabled population, which, as of 1998, numbers approximately 785. This reflects the number of persons officially registered for disability services on campus, not the total university-wide population of disabled persons.

BACKGROUND

The Accessibility Centre was initiated by Florence Thomlison, coordinator of the UW Office for Persons with Disabilities from 1984 to 1996, and Bruce McNeil, associate librarian, UW Library from 1975–96. Ms. Thomlison's plan involved directing a portion of the University of Waterloo allotment of the Ontario government funds targeted to colleges and universities to the library at the University of Waterloo. She worked with the library to arrange for space, acquire adaptive equipment, and hire a librarian who was sensitive to the needs of people with disabilities. Lacking the equivalent of the United States's ADA to serve as a guide, planners sought direction in the Canadian *Charter of Rights and Freedoms*, the Ontario Human Rights Code, and national and provincial building codes. Primary input, however, came from students with disabilities, vendors of adaptive equipment, the National Library of Canada, and other academic libraries. The center was fully realized in 1992; and in 1994, a satellite center was constructed in the Davis Centre Library, which houses science, math, and engineering collections.

POPULATION SERVED

Any student registered with the campus Office for Persons with Disabilities. Any faculty or staff member with a disability.
Any resident of the region of Waterloo with a disability who has obtained the library's permission to use the center.

PROJECT FUNDING

The center has been funded by the Province of Ontario, Ministry of Education and Training, with ongoing grants since 1992.

Physical Space, Equipment, and Services

PHYSICAL ARRANGEMENT

The center is an open space (30' x 30') located in a corner of the main floor of the arts Library. Although this openness helps to integrate the center with the rest of the floor, its contents are contained to allow concentrated staff assistance when required. The center offers nine workstations, including two study rooms large enough to accommodate two individuals at a time.

The center provides tables with adjustable height, table lamps that can be moved from station to station to provide task lighting, large windows for natural light, and a comfortable chair called The Rest Stop, which is used and appreciated by people with chronic fatigue syndrome, multiple sclerosis, arthritis, etc.

EQUIPMENT
- Voice recognition: Dragon NaturallySpeaking
- Voice Output: JAWS for Windows 95, ASAP for DOS
- Magnification software: ZoomText Xtra
- Scanners: Kurzweil 1000 and Xerox Reading Edge
- Braille translation software: Mega Dots
- Closed Circuit TV Enlarger: VTEK Voyager XL
- Four-track tape players and a TDD/TTY (kept at the reserve desk) are available for use within the library.

SERVICES
The Accessibility Centre emphasizes user independence. Recognizing that independence can often be achieved with training and orientation, the center offers the following services:
- Staff awareness is central to good service. Each new public services staff member receives a tour of the center, a review of its services and facilities, and a general overview of the library's approach to users with disabilities.
- A reference librarian oversees the center and is available for consultations regarding research needs and training in the use of specialized equipment.
- The center will obtain recorded, large-print and braille textbooks for eligible students from Recording for the Blind and Dyslexic and through a provincially funded service available through the W. Ross Macdonald School for the Blind in Brantford, Ontario.
- Students and other library users can get assistance with retrieval of books and other materials, campus book delivery, and term loan borrowing privileges.

FACULTY LIAISON
The librarian, Services for Persons with Disabilities, consults with faculty concerning disabled students' research needs. A library handout for faculty who have students requiring special library assistance offers guidelines for referrals to the center. This guide is available at www.lib.uwaterloo.ca/~jdforgay/faculty.html.

COOPERATION WITH THE CAMPUS OFFICE
FOR PERSONS WITH DISABILITIES
Each fall, a joint session called Campus solutions is offered in which an open house is held for new students to find out about the resources available to them on campus, but especially through the office and the library.

The center is involved with the yearly Employment Strategies workshop series in which students learn how to use the library to find information about prospective employers.

A team of part-time staff uses space in the center to work on jobs for the Office of Persons with Disabilities, particularly transcription (audiotape, scanning, or braille production of course-related materials). While in the center, team members also make themselves available to work with students with disabilities in a variety of ways, (e.g., retrieving books from the stacks, photocopying, etc).

The center is made available to students with disabilities for test-taking and writing of exams.

EVALUATION OF THE PROJECT
The Accessibility Centre provides disabled users a much-needed contact point in the library. Statistics for the 1997–98 term reveal that students met with the librarian, Services for Persons with Disabilities, 228 times for research assistance and/or training in the use of adaptive technology. During the same period, 196 titles in alternative formats were requested.

Michigan State University Libraries
Contact: Denise A. Forro, Head, Information and Referral Center
Assistive Technology Center
East Lansing, Michigan 48824-1048
E-mail: forro@mail.lib.msu.edu
Institutional URL: http://www.lib.msu.edu
Program-related URL: http://www.lib.msu.edu/atc/

INSTITUTIONAL PROFILE:
Michigan State University enrolls more than 43,000 students, and has an academic/faculty population of more than 4,000. With more than four million volumes and fifty-seven professional library staff members, the Michigan State University Libraries serve the many undergraduate and graduate programs and professional schools that comprise MSU.

More than six hundred students are registered for disability services on campus. The Assistive Technology Center is funded by the library budget and through special funding requested by the Accommodating Technology Committee of the Libraries, Computing and Technology Department. Denise A. Forro, who also serves as head of the Information and Referral Center, oversees the program, with the assistance of support staff.

ASSISTIVE TECHNOLOGY CENTER
The technology available in the Assistive Technology Center (ATC) is designed to accommodate patrons with visual and hearing impairments in using the facilities of the library through the electronic resources provided within the center. ATC also provides equipment that is designed to be used by pa-

trons throughout the library to increase their mobility through the shelves and to provide better hearing for discussions, conferences, and presentations with audio enhancement aids.

VISUAL DISABILITY TECHNOLOGY

The following list includes the equipment and software available in the Assistive Technology Center at the main library for patrons with visual impairments. Training in the use of assistive technologies involves one-on-one review of the equipment and each piece of software. As this book goes to press, print and online training materials are "in the works."

- ClearView Closed-Circuit TV
- Xerox Reading Edge
- Omni 1000 Kurzweil Reading System
- Jaws for Windows
- Alva ABT-340 Braille Terminal
- ZoomText for Win95
- Dragon Dictate
- Atlas Speaks

AUDITORY DISABILITY TECHNOLOGY

The Phonic Ear assists patrons with hearing disabilities who may experience difficulty in attending bibliographic instruction courses in the library or meetings in the building. The equipment consists of a transmitter and a receiver worn, respectively, by the speaker and the listener.

In addition, ATC provides a conference microphone that can be placed on a table, turning the table itself into a microphone to help hearing-impaired patrons fully participate in group discussions.

TTY

The Information and Referral Center maintains a 24-hour line with a TTY telecommunication device for the deaf. Incoming messages from hearing-impaired patrons can be received, and information queries are answered promptly.

MOBILITY TECHNOLOGY

For patrons with mobility difficulties, the main library provides an Amigo motorized cart. The Amigo was designed to assist people with walking difficulties, offering freedom, mobility, and a sense of security. The purchase was supported by the libraries and the Accommodating Technology Committee.

OTHER SERVICES PROVIDED BY ATC

- Retrieval of materials
- Special extended loan periods
- Mailing of library materials

- Renewal of library materials by phone
- Authorization of runners/readers to check out library materials in patron's name
- Training of professional and support staff in the form of in-house workshops

College of Staten Island
City University of New York (CUNY)
Installation of an Adaptive Workstation:
Platform Challenges

Contact: Prof. Rebecca Adler
Library 1L-219
College of Staten Island
2800 Victory Blvd.
Staten Island, New York 10314-6600
e-mail: adler@POSTBOX.CSI.CUNY.EDU
Institutional URL: www.csi.cuny.edu
Program-related URL: http://163.238.169.25/libserv/assistec.html

INTRODUCTION

The Library of the College of Staten Island (CSI), one of the campuses of the City University of New York (CUNY), serves an urban undergraduate population of 8,000+ students and a smaller group of graduate (master's degree) students. Like most other libraries nationally, the CSI library has been undergoing a process of integrating new digital technologies and resources. Thus, the CSI Library, with its link to a university-wide network, now includes some thirty computers providing access to the online catalog (OPAC) and to the Internet. At some stations, CD-ROM databases installed on a server can be accessed via a local network.

The student body of the college includes a population of approximately 450 students with disabilities who receive various services through the college's Office of Disability Services. In keeping with Section 504/ADA protocol, the college has been making every effort to integrate these students into the general student body and has begun to provide the means to facilitate that integration. What follows is an account of the CSI library's program to install, alongside its conventional terminals, two workstations to provide blind, visually impaired, and learning-disabled students access to all of the library's computer-accessible resources in a congenial, nonsegregated environment.

BRIEF HISTORY

Early ad hoc endeavors to assist the disabled student population in using the library's facilities came under general coordination with the convening of a campuswide meeting during the fall 1997 semester; attendees included members of the college's Office of Student Disabilities, a student with a disability, the acting chief librarian, a member of the college's Office of Information Technology (OIT), members of the library's technical staff, and myself, the library's liaison to the Office of Student Disabilities. The purpose of the meeting was to investigate ways to bring the library's facilities into compliance with 504/ADA standards in a timely fashion. Not that our library and staff had not previously made every effort to accommodate students and faculty who required special assistance in library use and information gathering. Indeed, as library liaison to the Disabilities Office, I have conducted regular classes for library users with disabilities for several semesters. These are designed to provide library patrons with the skills they need to utilize the full range of library services and resources. In addition to the imperatives of 504/ADA timetables for compliance, what made the necessity of putting a more systematic process in place was the college's move during 1992–94 from its earlier location on two separate, makeshift campuses into a single 200-acre campus occupied by a few old renovated buildings and a new library building—all connected by a state-of-the-art fibre-optic backbone. What emerged from the initial and follow-up meetings was a coordinated short- and long-range plan for the installation of facilities that would extend the library's information technology to the sizable population of students with disabilities.

FUNDING
The acquisition of equipment and facilities is funded by ADA allocations provided through CUNY's Central Office of Disability Services. Major planning decisions faced by the college included what kinds of hardware and software should be acquired as well as training of librarians and library staff who would assist users. The initial plan included the installation of two workstations accessible to the disabled; at this writing, one is already in place and the second is scheduled for installation.

THE OPERATIVE PROGRAM
Regarding the software, it was decided that a Windows environment is preferable to DOS because the college, in the computers already installed at other campus locations, was already wedded to the former and was also in the process of migrating existing DOS applications to that configuration. As it turned out, most of the disabled students were more comfortable with DOS, inasmuch as DOS consists essentially of text. However, with a view to the job market and the future, it was felt that retraining these students in the Windows environment was worth the extra effort.

On the other hand, the CD-ROM server in the library, presently consisting of some fifteen dozen databases in a variety of disciplines, is DOS based, and therefore any serviceable workstation had to allow DOS applications to run, thus consuming a great deal of conventional memory.

PRESENT SETUP

As of this writing (December 1998), a single workstation is in place, linked to a nondedicated network laser printer. Unlike other institutions that have a separate "accessibility" area for the disabled, the campus 504/ADA Committee strongly recommended that the facility be located alongside the conventional terminals in the library to avoid any sense on campus of a "segregated" group of students. The workstation, a Pentium 90, running DOS 6.22 and Windows 3.11, offers the following:

- MultiVoice 2.8 synthesizer;
- JAWS 2.83 for Windows;
- VocalEyes 3.0 for DOS;
- LP Deluxe 6.1;
- Netscape Navigator;
- CD-ROM server;
- TCP 3270 CUNY+PLUS (the online catalog);
- WordPerfect 5.1 for DOS;
- WordPerfect 6.1 for Windows;
- 21-inch monitor.

Although this configuration seems more of a mixed environment than planned, the idea was to gradually wean students from the more familiar DOS to the more ubiquitous Windows interface.

THE FUTURE

The second workstation, to be rendered operational during the spring 1999 semester, consists of a Windows 95 Pentium 300 system placed on a height-adjustable table, making the station, among other things, wheelchair-accessible. This station will include:

- a dedicated laser printer;
- Soundblaster (soundboard) with TextAssist (software), making a separate speech synthesizer unnecessary;
- the latest version of JAWS for Windows;
- Netscape Navigator;
- a TCP 3270 for CUNY+PLUS (the online catalog);
- a 21-inch monitor; and Microsoft Office—with the possibility, in addition, of Zoomtext Xtra level 2 (which synchronizes speech with screen magnification).

After the newer workstation is in place, the first workstation will be dedicated to DOS-based CD-ROMs. The migration of the second DOS-based CD-ROMs to a Windows configuration is a project currently under way.

STAFF TRAINING

No access project can rely entirely upon technology; it is equally important that personnel receive training in the use of these important technologies, including sensitivity or awareness training in the special needs and requirements of patrons with various disabilities. To accomplish this often-over-looked facet of the access program, the library collaborates with the Office of Disability Services, whose staff provide regular workshops in sensitivity training for all librarians and library staff who are in any way charged with assisting students in the use of the specialized workstations. In addition, the college's coordinator of Disability Services has conducted a workshop that included, among other issues, an overview of ADA, students' rights under the law, and the demographics of the students population, emphasizing special pointers to make the interactions and communications with disabled persons as natural and as free from possible misunderstandings as possible.

It should be noted that disabled students are expected to learn basic com-puter use outside the library. In New York, some of the options include The New York State Commission for the Blind, The Jewish Guild for the Blind, among others. In addition, a member of the staff of the Office of Disability Services may work with these students to refine their computer skills. It is the librarians' task, on the other hand, to assist disabled students—as well, of course, as nondisabled students—in the library applications of the equipment and the software.

Inevitably, however, training in the use of specialized technologies does occasionally fall on the librarian's shoulders. That is to say, as in any real-life operation, problems emerge that are not entirely foreseen in the planning or the implementation of a particular program. And, indeed, those problems are often not as simple to resolve as one would think—from the point of view of both the librarian and the student concerned.

TECHNOLOGICAL CHALLENGES

The library's CD-ROM server has a capacity of seventy disks. Moreover, many of the databases loaded in it derive from a variety of disciplines, all having different interface software; these include ProQuest, Silver Platter, and Eric Dialog. And inevitably, there are problems when the speech software interacts with the search software, problems that differ from one database to the next. Briefly stated, total compatibility among the different interfaces and the speech software cannot be universally achieved in the current setup. The resolution of the problem will un-doubtedly lie in the fact that as more commercial CD-ROM databases become available in HTML-accessible form, it will become easier to facilitate a client-use interface that will better serve the blind and the visually impaired. Migrating the CD-ROMS to a Windows environment will also help by presenting a unified user interface. Another consideration is that in using the computer-synthesized voice access, trouble arises when the online catalog is accessed. The online catalog is a mainframe application based on the NOTIS system whose screens were not de-signed with speech software in mind. For example, the voice tends to read every-thing on the screen—dashes, double lines, cursor position, etc. Thus, in the present circumstances students are well advised to learn the configuration of each kind of screen in order to bypass these petty annoyances.

EVALUATION AND OVERSIGHT

A special task force on technology was recently inaugurated by the president of the college. A subgroup of this task force is the Subcommittee on Technology and Disabilities. This committee will be reviewing the operation of the library's disabilities services and making, where necessary, the appropriate remedial recommendations.

Acknowledgments

The author wishes to thank Joe Nicolosi of the CSI Office of Disability Services and Arshad Jameel of the CSI Library technical staff for their assistance; and Mark Lewental of the CSI Library computer staff for his invaluable contribution to the design of the disability workstations.

University of Michigan
Campus Accessibility Guide

Contact: Pamela Hamblin, Manager, Facilities Information Center, and Michael Myatt, Draftsperson I, Accessibility Guide Coordinator
University of Michigan
Ann Arbor, Michigan 48109
Institutional url:www.umich.edu
Project-URL: www.fpd.bf.umich.edu/accguide/htm/files/imintens.htm

DESCRIPTION

With a student/faculty population exceeding 45,000, the University of Michigan is located on one of the largest, most sprawling campuses in the United States. As such, it offers immense navigational challenges to many of its students with disabilities. In 1998–99, the university had more than 450 individuals registered for disability services on campus, not to mention the countless unidentified students, faculty, and staff members with one or more disabilities.

To address the wayfinding needs of the university's considerable disabled population, the authors, in coordination with the university's Council for Disability Concerns, initiated the online "Campus Accessibility Guide." The Accessibility Guide Team was organized to develop a Web-based version of the campus accessibility map. The team's goal was to design the online guide with an eye toward providing greater depths of information while ensuring maximum ease of maintenance and updating.

The information presented on the original (print) map is highly visual and deals primarily with access issues encountered by those with physical disabilities. The accessibility guide is designed to be accessible to blind and visually impaired persons as well as those with mobility disabilities. In the past, the map had been printed on large paper which, because of its size, was cumbersome and offered a limited amount of content information. In this project, the accessibility of the campus is the main issue, but the accessibility of information is proving to be of equal importance.

The data collected for the accessibility guide, whenever possible, has been collected objectively with the idea that it could inform future decisions about the project. The building information was gathered, initially, from the perspective of those with mobility impairments as well as those with visual impairments, and was then placed into a database that is available to all involved.

Figure I

Computing Center Annex   http://www.fpd.bf.umich.edu/accguide/htm/bldgs/cmpanex.htm

Computing Center Annex

Link to text only page

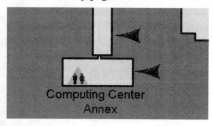

Nearest Thoroughfare: **Contact Number:**
Bonisteel Boulevard   SSD 763-3000

Building Information:

General:
The Computing Center Annex is located at 1071 Beal Avenue.
Number of Floors: 1
Parking:
The nearest accessible parking is in the lot southeast of the Computing Center next door.
Entrances:
There is an accessible entrance on the east side of the building.
Elevators:
No elevators.
Stairs:
No stairs.
Restrooms:
There are two accessible restrooms. Walk straight down the main corridor from the entrance, then turn right at the T-junction, then left, and the restrooms are on the left-hand side.
Rescue Assistance:

[Index Page] [Area Map] [Central Campus Map] [Access Guide Home]

The ultimate goal of this group is to provide valuable information to those who need it most. The physical structure of the accessibility guide itself is not the most important portion of our task; rather, helping to make everyday experiences at the university a little more predictable and enjoyable for persons with disabilities is the objective.

Figures 1 and 2 show the parallel graphical/textual versions of the accessibility guide. Note that people with limited vision who use screen-reading software, refreshable braille displays, or other adaptive technologies are provided with the same wayfinding information available to their sighted counterparts.

Figure 2

Computing Center Annex Info   http://www.fpd.bf.umich.edu/accguide/screen/srbldgs/cmpanex.htm

Computing Center Annex

Nearest Thoroughfare
Beal Avenue
Contact Number
SSD 763-3000

Building Information

General
The Computing Center Annex is located at 1071 Beal Avenue.
Number of Floors
1
Parking
The nearest accessible parking is in the lot southeast of the Computing Center next door.
Entrances
There is an accessible entrance on the east side of the building.
Elevators
No elevators.
Stairs
No stairs.
Restrooms
There are two accessible restrooms. Walk straight down the main corridor from the entrance, then turn right at the T-junction, then left, and the restrooms are on the left-hand side.
Rescue Assistance
Contact Building Coordinator for evacuation plan.

Hyperlink list with 4 choices
Hyperlink Number 1 is Go back to index of buildings beginning with the letter C
Hyperlink Number 2 is Go back to main building index
Hyperlink Number 3 is Go back to main accessguide page
Hyperlink Number 4 is to send comments through e mail

You have reached the end of this document

---

appendix B

Planning For Service: A Model Survey For Academic Libraries

Janet M. Bedney

Each academic year, librarians who serve our target population—those with one or more disabilities—meet a new group of students. Depending on the type of institution, this new patron base might include a combination of undergraduates, graduate and professional students, special students, and faculty and staff members with disabilities. Just as the disability-related demographics of our society at large change, so will the population of persons with disabilities enrolled in, or employed by, institutions of higher education.

The Americans with Disabilities Act was discussed throughout this book. Recall that the ADA requires colleges and universities to provide an environment that is free of architectural barriers as well as to remove less-tangible obstacles that can interfere with full access to higher education. In addition to the legal bases for accessibility, additional forces affect what librarians do and how they do it. Of course, this extends beyond the world of disability access. The general state of the economy, the library's own budget for materials and equipment, and a host of other factors dictate what is acquired and how funds are apportioned. All of these forces require today's academic librarian to become increasingly resourceful in managing financial and human resources.

To maximize their effective use of resources, libraries must obtain information that can guide their strategic planning efforts and help them to market their services properly. Surveys can provide the much-needed information required for informed planning and decision making. Following the lead of private industry, which increasingly uses surveys to reach out to customers and potential customers, libraries are well advised to consider this effective tool for planning and program assessment.

Patrons — whether students, faculty members, or the general public — are the library's customers. To plan for optimal service, librarians must somehow measure their patrons' expectations and satisfaction levels and assess which services, equipment, or other changes might improve their users' experience in the library. If done properly, this information can and does directly effect changes in policy, procedures, programs, choices of equipment, and other aspects of the library. Because our patrons are the library's primary concern, it is crucial to ensure customer satisfaction and also to keep abreast of emerging trends affecting library services.

The following generic survey is intended for use by academic librarians who want to assess their users' needs and expectations of the library. It might be included in initial mailings, discussed in orientations to the library and/or the college or university, or administered through other venues.

Library Services And Facilities Survey
PERSONAL INFORMATION

I am a(n) ☐ Graduate Student ☐ Undergraduate ☐ Faculty Member
☐ Staff Member ☐ Other (describe) _____

I am enrolled/employed ☐ Part-time ☐ Full-time

My disability/disabilities can best be described as (check all that apply):
☐ Visual impairment / blindness
☐ Hearing impairment / deafness
☐ Mobility / orthopedic
☐ Learning disability
☐ Chronic illness
☐ Psychological/emotional (including phobias)
☐ Other (Please describe if you are comfortable doing so)_____

_____

Which of the following do you have experience using (check all that apply):
☐ Online (computerized) library catalogs
☐ Internet
☐ CD-ROM / online research databases
☐ Card catalogs

Do you have your own computer? ☐ Yes ☐ No

If yes, what type of system?: ☐ Macintosh ☐ IBM-compatible PC

When you are on campus, where do you hope/plan to do the majority of your computing?
☐ At the university's main computing center   ☐ In the library
☐ Wherever I am, with my own laptop   ☐ Don't know yet

Which of the following *computer-related* accommodations do you hope to find in the library (check all that apply):
☐ Large-print software
☐ Speech output (talking computer)
☐ Voice input
☐ Braille printing capability
☐ Special keyboard (describe if you can):
☐ Other special input device (e.g., trackball mouse):
☐ Refreshable (soft) braille display
☐ Other (Please describe):_____

Depending upon your disability, any or all of the following will be available to you. Please rate each of the services in terms of their importance for you:

	Least				Most
1. Retrieval of books from stacks	1	2	3	4	5
2. Staff-assisted photocopying of library materials	1	2	3	4	5
3. Assistance in using computerized databases/catalogs	1	2	3	4	5
4. Individualized tour of the library, services, and collections	1	2	3	4	5
5. Training in the use of specialized technologies	1	2	3	4	5
6. Private consultation with reference or other librarian(s)	1	2	3	4	5
7. Receiving books and other materials through the mail	1	2	3	4	5
8. Reserving and renewing library materials over the phone	1	2	3	4	5
9. Reserving and renewing library materials via computer	1	2	3	4	5
10. Access to a cart for moving materials throughout the library	1	2	3	4	5
11. Ability to ask questions via e-mail	1	2	3	4	5
12. Reference help by telephone	1	2	3	4	5
13. Help in finding specialized materials (e.g., books on tape, braille)	1	2	3	4	5

14. Any other services not identified above (please describe): _____

_____

The library tries to provide the appropriate *facilities* to meet your needs. Please rate the importance of each of the following:

	Least				Most
1. Access to a private study room	1	2	3	4	5
2. Access to a room for small-group work	1	2	3	4	5
3. Special lighting	1	2	3	4	5
4. Adjustable-height desks/tables	1	2	3	4	5
5. Ergonomic chairs	1	2	3	4	5
6. Access to a TTY/TDD	1	2	3	4	5
7. Access to a closed-caption video player	1	2	3	4	5
8. Access to a CCTV (video enlarger)	1	2	3	4	5

9. Any other (Please describe to the extent you are comfortable doing so):_____

_____

_____

appendix c

Directory of Resources

Compiled by Nicole McKay

Books

Baldewijns, Jeroen. 1997. *Vision on Assistive Technology: A Guide for the Blind and Visually Impaired and their Assistants*. Leuven: Vlicht.

A very concise primer on assistive technologies. Each section includes very readable definitions, including tips for knowledgeable selection. Specific products are described briefly, and an appendix offers a comprehensive list of manufacturers with contact information.

Cunningham, Carmel, and Norman Coombs. 1997. *Information Access and Adaptive Technology*. Phoenix: American Council on Education and Oryx Press.

General overview of assistive technologies in higher education. Includes a great deal of practical advice on acquiring technology, designing work spaces for people with disabilities, and funding issues.

Deines-Jones, Courtney, and Connie Van Fleet. 1995. *Preparing Staff to Serve Patrons with Disabilities: A How-to-Do-It Manual for Librarians*. New York: Neal Schuman.

This book provides excellent resources and tips on how to aid nontraditional library patrons in the everyday library setting. Included are sample forms and problem/solution examples to aid librarians with providing the best possible library services.

Foos, Donald D., and Nancy C. Pack. 1992. *How Libraries Must Comply with the Americans with Disabilities Act (ADA)*. Phoenix, Arizona: Oryx Press.

Offers a comprehensive analysis of various aspects of the Americans with Disabilities Act and libraries' responsibilities under the law. Case studies, well-considered bibliographies, and resource directories make this a must-read for the administrator or librarian charged with serving patrons with disabilities.

Heyward, Salome M. 1992. *Access to Education for the Disabled: A Guide to Compliance with Section 504 of the Rehabilitation Act of 1973*. Jefferson, N. C.: McFarland.

A leading expert in the field of higher education and disability, attorney Salome Heyward provides a very concise and readable overview of Section 504 and its application in elementary, secondary, and postsecondary educational institutions.

Lazzarro, Joseph J. 1993. *Adaptive Technologies for Learning and Work Environments*. Chicago and London: ALA.

Intended for the user of assistive technologies and professionals who serve them, this book highlights the value of technology in the home, school, and workplace. Many adaptive products are introduced along with clear explanations and simple instructions on installation and use.

Mates, Barbara T. 1991. *Library Technology for Visually and Physically Impaired Persons*. Westport, Conn.: T. Meckler Publishing.

Good source of technical information for public and academic librarians serving disabled populations.

McNulty, Tom, and Dawn M. Suvino. 1993. *Access to Information: Materials, Technologies and Services for Print-Impaired Readers*. Chicago and London: ALA.

Examines the technology available to print-impaired readers, including blind, low-vision, and learning-disabled persons. A brief history provides a broader understanding of how technology has evolved. Focus is on braille, audio-recorded, and computerized texts.

Walling, Linda L., and Marilyn M. Irwin. 1995. *Information Services for People with Developmental Disabilities: The Library Manager's Handbook*. Westport, Conn. and London: Greenwood Press.

Provides a broad view of people with developmental disabilities from different library perspectives. The book is divided into three parts: developmental disabilities from a librarian's perspective; issues that affect information services for people with disabilities; and how people with developmental disabilities are affected by the Americans with Disabilities Act in libraries.

Electronic Resources
DISABILITY META-SITES

Apple/Macintosh Disabilities Information
http://www.apple.com/education/k12/disability

One-stop shopping for Macintosh access information, includes a software library with product information, shareware, and freeware for the Macintosh family of computers.

Assistive Technology On-Line
http://asel.udel.edu/at-online/assistive.html

Very nicely organized Web site offers information on assistive technologies for all disability groups. Includes a concise glossary of technical terminology; information on federal funding and legislation; links to electronic journals; papers, and conference schedules; and more.

Closing the Gap
http://www.closingthegap.com
    Provides a wealth of information on assistive technologies, with emphasis on learning environments. The Resources Directory allows the user to search for hardware and/or software products. The online Library contains a great many articles and papers on various aspects of disability, with some very good coverage of technology applications for learning-disabled persons.

EASI: Equal Access to Software and Information
http://www.rit.edu/~easi
    EASI provides information on adaptive technologies for individuals and institutions. This handy site includes links for K–12 educators, audio Web casts, EASI online seminars, and EASI's own electronic journal, *Information Technology and Disabilities*.

Geocities: Librarians' Connections
http://www.geocities.com/CapitolHill/1703/DRMlibs-message.html
    Particularly useful site for the neophyte to disability and library issues. Pointers to individual libraries' accessibility plans, programs, etc., serve as a good starting point for librarians new to the field.

LD Resources
http://www.ldresources.com/
    Includes information on various aspects of learning disability and technologies for instruction; heavily Macintosh oriented.

Microsoft Accessibility Web site
http://www.microsoft.com/enable/
    Provides lots of current, and useful information on accessibility of Microsoft's product line.

National Library Service for the Blind and Physically Handicapped
http://www.loc.gov/nls
    Provides information on NLS services, including a searchable online catalog of books in braille and/or audio-recorded formats.

NARIC: The National Rehabilitation Information Center
http://www.naric.com/naric
    Funded by the National Institute on Disability and Rehabilitation Research (NIDRR), NARIC provides a variety of services and information resources, including REHABDATA, the searchable database of rehabilitation literature.

Trace Research & Development Center
http://www.trace.wisc.edu/
    An excellent comprehensive disabilities Web site particularly rich in resources on universal design and Web accessibility.

LISTSERVS (DISCUSSION GROUPS)

Listservs, or e-mail-based discussion groups, are excellent sources of information. Several library-related listservs are devoted to services for people with disabilities. For information on specific technologies, service strategies, etc., for specific disability groups, locate more specialized listservs at:

CataList, the official catalog of LISTSERV lists
http://www.lsoft.com/lists/listref.html
    This searchable, Web-based inventory of listservs provides subscription instructions, addresses, and other information on more than 24,000 public listservs.

SELECTED LIBRARY/DISABILITY LISTSERVS

To subscribe to the following mailing lists, address an e-mail message to the LISTSERV address, e.g.:

listserv@maelstrom.stjohns.edu

In the message, enter the following text:
subscribe listserv name your name

for example:
subscribe able-job Joe Smith

ACCESS

Media Access Mailing List
Addresses: access@maelstrom.stjohns.edu (list)
listserv@maelstrom.stjohns.edu (listserv)
    The media access list discusses captioning, audio description, subtitling, dubbing, Web access, and other issues in making media of information accessible to people with disabilities and others.

Disability Access to Libraries (AXSLIB)
Addresses: axslib@maelstrom. stjohns.edu (list)
listserv@maelstrom.stjohns.edu (listserv)
    Sponsored by EASI (Equal Access to Software and Information), this list provides excellent contacts with other public, school, and academic librarians seeking information on access to libraries by persons with disabilities.

Disabled Student Services in Higher Education (DSSHE-L)
Addresses: dsshe-l@ubvm.cc.buffalo.edu (list)
listserv@ubvm.cc.buffalo.edu (listserv)

Provides a forum for administrators, disabled student services coordinators, and other professionals charged with providing service to disabled persons in institutions of higher education.

Library Adaptive Technology
addresses: adapt-l@american.edu (list)
listserv@american.edu (listserv)

Provides a forum for the exchange of information on library applications of adaptive technologies.

ONLINE LIBRARY CATALOGS OF ALTERNATIVE FORMAT MATERIALS

Recording for the Blind and Dyslexic
http://www.rfbd.org/catalog/

This Web-based catalog provides access to more than 75,000 recorded titles.

Library of Congress
http://www.loc.gov/nls/web-blnd/bphc.html

Provides author, subject, title, and keyword access to the holdings of the National Library Service for the Blind and Physically Handicapped of the Library of Congress.

American Printing House for the Blind
Louis (formerly CARL ET AL)
http://www.aph.org

Louis is a unique database of accessible materials for readers who are visually impaired or blind. It provides access to materials produced by hundreds of North American agencies.

Directories

AFB Directory of Services for Blind and Visually Impaired Persons in the US and Canada. 25th ed. 1997. New York: American Foundation for the Blind.

Offers directory information to a wide range of services for blind and low vision patrons, including contact information for schools, organizations, and programs. The directory is organized by state and further subdivided by category, (i.e., school, organization, program). Each category provides in-depth contact information and brief history.

Closing the Gap Directory. Henderson, Minn.: Closing the Gap, annual.

Perhaps the most exhaustive available listing of commercially produced hardware and software for special education and rehabilitation.

National Rehabilitation Information Center
REHABDATA
http://www.naric.com

REHABDATA, produced by the National Rehabilitation Information Center and made available free of charge on the Web, is the leading literature database on disability and rehabilitation. The REHABDATA database provides searchable access to materials covering physical, mental, and psychiatric disabilities; independent living; vocational rehabilitation; special education; assistive technology; law; employment; and other issues as they relate to people with disabilities. The types of documents described in REHABDATA include research reports, books, journal articles, and audiovisual materials.

Norlin, Dennis A, Gasque Cay, Christopher Lewis, Ruth O'Donnell, and Lawrence Webster. 1994. *A Directory of Adaptive Technologies: To Aid Library Patrons and Staff with Disabilities*. Chicago and London: Library and Information Technology Association.

Although somewhat dated, this directory includes a plethora of adaptive technology products, including items intended for users with visual, hearing and speech, and mobility impairments. Includes contact information for disability product vendors, manufacturers, and organizations.

Texas School for the Blind and Visually Impaired
Technology Manufacturers' Links
http://www.tsbvi.edu/technology/manufacture.htm

Well-organized directory to home pages of manufacturers and vendors of large print, speech access, scanners, reading machines, and more.

Manufacturers of Adaptive Computing Products (Hardware and Software)

This list is by no means exhaustive. However, it does include information for products described in this book, as well as a number of other major producers of adaptive technologies.

AI Squared

P.O. Box 669
Manchester Center, Vermont 05255
Phone: (802) 362-3612
Fax: (802) 362-1670
E-mail: zoomtext@aisquared.com
Products: Zoomtext, VisAbility

Arkenstone
NASA Ames Moffett Complex, Building 23
P.O. Box 215
Moffett Field, California 94035-0215
Phone: (800) 444-4443 (U.S. and Canada)
Fax: (650) 603-8887
TDD: (800) 833-2753
Product: Open Book Unbound

Artic Technologies
55 Park Street, Suite 2
Troy, Michigan 48083
Phone: (248) 588-7370
Fax: (248) 588-2650
Web site: www.artictech.com
Products: Business Vision, Magnum GT, Win Vision

Berkeley Systems
2095 Rose Street
Berkeley, California 94709
Phone: (510) 540-5535
Fax: (510) 540-5115
Web site: http://www.berksys.com
Products: outSPOKEN, inLARGE

Braille Planet, Inc.
408 South Baldwin Street
Madison Wisconsin 53703
Phone: (800) 347-9594
Fax: (608) 257-4143
Web site: www.brailleplanet.org
Products: MegaDots Braille production software

Dragon Systems
320 Nevada Street
Newton, Massachusetts 02460
Phone: (617) 965-5200
Fax: (617) 527-0372
Web site: http://www.dragonsystems.com
Products: DragonDictate, Dragon NaturallySpeaking